T0330652

Advances in Industrial Engineering in the Industry 4.0 Era

At the core of this book are several application areas where Industry 4.0 has been, or can be, applied. This book introduces the Fourth Industrial Revolution, with discussions and reflections that will lead the reader into a deeper understanding of the nature of the concept. This book also reveals various facets that can be applied and utilized for implementation of the concept in various sectors.

This book:

- Comprehensively discusses skills for Industry 4.0
- Provides insights into the application of Industry 4.0 in the healthcare sector
- Presents involvement of Industry 4.0 in current concepts such as supply chain and blockchain
- Showcases innovative additive manufacturing to enhance human–machine co-working
- Includes virtualization and simulation techniques for decision-making in manufacturing and assembly processes

This book is primarily written for graduate students and academic researchers in the fields of industrial engineering, manufacturing engineering, mechanical engineering, production engineering, and aerospace engineering.

Advances in Industrial Engineering in the Industry 4.0 Era

Edited by Kaushik Kumar

CRC Press
Taylor & Francis Group
Boca Raton London New York

CRC Press is an imprint of the
Taylor & Francis Group, an **informa** business

Contents

Preface

The editor is pleased to present the book *Advances in Industrial Engineering in the Industry 4.0 Era*. The title was chosen understanding the current importance of Industry 4.0 as well as familiarization and application for the industrial and service sector.

Industry 4.0 in industrial engineering emphasizes manufacturing and assembly systems that are modularly structured with cyber-physical systems, as "convertible machines", "smart assembly stations" and "smart part logistic". These elements communicate and cooperate with each other in real time, integrating the physical processes with virtual information in an augmented reality fashion to eliminate errors and maximize the production process efficiency. Furthermore, aided assembly improves the duration and safety of fastening and picking activities through several technologies, such as cobots (collaborative robots). CNC machines and reconfigurable tools are integrated through adequate controls in an open architecture environment to produce a particular family of customized parts, ensuring a scalable, convertible, and profitable manufacturing process. Manufacturing, like other industries, is rising to the challenges imposed by aggressive consumer demands and the need for cost-effective processing which delivers quality in the fastest possible time. Fierce competition means that keeping abreast of new developments and applications in technology is essential if companies are to meet market demands profitably and keep ahead of their competitors. The book investigates the design and management of industrial engineering for an efficient, flexible, and modular production of customized products exploiting the 4IR-enabling technologies.

In recent years, the development of advanced mechanical systems and manufacturing has been continuously pushed to fulfil a higher demand for specification because of the need for better and more consistent product quality, more product variability, reduced product cost, globally competitive products, and a shorter product life cycle. The advancement of data communication and storage through the Internet of Things (IoT) opens the possibilities of connecting sensors, robots, and devices. In other words, the human role in industry is decreasing due to the development of connected manufacturing floors allowing them to take more control over the manufacturing processes, decisions, and even maintenance. The big data generated by the manufacturing process is consistently growing and becoming more valuable than the hardware that it generates. However, to make use of it, manufacturers must distinguish the useful data from big data, after which the useful data must be correctly analyzed in order for it to be meaningfully interpreted and understood. Thus, the resource that manufacturers require is not only big data, but also the ability to manage the data and turn it into useful data that can be used for decision support and maximizing the profit margin. Several benefits can then be derived. By exploiting 4IR, manufacturing enterprises expect to achieve shortened product development, early validation of manufacturing processes, faster production ramp-up, faster time to market, reduced manufacturing costs, improved product quality, enhanced product knowledge dissemination, reduction in errors, increased flexibility, and so on.

At the core of this book are several application areas where 4IR has been or can be applied. Each is treated as a complete chapter. This book also provides an introduction to the Fourth Industrial Revolution, discussion and reflection that will lead the reader into a deeper understanding of the nature of the concept. This book also reveals various facets that can be applied and utilized for implementation of the concept in various different sectors.

The chapters of the book are grouped in five sections:

- Section I: Skills for Industry 4.0 (Chapter 1)
- Section II: Healthcare and Industry 4.0 (Chapter 2)
- Section III: Industrial Engineering and Industry 4.0 (Chapters 3 to 5)
- Section IV: Additive Manufacturing and Industry 4.0 (Chapters 6 to 8)
- Section V: Applications of Industry 4.0 (Chapters 9 and 10).

Section I of the book starts with Chapter 1, which discusses the skills required to navigate uncertainty produced by "digital convergence" manifest as Industry 4.0. Key skills for future working, such as identified by the World Economic Forum Global Risks Report 2023, include analytical thinking, creative thinking, systems thinking, curiosity, lifelong learning, and adaptability. These skills are increasingly needed because digital convergence, where the synergy of two or more digital technologies significantly change practice, combines technical aspects of computing with design and innovation requiring a different emphasis in skills development. The chapter provides a discussion on how new skills for digital convergence could help organisations better navigate the ambiguities of integrating Industry 4.0.

In Section II, Chapter 2 emphasizes the technologies associated with Industry 4.0 including the IoT, artificial intelligence (AI), robotics, big data analytics, cloud computing, and others towards offering new opportunities to collect, analyse, and leverage vast amounts of healthcare data, leading to improved diagnostics, personalized treatment plans, and enhanced patient monitoring. Additionally, these technologies enable automation of routine tasks, reducing human error and freeing up healthcare professionals to focus on more complex and critical care activities. On the other hand, Lean principles emphasize the identification and elimination of waste within processes. The chapter provides an insight into the integration of the Fourth Industrial Revolution and Lean concepts in the healthcare sector.

In Section III, Chapter 3 talks about the prediction of the devastating effects of disasters. The authors have developed a hypothetical humanitarian supply chain to provide food and water to people in need of emergency shelters. It is an agent-based simulation developed with the Python programming language choosing situational method engineering as a programming approach in the software development process. The developed software has the capability of identifying peoples as "parent", "mentally disabled", and so on. The chapter concludes with a note that panic among people can hinder the success rate of aid efforts, and relief operation plans that overlook individual differences are more likely to be unsuccessful.

Chapter 4 has amalgamated AI and Blockchain. Blockchain technology and AI have a significant impact on our daily lives. By combining these two technologies, decentralized AI might be enabled, allowing research, conclusions, and self-learning on trustworthy and pooled data on the blockchain network. The IoT makes it possible for virtual and physical devices to communicate with one another, giving us access to real-time digital services. It is true that each technology has its own disadvantage. This chapter demonstrates how combining Blockchain and AI can reduce the drawbacks of both technologies. The chapter also covers the fusion of AI, Blockchain with the cloud, and IoT.

Chapter 5 highlights the impact of renewable energy (RE) resources and Industry 4.0 on growth of economics and policy for developing nation countries. The chapter investigates the relationship between economic development and RE resources, as well as the adoption of Industry 4.0 for newly industrialized emerging nations. The impact of RE on employment is generally disputed. Hence, the influence of RE on economic growth, GDP, and employment is presented in this chapter. The chapter includes all the detailed analyses and information made by the project developers of RE and policymakers for the successful dissemination of RE policies. It also highlights the difficulties that developing nations have in adopting Industry 4.0, as opposed to the enormous potential of energy from renewable sources. The chapter concludes that incentive promotional policies and subsidies prove to be significantly vital factors that play an essential role in the improvement of RE use.

Industry 4.0 can be defined as "the integration of intelligent digital technologies into manufacturing and industrial processes". In the same line, Section IV is dedicated to additive manufacturing (AM). Chapter 6 provides in-depth exploration of AM technologies in the era of Industry 4.0. AM technologies, also known as layered manufacturing, solid free form fabrication, tool-less manufacturing, 3D printing, and rapid prototyping, represent a groundbreaking suite of methodologies reshaping the industrial landscape. These approaches diverge from traditional manufacturing methods by emphasizing the incremental construction of objects, layer upon layer. Solid free form fabrication specifically champions the creation of intricate designs, bypassing the limitations imposed by conventional tooling processes. Tool-less manufacturing stands out as a hallmark feature, enabling the production of components without the need for specialized tools. The term "3D printing", a more commonly recognized phrase, encapsulates the essence of these technologies, highlighting the additive nature of material deposition based on digital blueprints. Rapid prototyping, integral to this suite, underscores the accelerated pace at which prototypes can be conceptualized and materialized, streamlining the product development life cycle. Collectively, these terminologies underscore the diverse facets and far-reaching potential of AM technologies in reshaping industrial practices.

Similar to Chapter 6, Chapter 7 elaborates on AM technologies for on-demand production of customized goods in the era of the 4th Industrial Revolution. Customer demands for customized products and services that are more time- and cost-effective are leading to a resultant shift from Industry 3.0, mainly dominated by computerized machines, to a more robust and accommodating Industry 4.0. This comes with the development and harmonization of different forms of technologies aimed at providing a sustainable decentralized production environment to shorten the realization time in product development and service delivery. The AM technique is an advanced manufacturing technique currently employed in production of intricate engineering components with improved properties. It is one of the most valuable technologies enhancing the realization of the 4th Industrial revolution. This chapter discusses AM technologies, principles, types, and applications. The chapter further looks at the significance and relevance of AM to Industry 4.0 in the production of on-demand customized items in today's world and the future trend of AM in Industry 4.0.

The last chapter of the section, Chapter 8, provides computational analysis of the mechanical compression of additive manufactured lattice structures. The lattice structure is a unit cell that has the ability to fill space and can be tessellated along any axis without any interstices between the cells. AM is a highly effective manufacturing technique utilized for the fabrication of lattice structures due to its ability to accommodate complex geometries. These structures are a nascent solution to the reduction of weight, energy consumption, and advanced manufacturing time. This study focuses on the numerical investigation of the mechanical compression and deformation characteristics of various lattice structures produced through AM. The formation of a lattice structure involves the consideration of three distinct types of unit cell, namely the body-centered cubic (BCC), face-centered cubic (FCC), and fluorite. A linear finite element model has been established for the purpose of analyzing mechanical compression and deformation characteristics, utilizing the nTopology software. The chapter concludes that the BCC lattice configuration provides better compressive strength and deformation characteristics as compared to the FCC and fluorite lattice configurations.

The last section of the book, Section V, handles the applications of Industry 4.0. Chapter 9 discusses rethinking manufacturing workflows for digital convergence, with reference to the Royal Australian Air Force. A key challenge for advancing industrial engineering in the era of Industry 4.0 is to understand the changes to workflow that will be needed to support new ways of operating. Embedding digital technology into a production system creates opportunities not only for increasing efficiency, but also for supporting new production paradigms. However, as innovative workflows are created to maximize the new ways of working that digital technology brings (with the added complexities of digital convergence), it is still critical to recognize the importance of the role of effective people management within the process. This chapter considers changing workflows in the context of rethinking manufacturing within the Royal Australian Air Force for more flexibility, distributed production, and adaptable outcomes. The influence of the individual on practice is acknowledged and integrated into systems development.

The best practice to understand a system is to learn by imitating. The book concludes with Chapter 10, which describes the state of the art on hybrid harvesting for sustainable micro-energy generation in the Industry 4.0 era. Micro-energy harvesting has a crucial role in the modern wireless communication technology like the IoT and cloud computing concepts of Industry 4.0. It involves capturing and converting energy from various ambient sources to power small-scale electronic devices and systems. Industry 4.0 enables efficient data collection, analysis, management, and integration of these systems into industrial processes and grids, ultimately contributing to sustainability, cost savings, and improved overall efficiency in energy utilization. A specially designed cantilever oscillator with embedded piezoelectric or electromagnetic circuits is employed for such energy harvesting. However, it is difficult to tune the harvester with the surrounding vibrations, as most ambient vibrations are low-frequency signals. The chapter reports some developments in enhancing the output power of the harvester using hybrid piezoelectric and electromagnetic principles of energy conversion. Using some basic dynamic models of these harvesters, the structural response and the power output evaluations are discussed. Optimized design of harvesting system for power enhancement is described.

Acknowledgements

First and foremost, I would like to thank God. It was your blessing that provided me the strength to believe in passion and hard work and to pursue dreams. I thank my families for having the patience with me for taking yet another challenge, which decreased the amount of time I could spend with them. They were my inspiration and motivation. I would like to thank my parents and grandparents for allowing me to follow my ambitions. I would like to thank all the contributing authors, as they are the pillars of this structure. I would also like to thank them to have belief in me. I want to take this opportunity to thank all of my colleagues and friends in different parts of the world for sharing ideas in shaping my thoughts. My sincere efforts will come to a level of satisfaction if the students, researchers, and professionals concerned with all the fields related to Industry 4.0 thinking are benefitted.

I owe a huge thanks to each and every contributing author, reviewers, the editorial advisory board members, the book development editor, and the team of CRC Press for their availability to work on this huge project. All of their efforts were instrumental in compiling this book, and without their constant and consistent guidance, support, and cooperation I couldn't have reached this milestone.

Last, but definitely not least, I would like to thank all individuals who have taken time out to help me during the process of editing this book. Without their support and encouragement I would have probably given up on the project.

Kaushik Kumar

Contributors

Kamardeen O. Abdulrahman
University of Ilorin
Nigeria

C. J. Anderson
Griffith University
Australia

Rabiu Abdulkarim Baba
University of Ilorin
Nigeria

Luke Houghton
Griffith University
Australia

Matthew Jennings
Deakin University
Australia

Christopher Kourloufas
Air and Space Power Centre
Canberra
Australia

Deepak Kumar
National Institute of Technology
Jamshedpur, India

Kaushik Kumar
Birla Institute of Technology
Mesra, India

Kishore Kumar
Sri Ramakrishna Engineering
    College
Coimbatore, India

Rahul Kumar
National Institute of Technology
Jamshedpur, India

Christopher Larkin
Deakin University
Australia

Jennifer Loy
Griffith University
Australia

Mridula G. Narang
M S Ramaiah University of Applied
    Sciences Bangalore
India

T. Nivethitha
Hindusthan College of Engineering
    and Technology
Coimbatore, India

Subhransu Kumar Panda
National Institute of Technology
Rourkela, India

P. K. Poonguzhali
Hindusthan College of Engineering
    and Technology
Coimbatore, India

Chikesh Ranjan
Birla Institute of Technology
Mesra, India

Bernard Rolfe
Deakin University
Australia

Mumtaz Rizwee
National Institute of Technology
Jamshedpur, India

Arzu Eren Şeneras
Bursa Uludag University
Bursa, Turkey

Hayrettin Kemal Sezen
Altinbas University
Istanbul, Turkey

William Sowry
Phare Consulting
Australia

J. Srinivas
National Institute of Technology
Rourkela, India

Supriya M. S.
M.S. Ramaiah University of Applied
    Sciences
Bangalore, India

Balazs Szikszai
Deakin University
Australia

Furkan Onur Usluer
Bursa Uludag University
Bursa, Turkey

About the Editor

Kaushik Kumar holds a PhD in engineering from Jadavpur University, India; an MBA in marketing management from Indira Gandhi National Open University, India; and a bachelor of technology from Regional Engineering College (now the National Institute of Technology), Warangal, India. For 11 years, he worked in a manufacturing unit of global repute. He is currently working as an associate professor in the Department of Mechanical Engineering, Birla Institute of Technology, Mesra, Ranchi, India. He has 22 years of teaching and research experience. His research interests include composites, optimization, non-conventional machining, CAD/CAM, rapid prototyping, and quality management systems towards product development for societal and industrial usage; for these he has received 29 Patents. He has published more than 55 books (including 31 edited book volumes that serve as textbooks and reference books by more than 40 universities and institutes in their academic curriculum), 80 book chapters, and more than 200 research papers in peer-reviewed national and international journals of repute. He has also served as editor-in-chief, series editor, guest editor, editor, editorial board member, and reviewer for international and national journals. He has been felicitated with many awards and honours including the Distinguished Alumnus Award for Professional Excellence 2023 under Academic and Research from his alma mater, the National Institute of Technology, Warangal, India. He has also received sponsored research and consultancy projects of more than 1 crore from the government of India and abroad. He has delivered expert lectures as keynote speaker at international and national conferences, and has served as a resource person at various workshops, Faculty Development Programs, and short-term courses. He has guided many students of doctoral, masters, and undergraduate programmes of his home and other institutions in India and abroad. He also has served as reviewer and examiner of doctoral and master's dissertations for institutes in India and abroad.

Section 1

Skills for Industry 4.0

Chapter 1

Skills for Industry 4.0

Navigating Uncertainty in a Digital Era

Luke Houghton and Jennifer Loy

1.1 INTRODUCTION: DIGITAL SKILLS

A key problem facing those involved in workforce planning is the growing uncertainty around the roles and responsibilities of working with maturing digital technology innovations. One of the most significant of these is artificial intelligence (AI; Basu et al., 2023), which is replacing many aspects of work that were traditionally only thought possible for humans. Another is digital manufacturing, which is enabling remote management of processes and shared inventory, which demand new ways of working. When digital technologies are aggregated and added into a society that is increasingly networked (Barney, 2004; Castells, 2009), there is a noticeable convergence effect (Iosifidis, 2002). The impact of this digital convergence has been described as disruptive (Danneels, 2004). Digital convergence in this context refers to the integration of different types of media, technology, and platforms over a consistent and common digital ecosystem (Seo, 2017). Commonly the term 'digital convergence' is used to describe the coming together of digital applications to perform an outcome. This often includes telecommunications and media forming a unified and connected network, a digital environment facilitated by mobile devices and the Internet (Matt et al., 2023). Arguably, society is moving rapidly towards a constant state of disruptive digital convergence (Hinterhuber & Stroh, 2021; Vial, 2021).

An example that illustrates the paradigm shifts digital convergence is creating is found in the entertainment industry. Consider the way recorded entertainment has been, and now is, consumed. Fifty years ago, storytelling was only available through a limited number of formats and media. Now, on-demand television, film, and video content as well as audio can be accessed through multiple devices and platforms. A similar shift to prolific production and availability can be seen in other industries (Kapoor & Lee, 2013; Wei & Pardo, 2022), and in each case, the experience of the worker in that industry has changed. For the knowledge worker in particular, digital convergence has serious implications (Lenkenhoff et al., 2018). The ability to share information across and between organisations is creating challenges (Jiang et al., 2023), just as the responsibilities of managing those interactions is becoming increasingly complex.

DOI: 10.1201/9781003486244-2

1.2 TOWARDS INDUSTRY 4.0

Table 1.1 outlines the rapid technology cycles of the last 24 years that a knowledge worker would have to navigate.

Table 1.1 Technology Cycles

Technology Cycle	Date	Transformation
Dot com bubble burst	1999–2002	Internet enters the business world; the birth of Amazon and e-commerce platforms
Web 2.0	2005–2010	Web 2.0 introduces interactive web technologies, such as Digg, MySpace, YouTube, and Facebook
Web 3.0	2006	Web 3.0 content is available across apps and devices as a single web; artificial intelligence (AI) enables computers to distinguish results based on an understanding of the meaning of words, rather than purely recognisable words, described by Tim Berners-Lee as the rise of the 'semantic web'
Smartphones	2007	Personalised computing on a smartphone introduces the idea of portable handheld computing
Cloud computing	2008	New technologies run from the web drastically decrease the cost of infrastructure for businesses and increase flexibility, portability, and scalability
Big data and analytics	2008–2010	Introducing the idea of being able to use data for more meaningful predictions based on accurate representations collected from transactions
AI and machine learning	2010	Over the past decade, digital technologies have led to increased automations in businesses and the replacement of many jobs
Blockchain	2016	Disrupted supply chains and automated authentic identity verification
5G	2017	Although slow to be introduced in countries such as Australia with vast regional areas, wireless working becomes more reliable
Remote working (COVID-19)	2020–2023	Hybrid working introduced during the pandemic, with many businesses now focusing on developing semi-permanent remote working practices
Hacking and cybersecurity changes	2023	Massive investment required to prevent bad actors from breaking into digital systems
Rapid uptake of AI, the Metaverse, and beyond, Web 4.0	2023	Accessibility to AI through developments such as ChatGPT, the increased use of automation with AI, and the emergence of Web 4.0, including the Metaverse

Studying patterns of interaction over recent years, relationships between people and machines have become more intertwined. The skills base for a graduate 25 years ago from a specialist technology discipline, such as systems analysis, would be typically narrow. However, recent graduates are expected to work with machines in a collaborative manner as using the technology becomes more intuitive. Therefore, the skill set from an undergraduate degree now tends to be seen as less technical and more collaborative and creative. As society moves through Industry 4.0 and towards Industry 5.0—characterised by a human-centric use of technology (Maddikunta et al., 2022)—the human–machine interface is designed to be increasingly accessible.

Looking beyond Industry 4.0 brings with it the need to move technical proficiency back from the forefront of computer technology and into the world of enabling technologies, an era of innovation (Aslam et al., 2020). Industry 5.0 is envisaged as a world where humans are central and technologies therefore designed to be easier to use and developmental (Nahavandi, 2019). This shift in emphasis is illustrated through the evolving of communications, as outlined in Table 1.1. Consider the example of using a web interface to build an e-commerce website to be installed in the 1990s and in the early to mid-2000s. Logistically, this would have been a difficult exercise at the time. In 2023, however, it is possible for individuals to access high-end server technology from home. As argued in recent research publications (Boobalan et al., 2022; Kukreja & Kumar, 2021; Matt et al., 2023; Xu et al., 2021), because technology has become easier to use, it is therefore more readily adopted. One illustration of the growing ease of use of technology is the Metaverse. This is a user-centred, online immersive environment that is accessible across multiple devices without specialist equipment.

In the example of the Metaverse, whilst programming for the Metaverse is still an emerging skill, the usability of the interfaces involved is significantly more palatable than a COBOL interface was in the 1980s. The need for specialist skills diminishes in exchange for an adaptable set of skills, able to handle the disruptions these technologies bring (Danneels, 2004). As the capabilities of disruptive digital technologies (Robertsone & Lapiņa, 2023; Subramaniam et al., 2019) replace technical skills' requirements, the challenge then becomes, what are the new skills required for future practice? According to the latest World Economic Forum report, analytical thinking, creative thinking, systems thinking, curiosity, lifelong learning, and adaptability are key abilities for workers in 2023. When considering recent developments in AI and natural language processing (NLP) models, and their disruptive potential, the emphasis on creativity and imagination becomes clear. Analytical thinking and systems thinking are equally critical to build solutions within the complexity frameworks that curiosity, creative thinking, and digital convergence inspire. Given the rate of change in the field, as outlined in Table 1.1, and the uncertainties that digital convergence creates, lifelong learning and adaptability are fundamental to worker development for this era.

1.3 DISRUPTIVE AMBIGUITY AND THE NEED FOR INTEGRATED SKILLS

During the past 50 years of problem-solving research, the concepts of complexity and disruption have been a focus. One of the main areas of concern has been how to manage and harness ambiguity in complex problem-solving situations. Unfortunately, this research tended to be limited to group problem-solving interventions for organisations, instead of society-wide responses (Mingers & Rosenhead, 2004; Rosenhead, 2006; Houghton & Loy, 2023). In this section, these shortcomings will be briefly examined in the context of understanding the future of work on a broader scale. This section also scopes out a possible way forward for digital era skills integration—and integrated skills—for the future.

In historical problem-solving research the idea of ambiguity as a disruptive influence is a central concept (Checkland, 1994; Weick, 1993a). The term 'disruptive ambiguity' was coined by Karl Weick (Weick, 1993b). Seen through the lens of sociology and management, disruptive ambiguity is about the unanticipated disturbances that derail expected practice. Ambiguity is therefore argued by these authors as a 'sense of not knowing', characterised by an inability to understand how the activity had been derailed (Price, 2004). An example is the emergence of a new technology that upends the market, such as was the case with Blockbuster Video when streaming disrupted conventional business models. The uncertainty created by the emerging technology is frequently only understood after the fact, hence the term 'sense making' (Weick, 1993a, 1993b).

The scale of today's disruptive ambiguity is arguably creating cognitive dissonance in which the reality of the situation is so different to established practice that it is difficult to comprehend. Think of the rise in AI and data analytics over the last few years and trying to anticipate their impacts on markets and the reshaping notions of the future of work. This can be unsettling and inevitably has destructive side effects that can exclude particular groups.

With increasing cycles of technological change come increasing cycles of ambiguity. When considering the number of disruptions caused by technological innovations over the last 20 years, as per Table 1.1, it can be argued that the degree of ambiguity and uncertainty in the work environment is stronger (Kearney et al., 2022). The rate of technological change and the need for markets to adapt means that the average knowledge worker must adapt to more frequent cycles of ambiguity and change than in previous times in history.

An illustration of this increasing speed can be seen in a comparison between the time it took for VHS technology to be replaced by DVD, and then DVD to be supplanted by streaming. Four years ago, the online short form video provider TikTok was called music.ly and was an under-subscribed platform for teenagers to share music videos. In 2019, TikTok had approximately 219 million users worldwide. By September 2023, they had 1.6 billion. This type of exponential growth is possible because of changes in how people can consume their media. TikTok now hosts a wide variety of content that is selected by algorithms based on user input. The videos are now shorter and more tailored to people's needs, and the scrollable format enables faster consumption. So strong was this disruption to the market that other platforms, such as Facebook, Instagram, Snapchat, X (formerly Twitter), and YouTube, introduced a similar video format. This shift to consuming video content online took place over a relatively short time span, disrupting advertising budgets and conventional marketing plans.

Where does this leave the knowledge worker? With this pace of technological change disrupting the workplace, the core sets of skills that a knowledge worker is likely to need to be able to adapt have changed, as identified in the latest World Economic Forum report. Broadly speaking, these skills are less technical than before because technology has become easier to use and adopt (unless the worker is a specialist in enterprise architecture or other similar field, such as cybersecurity) and as such these skills fall under the heading of 'adaptability'. A knowledge worker needs to be able to have a core set of skills that give them the ability to be flexible and adaptable no matter what environments change around them, because one thing is certain: technological change is accelerating (Matt et al., 2023).

In the following section, skills under the broad heading of adaptability are discussed to provide a set of outcomes for the knowledge worker to work towards, given the ongoing pressures of digital convergence. In summary, this argument is twofold. First, a knowledge worker must respond to the constantly changing, increasingly complex technical environment caused by digital convergence. Second, the response to this complexity and disruption is not to learn more technologies or to learn them faster, but to build an underpinning set of skills that makes one more adaptable to change. Whilst this proposal is speculative in nature, it is based on established research, as discussed in the following section.

1.4 SKILLS FOR DIGITAL CONVERGENCE

It is unlikely that the pace of change will slow down or be rationalised because it is beyond the individual's ability to control (Maddikunta et al., 2022). Author Tim Harford (2016) argues that it is better to think of ambiguity as the beginning of a change process. The world is becoming so interconnected and complex, and the pace of change extremely rapid and at a large scale, that more progress needs to be achieved in supporting individuals to meet this challenge head-on. That is, a different way of thinking or operating is required to support the workforce in constructing meaning and acceptance in a time of ambiguity. Large international bodies, such as the World Economic Forum, have mapped this trend, putting technological literacy below curiosity, and including empathy, motivation, and self-awareness on the Top 10 Skills of 2023 list (Figure 1.1).

It is interesting to note that these are not 'skills of the future', so to speak, but skills of the present that are currently in demand by the myriad of companies surveyed for the report. As part of the research, the skills of the future that would-be employers thought were necessary are different, and it's interesting to compare the difference (Figure 1.2).

Top 10 Work Skills in 2023 According to the World Economic Forum			
1	Analytical thinking *(cognitive skills)*	6	Technological literacy *(technology skills)*
2	Creative thinking *(cognitive skills)*	7	Dependability and attention to detail *(self-efficacy)*
3	Resilience, flexibility, and agility *(self-efficacy)*	8	Empathy and active listening *(working with others)*
4	Motivation and self-awareness *(self-efficacy)*	9	Leadership and social influence *(working with others)*
5	Curiosity and lifelong learning *(self-efficacy)*	10	Quality control *(management skills)*
n.b. Skills judged as greatest importance to workers at time of survey.			

Figure 1.1 World Economic Forum most in-demand skills for 2023 (World Economic Forum, 2023).

Top 10 Skills on the Rise According to the World Economic Forum			
1	Creative thinking *(cognitive skills)*	6	Systems thinking *(working with others)* Technological literacy *(technology skills)*
2	Analytical thinking *(cognitive skills)*	7	AI and Big Data *(technology skills)* Dependability and attention to detail *(self-efficacy)*
3	Technological literacy *(technology skills)*	8	Motivation and self-awareness *(self-efficacy)* Empathy and active listening *(working with others)*
4	Curiosity and lifelong learning *(self-efficacy)*	9	Talent management *(Management skills)* Leadership and social influence *(working with others)*
5	Resilience, flexibility, and agility *(self-efficacy)*	10	Service orientation and customer service *(engagement skills)* Quality control *(management skills)*
n.b. Skills judged as increasing importance most rapidly from 2023 to 2027			

Figure 1.2 World Economic Forum skills on the rise for 2023–2027 (World Economic Forum, 2023).

Employers highlighted skills such as systems thinking, AI and big data, as well as talent management, service orientation, and customer service. Returning to the argument of this chapter that the skills of the future are embedded with the use of machines, it is interesting to note that the top skills in demand appear to be creative thinking, analytical thinking, technological literacy, curiosity and lifelong learning, and resilience, flexibility, and agility. Using these identified skills as a basis, the discussion then becomes why these skills are the most important to surviving the future.

1.5 THE CYBERNETIC KNOWLEDGE WORKER

The term 'cyborg' is used in public discourse to describe the melding of people with machines (as described in James Cameron's *Terminator* films). During the First Industrial Revolution, the nature of work changed with the move from an agricultural society to an industrial one. Centralised factories and mass production machines took over the processes of production. During the information age computers rose to the forefront. In the coming cybernetic age, following on from the current Industry 4.0 era, and increasingly referred to as Industry 5.0, machines and humans will integrate for a complex working arrangement (Novak & Loy, 2018). In fact, controversial entrepreneur Elon Musk has already argued that humans are increasingly cyborg because there are many different digital versions of people on various platforms.

As work moves into a more complex era, the human as a cybernetic organism becomes increasingly realistic. This thinking is not new, it was described in the work of UK theorist and cybernetician Stafford Beer (2002), who described humans and computers collaborating through work on the viable system model. In 2023 technology is converging in every aspect of human life, with the adoption curve increasing as the complexity of the user interface decreases. Embedding AI is also enabling greater ease of user interaction, opening to a wider group of users programs that were previously the domain of specialists, such as video production, image editing, and even academic writing. Businesses still need the different technologies that are converging to integrate effectively into a business model and system. The current challenge for businesses and the knowledge worker is which bespoke pieces of technology should be integrated—and can integrate—to address a specific challenge, and how can the effects of digital convergence be anticipated and problems mitigated before their introduction. For workers there is the added complication of which technologies they learn to keep pace of the changes, and how to learn new applications created by digital convergence if there is no existing expertise and body of knowledge to learn from.

Based on current trends, as illustrated by the World Economic Forum report previously cited, employers have the perception that technological literacy will not be as important as creative thinking over the next decade. This is because of the rise of machines and systems-embedded Industry 4.0 technology mean that human beings will interact with machines as augmentations to themselves, rather than as tools to be used. People are already dependent on access to the Internet and the use of personal supercomputers in the form of mobile phones (e.g., to use maps for wayfinding, and for communication). There is also an increasing uptake of portable wearable devices that monitor the individual, such as Apple Watches. Equally, workplaces are becoming increasingly dependent on a multitude of applications to run their enterprise. On the horizon is the more comprehensive integration of work with machines on a global level. The augmentation of humans with machines is an enabler that may in the short term alter humanity's priorities and behaviours but will ultimately underpin more economically viable, connected healthcare, new ways of working anywhere and anytime, and effectively upskill a generation to take on new roles. This approach gives rise to the need for different skill sets for schools and universities. For businesses, future graduates need to have investigated the new business models enabled by digital convergence and augmented human activities. In the following section, these potential skills are discussed in the context of how they will be used to support the augmented knowledge workers to live and thrive in the digital age.

1.6 THE HUMAN–MACHINE COMPLEX

Humans and machines have long been learning to work—and live—together. Taken to the extreme, this could point towards a future where neural chips or Internet of Things devices will be inserted into the bloodstream or under the skin as a matter of course (Haleem & Javaid, 2019). Researchers have proposed many times the possibility of transhumanism. However, before then, the knowledge worker will increasingly work with AI to augment their skills—and augmented intelligence—and access real-time intelligence through communication technology, such as augmented reality. In addition, tools are emerging for greater collaboration online, which in itself is a form of augmented intelligence. If a worker can access meaningful collaborative insights in real time—and becomes dependent on that information sharing, surely that is a stepping stone to transhumanism.

It is unlikely that in the near future, employers will ask employees to submit to communication and monitoring chips to be inserted into their brains. However, many organisations are using as 'software as a service' as a way of making their operations more visible, and integrating workers' everyday activities and interactive software solutions. Whatever the case, the knowledge worker is likely to become ever more integrated with the machine as time goes on, in essence becoming a cybernetic organism.

The augmentation of humanity by machines is a significant theme for this generation. The challenge for the next generation is developing a skill set that supports being cognitively flexible enough to work with machines akin to early-stage evolution for man-plus-machine. The 'human–machine concept' refers to work that includes integrated technological architecture that is relatively easy to use because of a reduction in complexity in interface design. For the knowledge worker of this generation, as is often the case within large organisations, they are faced with navigating a world where technology convergence is slowly adopted by large risk-averse corporations who have a focus on short-term profits to maintain shareholder commitment.

1.7 MELDING WITH THE MACHINE

In this section it is assumed that future knowledge workers will all be techno-logically literate. This assumes that in the future these devices and applications will become significantly easier to use, unless they are specialist applications that require a high degree of knowledge. As discussed, the World Economic Forum report highlights skills needed for future practice. The skills identified are ana-lytical thinking, creative thinking, curiosity and lifelong learning, adaptability and systems thinking (Table 1.2).

These skills are not separate but are part of an interlinked and interdependent set of skills that the future knowledge worker will need to succeed.

During the history of technology, as discussed earlier, technology has become easier to use. The classic story of the rise of Apple and the downfall of Nokia is often used to demonstrate the inability of large companies to adapt, but in reality, it is a story of technology adoption. As mentioned previously, theory has suggested for some time that when technology becomes easier to use, it becomes easier to

Table 1.2 Skills Rationale

Skill of the Future	Justification
Analytical thinking	Skill is needed to frame hypotheses for testing and the development of robust processes to measure the effectiveness of the proposals
Creative thinking	Skill is needed to craft creative solutions and work with machines to deliver those solutions
Curiosity and lifelong learning	Skills needed to identify the learnings required for emerging technology landscapes and changing practices/having an open-growth mindset to skills adoption and a positive attitude to change
Adaptability	A set of complex problem-solving skills, a growth mindset, the ability to adapt to new environments, stress and well-being management for the rapid onset, and relentless continuation of technological change
Systems thinking	Skills to understand 'big picture thinking' and the leverage points that make systems work

adopt (Mueller, 1999). When comparing the different offerings from the two communication giants back in the early 2000s, the iPhone was easier to use but had much the same functionality as the Nokia phone did. The ease of use (Pavlou & Fygenson, 2006) of the phone was arguably what made it a game changer for most people. These developments in the early 2000s led to a shift in how theorists thought about technology adoption. In most developing countries at the time, the use of mobile devices drastically outstripped the use of desktop devices. Android phones flooded the market, making it easy to connect even where the power supply was limited.

When considering the modern phone and the connectedness of humanity via apps, people have, arguably, begun to merge with machines. Perhaps it is not as science fiction would have predicted, but with developments in AI, less technical expertise will be needed to be a successful knowledge worker in the future. The interface will take care of the complexity and be an ever-present technical assistant that will help humans make decisions that are complex but also require creativity and critical thought.

In the next section, the term 'artificial heart of the enterprise' is used to extend this metaphor to discuss what this might look like. Of concern to the authors is how skills evolve when technology is much easier to use and adopt. At the time of writing, companies such as Ford have argued that traditional manufacturers can now be considered software companies. What does this mean for the future of the enterprise?

1.8 THE ARTIFICIAL HEART OF THE ENTERPRISE

In science fiction, such as *The Minority Report* by Philip K. Dick written in 1956, there has been an assumption that technology will drive decision-making and collaboration in the future. Early thinkers in this space, such as Stafford Beer (2002), described the need for corporations to create a practical set of cybernetic skills to be able to cope with the complexity that technology would bring to an enterprise. Beer designed an information system for the Chilean government in the 1970s that would run their entire government services and automate the majority of important decisions (Discussion & Beer, 2000). This experiment failed due to a political coup but held the promise of being an early example of what would now be termed e-government (Beer, 2002). For it to work, technology would need to be part of a managerial system that could automate key tasks and create a sense of intelligence inside the firm that would outlast any management group, the proposal being that complexity could be managed by a system that was designed to be cybernetic (Stephens & Haslett, 2005).

The introduction of AI and recent rise of NLP models suggest that this might be achievable in the not-too-distant future. The problem until now is that technology adds processes and does not necessarily bring the levels of automation or intelligence required for the system to be effective. Take, for example, the long history of research on enterprise resource planning (ERP). The level of work required to operate at a reliable level of efficiency has frequently made ERP software and systems unviable. Overall, systems holding the promise of intelligent automation assisting human decision-making in complex situations are only now realistically emerging.

Keeping track of numerous, interconnected, deployed software frameworks is challenging, particularly with respect to making sure that access to the knowledge contained therein can be controlled. The challenge is how to automate a layer of intelligence to differentiate the contexts and constraints.

An emerging solution is to build digital twins of the process library of software solutions and create user interfaces that mean authorised persons could inquire about capabilities inside the software framework. In a similar way to J.A.R.V.I.S. (Just a Rather Very Intelligent System) described in the *Iron Man* comic books and movies, the systems should provide an intelligent digital twin of multiple software frameworks. Digital twins are used as virtual replicas of objects, systems, and processes (Huang et al., 2022). Generally, they are used as a simulation to track operations, and, to a lesser extent, take control of the real-world version through networked inputs. An example would be the use of digital twins in Formula One car racing. A virtual model of each car is used for simulation testing. The replica is used to replace, augment, or even redesign physical processes. Data would be collected on the actual use of the software frameworks and how they are applied by an internal application program interface (API) whilst collecting data on each process and comparisons between cycles. This data could be anything from the application of a framework to a specific business problem, to the modelling of a certain piece of software to deliver a business process or how often data is sent to and from the cloud in any application. The digital twin can be programmed to perform analysis of the simulation and identify issues the company may not be aware of. For example, a simulation may highlight where business operations are related across multiple projects, highlighting the potential to add efficiencies into the system. The simulation the digital twin runs can uncover insights, to be actioned and turned into automated processes using other software tools. These are then applied back to the use and deployment of these frameworks, with machine learning and AI employed for analysis and synthesis of the processes involved.

Another use case of this system would be in the shared deployment of a software framework that is often used but adapted for clients. The digital twin could use the data provided to model out a simulation on the implications of deployment automated across different client bases, including time and resources. It could also theoretically provide suggestions for troubleshooting and optimising performance over time.

Digital twins, characteristic of Industry 4.0, provide an ongoing feedback loop that can be applied to the software frameworks over time and therefore help them to bring optimisations to both the allocation of resource and the development of future software frameworks. For example, the system deployed can analyse all the frameworks currently in use and look for similarities to model and simulate what would happen when those similarities were combined into one singular process, rather than a myriad of executable processes. The digital twin will learn from the data and make increasingly accurate predictions on how to identify issues before they happen. In the example of sharing software frameworks, it would be able to make new suggestions based on the existing patterns of work behaviour and data fed into it. This leads to continuous learning in which the digital twin takes the data it learns and uses it to improve real-world processes.

The goal for software companies is to build a complete AI-driven model that has comprehensive data from inside the corporation fed into both an NLP model and an inbuilt knowledge base to which data is consistently added. The adding of this data enables the improvement of results from the digital twin and a degree of intelligence to the use of searching for data and software frameworks from inside the business. By drawing on this API the company could ask questions of it in a similar way to how people can ask questions of the AI program, ChatGPT version 4 (the latest at the time of writing). This could be asking a question about which software framework would be used to develop what application for a basic example and how it might be deployed at the client site.

The total goal would be to make the heart of the corporation completely digital. Ultimately it would mean that a client could approach their business with a project idea on how to use the software. Within a short period of time, a basic framework could be built based on this input and the existing digital twin, plus data inside the company and a reasonable prediction of details, such as price, scope, and design to reduce time and personnel. Practically, it would mean that the machine would take control of the existing processes and with the input of data could build real-time predictions with a fraction of the time involved. With an 'artificial heart' in the company through a commitment to a comprehensive artificial intelligent system and digital twin, companies could build deployable frameworks to a client site in a fraction of the time and resources. Almost any enterprise where processes are used and automation is possible could employ a degree of AI and digital twin, and it is likely to become more prevalent in the future.

1.9 INTO THE METAVERSE

One interesting development in digital technology in recent times has been the proposition created by the Metaverse concept. In essence, this is a virtual platform in which 3D avatars are used to interact and perform certain tasks in the online world. Whilst this proposal was initially envisaged as a communication space, engineering and design tools are increasingly being developed and tested for the Metaverse. This is interesting not only from a technical perspective but also in relation to its impacts on workflow. The link between Industry 4.0 digital threads and digital twins, and now modelling practice within the Metaverse, is growing. This development is arguably a step change in practice for digital transformation illustrating the use of digital convergence as the basis for more flexible, accessible, and critically more autonomous enterprise mobility.

For a large country, such as Australia, where markets tend to be dispersed, the prospect of a more comprehensive shift to an immersive Industry 4.0 profile for an organisation, such as a connected Metaverse, has the potential to enable asymmetric advantage. This concept comes from finance, where asymmetry refers to an advantage that comes from multiple different angles in a network and returns are adjusted in relation to different points of view. For example, the concept of the 'loss leader' in business, that is a product that may be sold at a loss to attract attention in the market, refers to the concept of asymmetric returns. A company may also put out a product at break even or at a loss to sell second- and third-tier products, which give an asymmetric advantage. In the training industry, for example, this might be a master class that is offered at low cost so that more expensive training can be sold to the people who registered, without needing additional advertising. This raises the overall cost per acquisition but also provides asymmetric returns magnifying and multiplying the lifetime value of the customer. In the world of hedge funds, the term 'asymmetry' refers to using different funding sources that balance in favour of the investor. Insurance agencies often pay out small amounts to customers but receive an asymmetric return when customers keep paying premiums every year. The insurance business provides asymmetric returns through these payments because not every person who is a customer will make a claim.

The Metaverse combines digital technologies, the Internet, and 3D technology in increasingly interesting ways. People involved in the Metaverse can be located at strategic vantage points anywhere, and this can provide asymmetric advantage. Spreading resources across multiple locations on multiple fronts, each additional positional difference giving a small return, then their return compounds together could provide an advantage. This is still in its infancy, but the potential is interesting and the technology increasingly sophisticated, as is the thinking.

1.10 THE METAVERSE AND ASYMMETRIC WARFARE

The conflict between Ukraine and Russia that began in 2022, when Russia invaded its neighbour, has provided numerous examples of asymmetric warfare, where Ukraine's investment in agile thinking and digital technology has helped the country to defend against an arguably overwhelming force. Whilst Russia has relied on conventional warfare methods, with consolidated forces and heavy artillery, Ukraine has subverted the battlespace by employing a strategy of deploying distributed artillery, focusing on smaller armaments of lower cost as part of a more guerrilla warfare approach (Porter, 2023). In particular, Ukraine has invested heavily in the use of drones. According to the European Council on Foreign Relations

(Söderström & Franke, 2023), although drones have been used in multiple conflicts, including the Vietnam War, 'The Ukraine battlespace features the most intensive use of drones in a military conflict in history, marking a shift in warfare tactics and technology.' This approach allows the Ukraine military to build and deploy low-cost armaments from numerous sites for reconnaissance and to deliver missiles. The challenge for an opposing force is keeping track of a myriad of small groups of adversaries, rather than meeting a single force head-on. For the Ukrainians, the ability to move around reduces their vulnerability. This does, however, create communication and tracking difficulties from their side.

In other countries there is an awareness of the vulnerability of centralised forces. Large bases are inevitable targets and therefore vulnerable. For some countries, such as Australia which is a very large country, the prospect of introducing agile basing could reduce those vulnerabilities and, at the very least, provide outposts of resistance should they be required. Taken to its extreme for the future, it may be that fully mobile and flexible basing would provide an asymmetric advantage against a larger foe. In such a scenario, effective, comprehensive communication strategies would need to be in place. Conventional communication platforms at this time tend to be generic and do little to add value to distributed practice specifically. There is no sense of place or relative position, or inventory or operational dependencies or efficiencies articulated by a conventional communication platform. However, if a Metaverse, supported by a digital twin, was strategically developed for agile basing, then it may be able to provide the means to frame, visualise and manage facilities that were constantly on the move. This would support logistics and decision-making and provide the organisation overall with a virtual sense of place where a physical base was missing.

Building real estate within the Metaverse involves creating connected spaces, which can be visualised and navigated using a map. The spaces themselves can be created bespoke to the organisation's needs, and can include areas to socialise and break into smaller meetings. It is possible to use cameras so that an individual's face can be seen overlaid on their avatar and sound works as in the real world, whereas as a person moves away, their voice becomes fainter. If Australia were to adopt a drone manufacturing, agile-based approach using the Metaverse and digital twins combined with digital manufacturing, then it would be possible to have the designers in one location and manufacturers in another, and even the operators in yet another, driving using augmented reality. This is a totally networked, immersive approach enabled by digital convergence that represents a paradigm shift in practice. It is only now a possibility because of Industry 4.0 and Web 4.0 and has the potential to provide asymmetric advantage if the investment in processes and organisational reform is made now.

Drawing on the skills argument from earlier, the move towards the Metaverse being a totally networked and immersive approach requires the person operating in it to think critically and creatively. For example, how would a design team create in such an environment if they're used to working in an office? If a threat emerged, how quickly can people assemble into the Metaverse and build a drone, and from that, how quickly can it be deployed if the key people involved are dispersed across wide geographical areas?

In the Ukraine example, they didn't solve this problem by having heavy technical skills, although that was a part of it to some extent. They used networked thinking. Instead of relying on traditional military techniques that are often used in battle, they relied on hiring a chief technology officer (CTO) from a start-up to run the technological infrastructure behind their resistance. The agile thinking required to be a CTO is usually focused on a combination of what technical stack to use to reach a business goal and the best methods of deployment of using that technology, as well as what specialists to use. This is a strategic position that uses systems thinking but also draws on the concepts of a networked and integrated workplace.

The CTO in this situation coordinates responses built on the assets in the network. If the Metaverse was active during this time, the CTO or advanced knowledge worker would have access to the assets required to deploy a response and be able to marshal the team together online to make that happen. In theory, future technology could be used to autonomously build a missile to respond to a threat or create a specialised drone to be deployed on demand after being specified by an online group of workers acting in concert in a Metaverse environment. What underpins this is the idea of a dispersed community working across the broad geographical distance, thinking creatively and knowing how to deploy that technology in a networked environment.

1.11 THE NETWORK

The network for any organisation adopting the possibilities this immersive approach allows would contain a variety of activity hubs and spokes, but these would be virtual based rather than physical, and therefore able to move locations in the real world whilst remaining in contact in the virtual one. Employees can operate within a Metaverse with very little additional equipment. Unlike virtual or augmented reality, the Metaverse does not require headsets or projectors. It is possible to access through most standard devices, such as desktop computer, laptop, tablet, or phone, though interacting within the Metaverse is currently easier using a computer with a wired mouse, mostly for latency reasons. The Metaverse does need to have seats booked in a particular location (though this can be a country-wide location) with whoever is hosting the service. Service providers currently include Amazon and Azure.

Distributed manufacturing hubs themselves can be very small units if the application allows. Unlike traditional manufacturing, a small number of digital manufacturing machines are needed to take the object from concept to production—within the limitations of those processes. With digital fabrication and digital twins, the blueprint of an object can be contained in a digital inventory, which can be updated or adapted in one location, and sent digitally to another for production. This does create vulnerabilities, particularly with respect to cybercrime, but it also allows for continuous updating of a product for a genuinely adaptable manufacturing strategy. This creates a short-run strategy over a conventional mass production one.

Another interesting development in the Metaverse is the ability to bring real-world data relatively easily into the space. 3D scans can be used to build an accurate environmental model as the basis for the Metaverse, and increasingly sophisticated technology for converting 2D data to 3D is making highly detailed 3D views accessible. At the time of writing, Gaussian splatting enables nanites in software, such as Epic's Unreal Engine, to enable building high-resolution 3D models. As Gaussian Splatting and similar applications evolve, the Metaverse environment will become increasing accessible and realistic. This suggests that business and organisations need to invest in this now to be better prepared for the future of work. For Defence, the most interesting promise of this technology is the idea that people can be immersed in a 3D environment and not be on the battlefield but be creating responses to emerging threats as they happen, because they can network with others in the virtual environment across military silos.

Early examples of this can be seen in the recent skirmishes in Ukraine and Russia. If the Metaverse was involved, then it could have given an advantage in terms of networking, collaboration, and dispersal. In theory it could allow for conventionally divided silos across Defence to coexist but also to deploy resources in a horizontally integrated manner. For example, if there were personnel on the eastern side talking to personnel on the western side, then they could converse within the Metaverse, sharing virtual resources is and talking about strategy in real time—even whilst their forces were active. In the Metaverse they could design, model products, and schedule for deployment. The complexity of engaging online is reduced because the interface is more instinctive than traditional online collaboration tools, enabling more freedom in creative thinking and allowing for a desperate group to be more adaptable.

1.12 TRAINED TO THINK RATHER THAN TO USE

These kinds of digital technologies move the idea of a use case from the end of the process towards the beginning of it. That is, designers and others involved in bringing this kind of technology into practice can start to think about the advantage the technology and test that advantage quickly, rather than wait years for it to be developed as in conventional practice. Software in organisations such as customer relationship management is becoming intuitive because of the development of intelligence technology. This moves the thinking from looking at the machine as framing the process to thinking about what might be achieved if one worked with the machine. As Industry 4.0 technology becomes more integrated into practice, and digital convergence adds layers of capability, thinking increasingly revolves around what can be achieved creatively with machines, rather than mimicking existing practices but more efficiently with the aid of the technology. This returns to preparing for the use of these technologies to the central thesis of this enquiry, what will the world look like once machines are fully 'intelligent' and autonomous, and what are the challenges for the future in developing skills for humans to maximise these capabilities and not be replaced by them?

1.13 REFRAMING DIGITAL UPSKILLING

So far in this chapter it has been argued that there is a new set of skills required due to the fact that machines and humans will need to work together in some kind of cybernetic fashion. What has happened in the past is that organisations have relied on technology training to cover this gap. As society moves into the newer world in which humans and machines will work together, the way these skills are developed and trained will have to change. Google certification, for example, now allows people to pick up a skill in six weeks that they can then use in their careers (e.g., https://grow.google/intl/ALL_au/certificates/). Traditionally, universities and higher education institutions have filled this gap. Admittedly, most of these courses are technical in nature and aimed towards filling gaps in the professional information technology sector. However, in preparation for Industry 4.0 and 5.0, these skills could be out of date as soon as five years.

In fact, early signs of this are on the horizon. Consider the aforementioned World Economic Forum Report on Skills (World Economic Forum, 2023). The pipeline problem mentioned in this report refers to the problem modern organisations are having with retaining and recruiting Generation Z talent. Although many companies perhaps did not invest in this past the pandemic, good-quality talent are objecting to a return to the office, even now the threat of the pandemic has passed. Employees want the lifestyle of choosing when and how they want to work, and the pandemic has demonstrated that this can be possible. Given the current talent shortages, certainly in Australia, companies are forced to offer remote or hybrid working as an option. As time goes on, these workplaces are likely to become more hybrid (Haan, 2023). The Metaverse is a complex an as yet untested environment for remote communications and real-time work. Digital upskilling therefore needs to be thought of as learning to work with machines not only for practical tasks, but for communication and engagement. The learning curve required to successfully adapt to this environment is not technical, rather it is social and practical. For example, when moving into the world of creative thinking and finding useful ways to deploy new technologies using a hybrid networked Metaverse environment, the question is how can it be used to make employees more productive instead of simply replicating existing outputs? Digital upskilling would therefore not be how to use the Metaverse effectively to leverage teamwork where it is not possible for everyone to be in the same room together.

Google runs a course on the technical skills required to run a successful e-commerce business. These skills point towards the use of Google's product to encourage more people into a business, such as a store. The skill set required to run ads on Google is a technical skill set, but arguably absent are elements such as designing customer discovery, concept testing, and the use of creative thinking and adaptability for mapping, for example for seasonal offers and fluctuations in the market. Current certificate skills programs are frequently framed as the future for education, but these tend to lack the additional aspects of education that will help the individual to be successful. Technical skills in a digital environment are not enough. Additional skills include how to create lifetime value by building a relationship with the customer and exploiting emerging technology to better serve the customer journey. The world of digital upskilling needs to change.

Cybersecurity is inevitably a key issue in this realm. As hackers become better at breaking into systems, it could reach a point where a small number of people engage in creating protective computer science models, whilst most of the team have to think creatively about working around a breach. Addressing a network exploit involves technical skills, but it also requires imagination and lateral thinking to recognise or anticipate possible vulnerabilities. For example, consider the unexpected threat to solar rooftop panels. According to a recent report (ACSM_Editor, 2023), solar panels are a leading cause of breaches for many organisations because hackers understand they operate on a networked environment, and it is possible to use the same network access to breach the company operating systems.

A leading skill in the future of any cybersecurity analyst will be understanding bridge patterns and their use to divide a system into several hierarchies. Creative thinking and an agile mindset will be needed to help employees adapt the workings of a company to avoid potential breaches on a continuous basis. In addition, companies need to be able to adapt to significant disruptions such as COVID-19. No amount of technical knowledge or technical literacy on its own will help them create step-change innovation in the face of challenges such as supply chain disruption. It is key that the future workforce be imaginative, collaborative, and resilient in a rapidly changing digital era.

1.14 DISCUSSION

In Table 1.3, the skills from Table 1.2 are shown with possible approaches as to how these could be applied to adapt to the use of emerging technologies.

It is clear that skills development needs to be considered from a new perspective. It is interesting to consider how sets of skills need to evolve to support the development of coherent models of original thought for dealing with digital convergence. The skills to work effectively with machines in the future need to enable the user to move between different states and to consider different angles of a

Table 1.3 Applications

Skill of the Future	Application
Analytical thinking	Using artificial intelligence to find interesting ways to solve old problems, such as finding new chains of reasoning and programming design
Creative thinking	Responding to the possibilities of digital convergence with original solutions
Curiosity and lifelong learning	Exploring new angles to create programmes and finding ways to develop asymmetric advantages by using technology in new and interesting ways to support creative innovation
Adaptability	Adjusting thinking to automated human thinking through the use of intelligent machines that can suggest new programmatic structures
Systems thinking	Seeing how the systems can be built together to create outcomes to solve complex issues at a strategic level; that is, building automated and digitally enhanced systems to create new programmes and connectivity

problem. For example, they will need to understand how AI and machine learning could be applied to a new scenario, and to build an innovative framework and prompts for this approach. This is largely because the complexity of programming machines has become foundational rather than at the interface, and the design of what might be achieved using these machines leads to more creative thinking. This creative thinking might be about synthesis, bringing together disparate parts of a system previously not thought of as connected. It is likely to involve agile working and continuous adaptation. History has demonstrated that when technologies become easier to use and their level of AI integration increases, humans will find creative and useful ways to exploit them.

The challenge now is what to build with the synergistic technologies now available. This is a question for society, but at an organisational sector level, how can a company future-proof by exploiting these technologies, and what skills should they develop in their workforce in preparation? Do those projected by the World Economic Forum report go far enough? Should companies be thinking about other skills? Or could it be that the value placed on the different skills should be weighted to emphasise aspects such as curiosity at this time of transition?

The central point is the design of a human future that goes beyond continuing along the same paths that society has walked previously, with the same problems, such as unsustainability. Could digital convergence be used to bring advantage to a greater whole, rather than perpetuating current issues and inequalities? The skills referenced in this chapter are arguably the foundational skills needed in the new world of digital convergence. This is because the methods of working with machines when AI is incorporated are evident, but the direction is not. People need to question practice to see a big picture to exploit the potential of these machines. Even now, there are AI-driven machines that are intelligent, but their applications are uncertain, especially when creating a positive picture for society is a factor. Skills for a future living with digital technology therefore need to be framed as intellectual rather than technical. Industry 4.0 is the first opportunity humanity has had to reimagine the world of work enabled by the paradigm shifts that digital convergence allows. It is therefore arguably the right time to rethink the relationship of workers and technology, and the priorities for the skills needed to effectively and humanely operate emerging digital systems.

1.15 CONCLUSION

This chapter discussed the changing skills required for businesses adapting to the opportunities and challenges that Industry 4.0 provides. Over the last decade, digital technologies have converged to create a digital era, where Industry 4.0 and digital skills have combined to create step-change in practice across industries. In many ways, the headlong development of digital technologies has itself been disrupted with the realisation that convergence and layering of digital technology is creating such radically new ways of working that it is the thinking that needs to catch up. It is no longer enough to upskill workers technically; there needs to be a mindset change to be able to shape businesses to exploit the technology available. In addition, the ability to continuously adapt, both in terms of business model development and in thinking about practice and operations, is as critical as building the system itself. Core skills for the future were considered in relation to digital convergence and the differences between being a knowledge worker in the past to the near future. Finally, it was suggested that the use of digital technologies described within an Industry 4.0 framework require a vision and a deeper sense of purpose in relation to their contribution to human achievement. This arguably leads society beyond Industry 4.0 and the capabilities it creates, towards what is defined as Industry 5.0, where humans are at the centre of the machine-enabled environment. The point made is that the future should not involve workers adapting to single machines, but collaborations where people and digital capabilities merge in new ways to create positive benefit for all stakeholders, not inhibited by past actions and assumptions. The question remains what to do with digital technological capabilities to redirect the future.

REFERENCES

ACSM_Editor. (2023, August 13). Cyber vulnerabilities identified in Australia's rooftop solar systems. *Australian Cybersecurity Magazine.* https://australiancybersecuritymagazine.com.au/cyber-vulnerabilities-identified-in-australias-rooftop-solar-systems/
Aslam, F., Aimin, W., Li, M., & Rehman, K. U. (2020). Innovation in the era of IoT and industry 5.0: Absolute innovation management (AIM) framework. *Information (Switzerland)*, *11*(2). https://doi.org/10.3390/INFO11020124

Barney, D. D. (2004). *The Network Society*. Polity Press.

Basu, S., Majumdar, B., Mukherjee, K., Munjal, S., & Palaksha, C. (2023). Artificial intelligence–HRM interactions and outcomes: A systematic review and causal configurational explanation. *Human Resource Management Review*, *33*(1), 100893. https://doi.org/10.1016/J.HRMR.2022.100893

Beer, S. (2002). What is cybernetics? *Kybernetes*, *31*(2), 209–219. https://doi.org/10.1108/03684920210417283/FULL/HTML

Boobalan, P., Ramu, S. P., Pham, Q. V., Dev, K., Pandya, S., Maddikunta, P. K. R., Gadekallu, T. R., & Huynh-The, T. (2022). Fusion of federated learning and industrial internet of things: A survey. *Computer Networks*, *212*. https://doi.org/10.1016/j.comnet.2022.109048

Castells, M. (2009). *The Rise of the Network Society*. John Wiley & Sons.

Checkland, P. (1994). Systems theory and management thinking. *American Behavioral Scientist*, *38*(1), 75–91. https://doi.org/10.1177/0002764294038001007

Danneels, E. (2004). Disruptive technology reconsidered: A critique and research agenda. *Journal of Product Innovation Management*, *21*(4), 246–258. https://doi.org/10.1111/J.0737-6782.2004.00076.X

Discussion and Beer, S. (2000). Ten pints of Beer: The rationale of Stafford Beer's cybernetic books (1959-94). *Kybernetes*, *29*(5/6), 558–572. https://doi.org/10.1108/03684920010333044

Haan, K. (2023, June 12). Remote work statistics and trends in 2023. *Forbes*. https://www.forbes.com/advisor/business/remote-work-statistics/

Haleem, A., & Javaid, M. (2019). Industry 5.0 and its expected applications in medical field. *Current Medicine Research and Practice*, *9*(4), 167–169. https://doi.org/10.1016/j.cmrp.2019.07.002

Harford, T. (2016). *Messy*. Little Brown Book Group.

Hinterhuber, A., & Stroh, S. (2021). The three pillars of digital transformation. *Managing Digital Transformation*, 67–72. https://doi.org/10.4324/9781003008637-5/THREE-PILLARS-DIGITAL-TRANSFORMATION-ANDREAS-HINTERHUBER-STEFAN-STROH

Houghton, L., & Loy, J. (2023). Living and thriving under ambiguity. *Air/Space*, 33146637. http://doi.org/58930/bp33146637

Huang, P. H., Kim, K. H., & Schermer, M. (2022). Ethical issues of digital twins for personalized health care service: Preliminary mapping study. *Journal of Medical Internet Research*, *24*(1). https://doi.org/10.2196/33081 WE—Science Citation Index Expanded (SCI-EXPANDED) WE—Social Science Citation Index (SSCI)

Iosifidis, P. (2002). Digital convergence: Challenges for European regulation. *Javnost*, *9*(3), 27–47. https://doi.org/10.1080/13183222.2002.11008805

Jiang, H., Yang, J., & Gai, J. (2023). How digital platform capability affects the innovation performance of SMEs—Evidence from China. *Technology in Society*, *72*. https://doi.org/10.1016/j.techsoc.2022.102187

Kapoor, R., & Lee, J. M. (2013). Coordinating and competing in ecosystems: How organizational forms shape new technology investments. *Strategic Management Journal*, *34*(3), 274–296. https://doi.org/10.1002/SMJ.2010

Kearney, A., Harrington, D., & Rajwani, T. (2022). Strategy making in hyper uncertainty: towards a conceptual framework from the seaport industry during Brexit. *International Journal of Organizational Analysis*. https://doi.org/10.1108/IJOA-04-2022-3255/FULL/PDF

Kukreja, R., & Kumar, R. (2021). Catalytic agents for easy adoption of industry 5.0—Indian context. *2021 9th International Conference on Reliability, Infocom Technologies and Optimization (Trends and Future Directions), ICRITO 2021.* https://doi.org/10.1109/ICRITO51393.2021.9596187

Lenkenhoff, K., Wilkens, U., Zheng, M., Süße, T., Kuhlenkötter, B., & Ming, X. (2018). Key challenges of digital business ecosystem development and how to cope with them. *Procedia CIRP, 73,* 167–172. https://doi.org/10.1016/j.procir.2018.04.082

Maddikunta, P. K. R., Pham, Q. V. B. P., Deepa, N., Dev, K., Gadekallu, T. R., Ruby, R., & Liyanage, M. (2022). Industry 5.0: A survey on enabling technologies and potential applications. *Journal of Industrial Information Integration, 26,* 100257. https://doi.org/10.1016/J.JII.2021.100257

Matt, D. T., Pedrini, G., Bonfanti, A., & Orzes, G. (2023). Industrial digitalization. A systematic literature review and research agenda. *European Management Journal, 41*(1), 47–78. https://doi.org/10.1016/j.emj.2022.01.001

Mingers, J., & Rosenhead, J. (2004). Problem structuring methods in action. *European Journal of Operational Research, 152*(3), 530–554. https://doi.org/10.1016/S0377-2217(03)00056-0

Mueller, M. (1999). Digital convergence and its consequences. *Javnost—The Public, 6*(3), 11–27. https://doi.org/10.1080/13183222.1999.11008716

Nahavandi, S. (2019). Industry 5.0-a human-centric solution. *Sustainability (Switzerland), 11*(16). https://doi.org/10.3390/SU11164371

Novak, J., & Loy, J. (2018). Digital technologies and 4D customized design: Challenging conventions with responsive design. Eds. V. C. Bryan, A. T. Musgrove, & Jillian R. Powers, *The Handbook of Research on Human Development in the Digital Age,* pp 403–406. IGI Global. https://doi.org/10.4018/978-1-5225-2838-8.ch018

Pavlou, P. A., & Fygenson, M. (2006). Understanding and predicting electronic commerce adoption: An extension of the theory of planned behavior. *MIS Quarterly: Management Information Systems, 30*(1), 115–143. https://doi.org/10.2307/25148720

Porter, P. (2023). Out of the shadows: Ukraine and the shock of non-hybrid war. *Journal of Global Security Studies, 8*(3), ogad014.

Price, I. (2004). Complexity, complicatedness and complexity: A new science behind organizational intervention? *E:CO, 6*(1–2), 40–48.

Robertsone, G., & Lapiņa, I. (2023). Digital transformation as a catalyst for sustainability and open innovation. *Journal of Open Innovation: Technology, Market, and Complexity, 9*(1). https://doi.org/10.1016/j.joitmc.2023.100017

Rosenhead, J. (2006). Past, present and future of problem structuring methods. *Journal of the Operational Research Society, 57*(7), 759–765. https://doi.org/10.1057/PALGRAVE.JORS.2602206

Seo, D. B. (2017). Digital business convergence and emerging contested fields: A conceptual framework. *Journal of the Association for Information Systems, 18*(10), 3. https://doi.org/10.17705/1jais.00471

Söderström, J., & Franke, U. (2023, September 5). Star tech enterprise: Emerging technologies in Russia's war on Ukraine. *ECFR.* https://ecfr.eu/publication/star-tech-enterprise-emerging-technologies-in-russias-war-on-ukraine/

Stephens, J. R., & Haslett, T. (2005). Peirce and Beer. *Systemic Practice and Action Research, 18*(5), 519–530. https://doi.org/10.1007/S11213-005-8486-2/METRICS

Subramaniam, M., Iyer, B., & Venkatraman, V. (2019). Competing in digital ecosystems. *Business Horizons*, *62*(1), 83–94. https://doi.org/10.1016/J.BUSHOR.2018.08.013

Vial, G. (2021). Understanding digital transformation: A review and a research agenda. *Managing Digital Transformation*, 13–66. https://doi.org/10.4324/9781003008637-4

Wei, R., & Pardo, C. (2022). Artificial intelligence and SMEs: How can B2B SMEs leverage AI platforms to integrate AI technologies? *Industrial Marketing Management*, *107*, 466–483. https://doi.org/10.1016/j.indmarman.2022.10.008

Weick, K. (1993a). Collective mind in organizations: Heedful interrelating on flight decks. *Administrative Science Quarterly*, *38*(3), 357–381. www.jstor.org/stable/10.2307/2393372

Weick, K. (1993b). The collapse of sensemaking in the organizations: Mann Gulch disaster. *Administrative Science Quarterly*, *38*(4), 628–652. www.jstor.org/stable/10.2307/2393339

World Economic Forum. (2023, April 30). The future of jobs report 2023. *World Economic Forum*. https://www.weforum.org/publications/the-future-of-jobs-report-2023/

Xu, X., Lu, Y., Vogel-Heuser, B., & Wang, L. (2021). Industry 4.0 and industry 5.0–inception, conception and perception. *Journal of Manufacturing Systems*, *61*, 530–535. https://doi.org/10.1016/J.JMSY.2021.10.006

Section II

Healthcare and Industry 4.0

Chapter 2

Comprehensive Insights and Systematic Integration of the Fourth Industrial Revolution and Lean Concepts in the Healthcare Sector

T. Nivethitha, Kishore Kumar, and P. K. Poonguzhali

2.1 INTRODUCTION

The Fourth Industrial Revolution encompasses a wide range of technologies, including the Internet of Things (IoT), artificial intelligence (AI), robotics, big data analytics, and cloud computing [1]. These technologies offer new opportunities to collect, analyse, and leverage vast amounts of healthcare data [2], leading to improved diagnostics, personalized treatment plans, and enhanced patient monitoring. Additionally, the Fourth Industrial Revolution enables the automation of routine tasks, reducing human error and freeing up healthcare professionals to focus on more complex and critical care activities.

On the other hand, Lean principles, derived from the Toyota Production System, emphasize the identification and elimination of waste within processes. By applying Lean concepts to healthcare, organizations can streamline workflows, reduce waiting times, optimize inventory management, and enhance patient flow. Lean thinking promotes a culture of continuous improvement, empowering frontline staff to identify areas for enhancement and implement changes that positively impact patient care.

The integration of the Fourth Industrial Revolution [3] and Lean concepts in the healthcare sector holds tremendous potential. By combining the power of digital technologies with a systematic approach to process optimization, healthcare organizations can create a more efficient and patient-centric environment. For instance, implementing IoT-enabled devices and wearables can provide real-time patient data, enabling healthcare professionals to make timely decisions and intervene proactively. AI algorithms can assist in analysing medical images, helping radiologists detect abnormalities with greater accuracy and efficiency.

Furthermore, the application of Lean principles can lead to significant improvements in the delivery of care. Lean methodologies such as value-stream mapping (VSM) and standardized work can help identify bottlenecks, reduce variation, and eliminate non–value-added activities. By implementing Lean practices, healthcare organizations can improve patient satisfaction, reduce medical errors, optimize resource allocation, and ultimately enhance the overall quality of care.

DOI: 10.1201/9781003486244-4

In this comprehensive study, we aim to explore the integration of the Fourth Industrial Revolution and Lean concepts in the healthcare sector. We will examine real-world case studies, research findings, and best practices from various healthcare settings to provide a holistic understanding of the potential benefits and challenges associated with this integration. By gaining insights into this transformative approach, healthcare leaders, policymakers, and practitioners can make informed decisions to drive positive change and leverage the full potential of the Fourth Industrial Revolution and Lean concepts in the healthcare sector.

2.2 THEORETICAL BACKGROUND

The integration of the Fourth Industrial Revolution and Lean concepts in the healthcare sector builds upon a strong theoretical background in both fields. Here we present a comprehensive overview of the theoretical foundations supporting the integration of these methodologies in the healthcare sector.

2.2.1 Fourth Industrial Revolution Theoretical Background [4]

2.2.1.1 Cyber-Physical Systems

The Fourth Industrial Revolution is based on the concept of cyber-physical systems (CPS), which refers to the integration of physical systems with digital technologies and data-driven intelligence. CPS enables the seamless interaction between physical devices, sensors, and digital systems, forming the foundation for automation, connectivity, and real-time data exchange in the healthcare sector.

2.2.1.2 Internet of Things

The IoT is a key component of the Fourth Industrial Revolution and is based on the idea of interconnected devices that communicate and exchange data with each other. IoT enables healthcare organizations to collect real-time patient data, monitor medical equipment, and facilitate remote patient monitoring. The theoretical foundations of IoT encompass communication protocols, data analytics, and sensor technologies.

2.2.1.3 Artificial Intelligence

AI plays a crucial role in the Fourth Industrial Revolution by enabling machines to perform intelligent tasks that typically require human intelligence. The theoretical underpinnings of AI include machine learning (ML), neural networks, and cognitive computing. AI algorithms can analyse complex healthcare data, support clinical decision-making, and optimize healthcare processes.

2.2.1.4 Big Data Analytics

The Fourth Industrial Revolution generates large volumes of data, and the theoretical foundations of big data analytics provide the framework to extract valuable insights from this data. Theoretical concepts include data management, data mining, ML, and statistical analysis. Big data analytics enables healthcare organizations to identify patterns, trends, and correlations in healthcare data for decision-making and process optimization.

2.2.2 Lean Theoretical Background

2.2.2.1 Toyota Production System

Lean concepts originated from the Toyota Production System (TPS) [5], which is centred on the philosophy of continuous improvement and waste reduction. The theoretical foundations of Lean are based on principles such as just-in-time production, eliminating waste, and empowering frontline staff to drive improvement. TPS focuses on creating value for the customer, optimizing flow, and enhancing quality.

2.2.2.2 Waste Reduction

Lean thinking emphasizes the identification and elimination of waste in processes. Theoretical concepts related to waste reduction include the seven types of waste (*muda*), such as overproduction, waiting time, defects, and unnecessary movement. Lean provides tools and methodologies, such as VSM, standardized work, and 5S (sort, set in order, shine, standardize, sustain), to systematically identify and eliminate waste in healthcare processes.

2.2.2.3 Continuous Improvement

Kaizen, also referred to as continuous improvement, forms a fundamental tenet of Lean methodology. The underpinnings of continuous improvement encompass PDCA (plan-do-check-act) cycles [6], root cause analysis, and the philosophy of gradual and repetitive enhancement. Within the realm of healthcare, Lean fosters a culture of perpetual learning and advancement, enabling healthcare practitioners to pinpoint and apply modifications that augment both patient care and operational efficiency.

By integrating the theoretical foundations of the Fourth Industrial Revolution and Lean concepts, healthcare organizations can leverage the power of digital technologies, data-driven decision-making, waste reduction, and continuous improvement. This integration enables the optimization of healthcare processes, enhanced patient outcomes, and the delivery of patient-centric care in an efficient and effective manner.

2.3 TECHNOLOGIES RELATED TO THE FOURTH INDUSTRIAL REVOLUTION

The Fourth Industrial Revolution encompasses various technologies that are revolutionizing manufacturing processes and transforming industries across the board. The following are some key technologies related to the Fourth Industrial Revolution.

2.3.1 Internet of Things

The IoT comprises a network of interconnected devices equipped with sensors, software, and connectivity capabilities. In the context of the Fourth Industrial Revolution, IoT enables machines, equipment, and products to communicate and exchange data with each other and with humans, creating a smart and interconnected ecosystem. IoT facilitates real-time data collection, monitoring, and analysis, leading to improved efficiency, predictive maintenance, and enhanced decision-making.

2.3.2 Artificial Intelligence and Machine Learning

AI and ML technologies enable machines and systems to learn, adapt, and perform tasks that traditionally required human intelligence. In the Fourth Industrial Revolution, AI and ML algorithms are used for data analysis, pattern recognition, predictive analytics, and automation. They can optimize production processes, detect anomalies, and enable autonomous decision-making, improving productivity and quality.

2.3.3 Robotics and Automation

Robotics exerts a profound influence by automating monotonous tasks and augmenting production efficiency [7]. Industrial robots can handle complex operations with precision and speed, leading to increased productivity and reduced errors. Collaborative robots, known as cobots, work alongside humans, assisting in tasks that require both human dexterity and robot strength. Automation technologies streamline processes, reduce manual labour, and enable flexible and agile manufacturing.

2.3.4 Big Data Analytics

The Fourth Industrial Revolution generates vast amounts of data from sensors, machines, and systems. Big data analytics involves capturing, storing, and analysing this data to derive valuable insights. Advanced analytics techniques, such as data mining, predictive modelling, and real-time monitoring, enable organizations to optimize processes, identify trends, and make data-driven decisions. Big data analytics facilitates predictive maintenance, quality control, and supply chain optimization [8].

2.3.5 Cloud Computing

Cloud computing facilitates flexible and readily available access to computing resources and services via the Internet. In the context of the Fourth Industrial Revolution, it plays a crucial role by empowering the storage, processing, and exchange of vast amounts of data originating from various sources. It supports real-time data analytics, remote monitoring, and collaboration across geographically dispersed teams. Cloud-based solutions enhance scalability, agility, and cost-effectiveness for organizations adopting Fourth Industrial Revolution technologies.

2.3.6 Cybersecurity

As the Fourth Industrial Revolution relies heavily on interconnected devices and networks, ensuring robust cybersecurity is crucial. With increased connectivity comes an elevated risk of cyber threats and data breaches. Protecting sensitive data, securing networks, and implementing robust cybersecurity measures are essential to maintaining the integrity and trustworthiness of Fourth Industrial Revolution systems.

These technologies, when combined and integrated effectively, empower organizations to transform their manufacturing processes, enhance productivity, optimize resource utilization, and drive innovation. In the healthcare sector, these technologies have the potential to improve patient care, enable personalized medicine, and enhance operational efficiency.

2.4 LEAN CONCEPTS

Lean concepts, when integrated with Fourth Industrial Revolution technologies, can bring significant benefits to the healthcare sector. The following is a comprehensive insight into the systematic integration of the Fourth Industrial Revolution and Lean concepts in the healthcare sector.

2.4.1 Value-Stream Mapping

VSM is a Lean tool that helps visualize and analyse the flow of processes in healthcare organizations. By mapping out the current state of processes, organizations can identify areas of waste, such as waiting times, redundant tasks, and excessive inventory. Integrating Fourth Industrial Revolution technologies, such as IoT-enabled devices and real-time data analytics, can provide valuable insights into process performance and enable continuous improvement efforts.

2.4.2 Real-Time Data Analytics

Fourth Industrial Revolution technologies in healthcare settings aim to streamline the gathering and examination of real-time data. By leveraging advanced analytics tools, healthcare organizations can gain actionable insights into patient care, operational efficiency, and resource utilization. Real-time data analytics enable proactive decision-making, early identification of bottlenecks, and predictive maintenance, leading to improved patient outcomes and streamlined processes.

2.4.3 Process Automation

Fourth Industrial Revolution technologies, such as robotics and automation, can automate repetitive and time-consuming tasks in healthcare [9]. By integrating robotics and automation into healthcare processes, organizations can minimize human error, reduce variation, and improve process efficiency. This integration allows healthcare professionals to focus on higher-value tasks, such as patient care and complex procedures.

2.4.4 Patient-Centric Care

Lean concepts emphasize delivering value to the customer, who is the patient in this case. By integrating Fourth Industrial Revolution technologies, healthcare organizations can gather patient data through wearables, sensors, and IoT devices, enabling personalized and proactive care. Real-time monitoring and remote patient management systems can enhance patient engagement, improve health outcomes, and reduce hospital readmissions.

2.4.5 Continuous Improvement

Lean thinking fosters a culture that values constant improvement and empowers frontline staff to identify opportunities for enhancement. By combining Lean principles with Fourth Industrial Revolution technologies [10], organizations can gather data-driven insights and facilitate continuous improvement initiatives. Teams can use real-time data analytics to monitor key performance indicators, implement Lean methodologies like PDCA cycles, and make data-based decisions to drive operational excellence.

2.4.6 Quality and Safety

Lean concepts emphasize the importance of quality and safety in healthcare. By integrating Fourth Industrial Revolution technologies, organizations can implement real-time monitoring systems, automate quality control processes, and enhance patient safety measures. For example, AI algorithms can assist in detecting anomalies in medical imaging, reducing diagnostic errors and improving patient safety.

The systematic integration of the Fourth Industrial Revolution and Lean concepts [11] in the healthcare sector has the potential to revolutionize patient care, optimize processes, and improve overall operational efficiency. By leveraging the power of digital technologies, real-time data analytics, and Lean methodologies, healthcare organizations can achieve higher levels of quality, patient satisfaction, and cost-effectiveness. This integration requires a collaborative approach involving healthcare professionals, technology experts, and stakeholders to drive transformative change in the healthcare industry.

2.5 HEALTHCARE SECTOR

The healthcare industry comprises a wide range of subindustries and enterprises that provide goods and services related to health and medical care. It can be categorized into six primary sectors, including pharmaceuticals, biotechnology, equipment, distribution, facilities, and managed healthcare. The value of the biotechnology industry lies in its ability to develop, manufacture, and market innovative patented medicines, generating substantial revenues. Biotech firms are often considered younger, more rapidly growing, and more innovative compared to pharmaceutical companies. Unlike pharmaceutical companies, biotech companies focus on developing new drug therapies using biological processes rather than chemical processes. These processes involve genetically modified living factories such as microbes or cell lines to produce treatments. Examples of such treatments range from common insulin injections to complex gene therapy for replacing defective genes in patients.

The healthcare sector has risen to become one of the largest revenue-generating and employment industries. It encompasses a wide array of components, including hospitals, medical devices, clinical trials, telemedicine, medical tourism, health insurance, and medical equipment. This rapid growth is attributed to expanded coverage, improved services, and increased expenditures from both public and private entities. Healthcare facilities serve as vital healthcare providers, delivering medicines and serving as primary locations for medical practice. These facilities offer diverse healthcare and social services through hospitals, doctors' offices, nursing homes, outpatient surgery centres, and more. Despite recent lower growth compared to the healthcare sector's average, healthcare facilities face substantial pressure to increase revenue. The healthcare and public health sector plays a critical role in safeguarding all sectors of the economy against various hazards like terrorism, infectious disease outbreaks, and natural disasters. Collaboration and information sharing between the public and private sectors are essential for enhancing the resilience of the nation's critical infrastructure in healthcare and public health, considering that most of the sector's assets are privately owned and operated. The healthcare and public health sector relies heavily on other sectors to ensure uninterrupted operations and service delivery.

2.6 ROLE OF ROBOTICS IN HEALTHCARE 4.0

Healthcare 4.0, the fourth medical revolution, is emerging as a transformative concept in healthcare. It encompasses the integration of electronically supported information technology, microsystems, automation, personalized therapy, and AI through the Internet of Medical Things. The ongoing COVID-19 pandemic has had a profound impact on global healthcare and related fields, highlighting the need for effective telehealth management and remote monitoring systems. Healthcare 4.0 presents an opportunity to address the challenges posed by the pandemic through the application of advanced technologies. This chapter provides an overview of previous medical revolutions and identifies the key supporting technologies of Healthcare 4.0.

While the development and mass production of intelligent medical devices have not progressed at the same pace as smart electronic devices, engineers have a crucial role to play in tackling healthcare challenges by incorporating Lean concepts. Similar to how the Fourth Industrial Revolution has transformed manufacturing, the Healthcare Fourth Industrial Revolution aims to revolutionize healthcare delivery by leveraging innovative technologies. The continuous introduction of diagnostic and treatment options, the generation of extensive data, and the deployment of wired and wireless equipment, sensors, and devices in various care environments are driving this paradigm shift. Advancements in computation power, ML, statistics, AI algorithms, modelling, and optimization techniques [12], and the integration of human factors methods contribute to the expanding capabilities of care delivery. Well-designed, implemented, and utilized innovations in Healthcare 4.0 have the potential to significantly improve care quality, patient experience, outcomes, population health, and clinician satisfaction. Robots are already transforming the medical field by streamlining supply delivery and disinfection processes, and freeing up time for healthcare providers to interact with patients. Their role has expanded during the COVID-19 pandemic [13], where they are employed for a broader range of tasks to reduce pathogen exposure and enhance operational efficiencies.

Medical robotics, with applications in minimally invasive procedures, personalized monitoring for chronic diseases, intelligent therapeutics, and social engagement for the elderly, holds great potential for revolutionizing the healthcare sector. Nurse robots can assist with non-urgent tasks, allowing human nurses to focus on more critical responsibilities and human interaction. These robots also mitigate workplace hazards, such as heavy lifting, for healthcare workers. Autonomous mobile robots contribute to reducing physical demands, addressing staffing challenges, and ensuring consistent processes by tracking inventory and performing timely orders. Disinfection and cleaning robots help minimize hospital-acquired infections while allowing healthcare workers to concentrate on value-driven patient care. The adoption of robots in surgical settings has improved precision, flexibility, vision, and control for surgeons, resulting in reduced infection risks, shorter hospital stays, less blood loss, and improved patient recovery times. Robotics in healthcare has the potential to enhance various aspects of patient care and is continually advancing in its capabilities and applications. To achieve Healthcare 4.0, further research, innovation, dissemination, and impact are required. The transition to smart and interconnected healthcare systems necessitates interdisciplinary collaboration among fields such as CPS, information technology, AI, robotics, security, modelling and optimization, and health sciences. Patient-centric care should be at the forefront, supported by all elements, interactions, and activities within the complex sociotechnical system of smart and interconnected healthcare.

2.7 THE FOURTH INDUSTRIAL REVOLUTION AND LEAN INTEGRATION

The seamless integration of data, models, and methodologies is of utmost importance for system connectivity. Each interconnected element operates with its own distinct model, focusing on specific objectives and priorities, which can sometimes diverge or clash. These models and methodologies encompass a range of quantitative, empirical, and experimental approaches. The challenge lies in effectively merging them with relevant datasets and harnessing their synergies to converge toward patient care goals while satisfying individual objectives. During this integration process, it is crucial to address underlying issues of health disparities and inequities. Therefore, prioritizing health equity in technological development and research becomes essential, especially by directing efforts toward vulnerable patient populations facing socioeconomic disadvantages and limited access to technologies.

The goal of healthcare performance improvement is to boost output, improve process effectiveness, and guarantee high levels of customer satisfaction. It works as a strategy within the overall performance management framework, assisting patients and healthcare service providers in receiving timely, high-quality care. Stakeholders throughout the world put a lot of pressure on hospitals and medical facilities to improve their performance. Organizations can examine their operational performance to find their strengths and shortcomings and launch initiatives to enhance their overall performance. Due to its complex entities, resources, activities, and processes, the healthcare industry largely depends on high-quality services for the welfare of society.

The Fourth Industrial Revolution, which includes technologies like the IoT, CPS [14, 15], big data analytics, enhanced communication infrastructure, and smart factories, serves as the foundation for digitalization. With greater automation and digitalization, these technologies enable the growth of supply chains and production processes. Fourth Industrial Revolution technologies push the boundaries by fusing the real and virtual worlds, with a focus on CPS and integration with IoT, RFID, cloud and fog computing, and big data analytics. These technologies enable next-generation systems to communicate with people via a variety of modalities and have integrated computational and physical capabilities.

While Fourth Industrial Revolution ideas and technologies are developing quickly in the industrial industry, their uptake in the service sector, including healthcare, is currently less common. Healthcare, or Fourth Industrial Revolution technologies, are being steadily adopted by the healthcare industry. The healthcare ecosystem is evolving toward this new paradigm thanks to IoT, cloud and fog computing, and big data technologies. Healthcare providers are looking for ways to provide high-quality, intelligent, and cost-effective care as the demand for smart healthcare services rises. To expedite medical advancement and guarantee financial effectiveness, the healthcare industry has already adopted cutting-edge digital equipment. Digital technology has not yet been completely utilized in several aspects of the healthcare industry, such as home-based rehabilitation and personalized healthcare.

2.8 CONCLUSION

The healthcare industry plays a vital role in ensuring society's wellbeing, demanding top-notch services. The need for healthcare services is rapidly growing due to factors such as an aging population, rapid urbanization, changing diets, sedentary lifestyles, and increasing obesity rates. Enhancing the operational efficiency of the healthcare supply chain and patient flow requires the strategic utilization of Fourth Industrial Revolution technologies and Lean practices. While the healthcare sector offers opportunities for health systems engineering, it also presents challenges. Innovations such as robotics are already improving basic agricultural procedures like increasing yield performance and reducing hazardous pesticide use [7]. To achieve smart and connected healthcare, it is imperative to integrate the healthcare sector with the Fourth Industrial Revolution and Lean concepts, prioritizing the involvement of patients, caregivers, and healthcare workers. Their characteristics, needs, abilities, and constraints should be considered during the design and implementation of smart and interconnected healthcare. To optimize performance, a strong synergy between Fourth Industrial Revolution technologies and Lean principles is crucial. Integrating pre-medical disease diagnostics, embracing Fourth Industrial Revolution technology, and adopting Lean practices can lead to improved patient flow, reduced wait times, and more effective resource management by healthcare professionals and ancillary services.

REFERENCES

[1] Lasi, H.; Fettke, P.; Kemper, H.-G.; Feld, T.; Hoffmann, M. Fourth industrial revolution. *Bus. Inf. Syst. Eng.* 2014, *6*, 239–242.

[2] Dalenogare, L.S.; Benitez, G.B.; Ayala, N.F.; Frank, A.G. The expected contribution of fourth industrial revolution technologies for industrial performance. *Int. J. Prod. Econ.* 2018, *204*, 383–394.

[3] Vaidya, S.; Ambad, P.; Bhosle, S. Fourth industrial revolution–a glimpse. *Procedia. Manuf.* 2018, *20*, 233–238.

[4] Kagermann, H.; Helbig, J.; Hellinger, A.; Wahlster, W. *Recommendations for Implementing the Strategic Initiative Industrie 4.0: Securing the Future of German Manufacturing Industry*; Final Report of the Industrie 4.0 Working Group; Forschungsunion: Berlin, 2013.

[5] Hermann, M.; Pentek, T.; Otto, B. (Eds.). *Design Principles for Industrie 4.0 Scenarios*; IEEE: Washington, DC, 2016.

[6] Bittencourt, V.L.; Alves, A.C.; Leão, C.P. Fourth industrial revolution triggered by Lean thinking: Insights from a systematic literature review. *Int. J. Prod. Res.* 2021, *59*, 1496–1510.

[7] Kishore Kumar, A.; Poonguzhali, P.K.; Nivethitha, T.; et al. *Industrial Automation and Robotics Techniques and Applications—Chapter 9: Robotics Applications and Its Impact in the Global Agricultural Sectors for Advancing Automation*; CRC Press, Taylor & Francis Group: London, 2022.

[8] Luthra, S.; Kumar, A.; Zavadskas, E.K.; Mangla, S.K.; Garza-Reyes, J.A. Fourth industrial revolution as an enabler of sustainability diffusion in supply chain: An analysis of influential strength of drivers in an emerging economy. *Int. J. Prod. Res.* 2020, *58*, 1505–1521.

[9] Ghobakhloo, M.; Fathi, M.; Iranmanesh, M.; Maroufkhani, P.; Morales, M.E. Fourth industrial revolution ten years on: A bibliometric and systematic review of concepts, sustainability value drivers, and success determinants. *J. Clean. Prod.* 2021, *302*, 127052.

[10] Luz Tortorella, G.; Cauchick-Miguel, P.A.; Li, W.; Staines, J.; McFarlane, D. What does operational excellence mean in the fourth industrial revolution era? *Int. J. Prod. Res.* 2021, 1–17.

[11] Kamble, S.; Gunasekaran, A.; Dhone, N.C. Fourth industrial revolution and Lean manufacturing practices for sustainable organisational performance in Indian manufacturing companies. *Int. J. Prod. Res.* 2020, *58*, 1319–1337.

[12] Blunck, E.; Werthmann, H. (Eds.). *Fourth Industrial Revolution-An Opportunity to Realize Sustainable Manufacturing and Its Potential for A Circular Economy*; Sveučilište u Dubrovniku: Dubrovnik, 2017.

[13] Magid, E.; Zakiev, A.; Tsoy, T.; Lavrenov, R.; Rizvanov, A. Automating pandemic mitigation. *Adv. Rob.* 2021, *35*, 1–8.

[14] Sobb, T.; Turnbull, B.; Moustafa, N. Supply chain 4.0: A survey of cyber security challenges, solutions and future directions. *Electronics* 2020, *9*, 1864.

[15] Mohebbi, S.; Zhang, Q.; Wells, E.C.; Zhao, T.; Nguyen, H.; Li, M.; Abdel-Mottaleb, N.; Uddin, S.; Lu, Q.; Wakhungu, M.; et al. Cyber-physical-social interdependencies and organizational resilience: A review of water, transportation, and cyber infrastructure systems and processes. *Sustain. Cities Soc.* 2020, *62*, 102327.

Section III

Industrial Engineering
and Industry 4.0

Chapter 3

Analysis of a Hypothetical Humanitarian Supply Chain with Agent-Based Simulation

The Expected Istanbul Earthquake

Furkan Onur Usluer, Hayrettin Kemal Sezen, and Arzu Eren Şenaras

3.1 INTRODUCTION

All humanity has tragic memories and experiences of disasters. In order to contribute to the research field of disaster studies, it is important to define the "disaster" phenomenon. It's hard to define all kinds of disasters as they can be classified with many different features such as size, magnitude, and time. However, organizations such as governments and non-governmental institutions need a definition of disaster to define operational steps [1, 2]. In a study in which worldwide disaster definitions were investigated, 128 different disaster definitions were found [3].

Preventing all disasters is impossible. It is also impossible to be fully prepared and eliminate the destructive effects of every disaster. However, every preparation to decrease the devastation of a disaster may prevent loss of life or injuries and reduce property damage.

There has been a rise in literature related to disasters, with the starting point of this trend traced back to the 1950s. This phenomenon can be attributed to the increased visibility of disasters [4].

Earthquakes are sudden and severe natural disasters. The energy released from tectonic movements causes the ground to shake. Earthquakes mainly occur where plates of the Earth's outermost layer converge or move against one another [5].

There are four components of disaster management [6], and there are studies that regard this operational cycle as "questionable" [7]. The four stages of the disaster management cycle are as follows:

Mitigation: This stage can be defined as evading or eliminating existing risks. Building substantial constructions according to the expected earthquake's magnitude can be given as an example. These are any acts to decrease long-term effects of natural or unnatural disasters [6]. Mitigation can also be described as reducing the possibility of disaster occurrence or protecting against the effects of unpreventable disasters [8].

DOI: 10.1201/9781003486244-6

Preparedness: This stage entails accepting and managing the inherent risks, rather than attempting to eliminate or avoid them altogether. In courses given to teach what should be done during an earthquake, evacuation plans can be given as examples. Preparedness consists of activities for developing operational capabilities [6].

Response: This stage consists of what should be done in the event of a disaster. These are measures that would be taken before, during, and right after the disaster [6]. The stage covers problems such as how to help earthquake victims under debris, which teams would go to which regions and when, how to create a humanitarian aid supply chain to deliver supplies such as food water, and so forth.

Recovery: This stage consists of activities related to returning society to its normal state after the disaster [6]. The recovery phase generally begins after the immediate response has ended [9].

The study area of this work is Istanbul, Turkey. The Northern Anatolian fault line passes through this area and has the potential to create an earthquake [10]. There have been devastating earthquakes in Turkey. One of these is the Gölcük earthquake of 17 August 1999. This 7.6 MW earthquake caused more than 17,000 deaths and 40,000 injuries [11]. Many studies indicate that there will be a powerful earthquake in Istanbul [12]. The magnitude of the expected earthquake is 7.7 MW in the worst-case scenario [13]. Estimates show that 2.5 million people would need emergency shelter after this potential earthquake [13].

The focus of this study is a hypothetical humanitarian supply chain which has a goal of providing food and water to people in need of emergency shelters. A significant aspect of this study is to investigate the effect of panic on the humanitarian supply chain. In many analyses, disaster victims have been considered standard phenotypes. Any distinction among people which can affect relief operations is limited. In this study, distinctions among people and the possible effects of these distinctions are important. Agent types such as "opportunist", "parent", "child", and "disabled" are in the model for this reason. All elements of the model such as agents and their features, topology, and system of relief operations are hypothetical.

Panic is an important factor and should be considered in disaster management. People's compliance with disaster plans is crucial for effective disaster management. However, the exceptional environment of disasters may constrain this. Although panic has been frequently reported in disaster environments, there is a limited number of quantitative studies specifically addressing this phenomenon. For instance, a study focused on disaster evacuation emphasized the importance of the panic element in its analysis [14].

Panic is an important element in this work. It is associated with passing time while waiting for humanitarian aid in the model. There are studies that show waiting has a cost and can increase the risk of anxiety [15].

Although many studies investigate disaster management on the scope of different perspectives, only a few studies are investigating the effects of disasters on people with disabilities [16–18]. According to the World Health Organization, more than 1 billion people have a disability [19]. Only a few works may aim to highlight the needs of disabled people during disasters [20]. However, there is a rise in studies that accept disabled people as a social group [16, 21, 22].

Two agent types represent disabled people in the model: "mentally disabled" and "physically disabled". The physically disabled agent type is the slowest agent type, meaning that it takes longer for these people to reach gathering places than other agent types. This situation makes accessing humanitarian aid more challenging for them. The mentally disabled agent type lacks the capability to make decisions regarding "location change" and "enter supply queue". To address this, a "guardian" agent is assigned to assist and guide these agents. Whenever the guardian agent changes its location, the mentally disabled agent also adjusts its position. The mentally disabled agent type can obtain humanitarian aid through these agents. People who need help with their daily routine are represented in this way in the model. According to one study, 20 percent of disabled people need help with their daily routine [23].

According to the United Nations Declaration of the Rights of the Child, every individual under the age of 18 is a child [24]. Representation of children in disaster management studies is very significant. Generally, children are classified as "under risk" and having have "special needs" in related disaster studies works [25].

Children are represented with the child agent type in this work. Although the child agent types are able to perform some behavioral activities of other agent types, they have a dependency on the parent agent type, which is appointed by the software, for location change decisions.

3.2 LITERATURE REVIEW

This section starts with studies that analyze the expected Istanbul earthquake regardless of their approach. Then the review continues with agent-based simulation (ABS) analysis examples for disaster management.

Studies focusing on the expected Istanbul earthquake generally employ mathematical models. However, it is possible to see examples in which discrete event simulation is utilized as a method. Barbarosoğlu Arda [26] developed a two-stage stochastic programming model for analyzing transportation in disaster response. Their analysis concerned the problem of satisfying demand nodes in the Istanbul–Avcılar district after the expected Istanbul earthquake. They used different disaster management operational circles consisting of phases such as the pre-event, early response, and response. Güler [27] developed a two-stage stochastic, multi-period, multimodal, and multi-commodity model for the disaster relief supply chain in Istanbul. The inventory model was solved with two approach styles named "equitable" and "pragmatic", and the results were statistically analyzed. Concerning the problem of locating response facilities in the expected Istanbul earthquake, Görmez et al. [28] propose a two-tier distribution system. There is a study investigating the state of health facilities' emergency departments after the expected Istanbul earthquake. A discrete event simulation model was developed in the study [29].

Disaster management studies that employ ABS as a method have many examples focusing on the "response" stage. Hashemi and Alesheikh [30] developed an ABS model with a geographic information system to analyze disaster response in a possible earthquake in Tehran. Their model has agents such as "street opener", "paramedic", and "citizen". They also developed software that can obtain statistical data to be used in disaster response. Fikar et al. [31] created an ABS model to analyze the humanitarian supply chain in the aftermath of the Nepal 2015 earthquake. There is a study that focuses on rescue missions with helicopters after an earthquake [32]. The authors of that study developed an ABS model for analysis. Cimellaro et al. [33] can be given as an example of studies that analyze the psychology of crowds. Their ABS model considers the anxiety effects generated by the crowd and their influence on the evacuation. Coordinating volunteers in disaster response is a very important topic. Paret et al. [34] address the topic. They developed an ABS model of spontaneous volunteer convergence to help the planning stage of disaster management. Wang and Zhang [35] developed an ABS model to analyze the supply of refined oil to areas affected by the 2008 Wenchuan earthquake in China.

ABS studies that focus on disaster management generally consist of evacuation analysis. Many evacuation studies which have earthquake scenarios try to find the best way to evacuate people from a location before a tsunami. In one study, an ABS model was developed to analyze a hypothetical evacuation scenario after an earthquake [36]. In order to analyze possible problems in evacuation for tsunami, Takahashi [37] developed an ABS model for the solution. In another study, evacuation for a tsunami at night in Aceh was investigated and analyzed with an ABS model [38]. Communication is a significant element in the model. Hardiansyah et al. [39] conducted a study that aims to analyze the earthquake evacuation of the Faculty of Engineering building, University of Bengkulu, Indonesia. They created an ABS model for analysis. In the case study in Indonesia, a model was developed using the ABS method to describe occupant behavior during the evacuation after a disaster [40].

ABS studies that focus on disaster management are not only conducted for the "response" stage of the disaster management circle. There are works which focus on the "recovery" stage of disaster management. Unequal housing recovery for different economic groups is a widely reported issue in the recovery stage of disaster management. To address the issue, Alisjahbana et al. [41] developed an agent-based financing model for post-earthquake housing recovery.

3.3 METHOD

3.3.1 Agent-Based Simulation

Simulation gives an analytical representation of a system. The representation created by the computer is a scene based on predetermined analytical rules. Simulations of scenarios about social subjects give new perspectives [42]. In the ABS method, units that form the system have autonomy and make decisions. These decisions affect the system.

Application areas of ABS vary from biology to management sciences [43]. Although some researchers have traced the roots of ABS back to the 1940s, the introduction of the SWARM language in the 1990s can be chosen as the real starting point of the ABS [44]. ABS allows some systems to be represented in a more comprehensible way than would be the case with other modeling and simulation techniques [45]. An employable method for representing the dynamism of complex systems [43, 45], ABS can be used for "complex tasks" such as disaster relief [46]. Agent-based systems are decentralized systems [43].

In the ABS methodology, units that form the system are called agents (smart objects). Agents have attributes, and they are dynamic elements. They can make their own decisions, and they are relatively independent [43, 45].

Frequently, agents' behaviors are defined with simple rules [43]. Agents must be functional in order to make their own decisions and exercise their autonomy [45]. An agent functions by interacting with other agents and their environment [43, 45, 47]. They can affect other agents. Their statuses and attributes may change as a result of interacting with other agents and their environment (topology). Additionally, agents are heterogeneous elements that are capable of adapting [43, 45].

Agent-based modeling involves the development of rules for all entities and the topology [44]. A set of agents, interaction rules among agents, and topology are fundamental elements of ABS [43, 45, 48]. Agent behaviors can be designed with collections of if-then-else rules, or artificial intelligence techniques [43, 49].

Topologies are analytic representations of the environment where agents interact. Topologies are classified as cellular automata, Euclidean, network, graphic information system, and soup [43]. The model of this study has network topology. Movements of agents occur between nodes of the network. Nodes represent gathering places. Agents' movements are limited to movement between these nodes.

3.3.2 Data

This model is hypothetical. The Istanbul Master Plan is the source of any prediction regarding the aftermath of the 7.5 MW earthquake [13]. According to the report, 2.5 million people may be in need of emergency shelter.

Demographic attributes of the agents, such as old, young, and disabled, have been obtained from TurkStat [50, 51]. The locations of gathering places selected randomly from the map had been published on the website of the municipality [52].

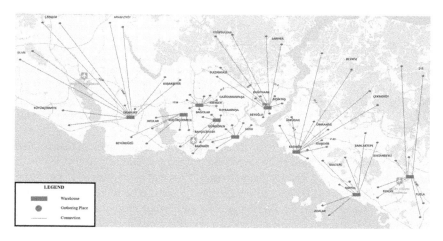

Figure 3.1 The node map.

The actual number of gathering places is too high for this work, because 1000 agents were used. Two gathering places were selected for every distribution zone for this reason. Distances between these gathering places and their zone's warehouses were obtained from Google Maps.

The node map contains all distribution zones. The study made an assumption that transportation from Kartal distribution center to Adalar could be conducted by land, although in reality, transportation to Adalar is only possible by sea.

Interviews were conducted with relevant institutions and experienced professionals to gather information about the distribution plan following a possible earthquake. Based on the insights obtained from these efforts, a hypothetical distribution plan was created.

The hypothetical distribution plan has warehouses responsible for specific districts. Every warehouse has specific inventory status and distribution teams.

3.3.2.1 Demographics

According to data obtained from TurkStat, the created agents should be classified as follows: 9.5 percent as "old", 67.3 percent as "adult", and 23.2 percent as "child" [51]. The data document related to the number of disabled people in society makes no distinction between "mentally" and "physically" [50]. The document reports a total of 2.6 percent, which is further divided as 1.3 percent for the mentally disabled and 1.3 percent for the physically disabled.

The stratified sampling method was used as the sampling method, in which 2.5 million people were represented with 1000 agents. Demographic attributes were divided among agents according to data and sampling ratio.

3.3.3 Software

ABS can be applied with general programming languages, such as Python, java, C++, and C, as well as through special applications [43].

Software is developed for the analysis in this study. There are goals for developing private software for this work rather than using software on the market. One of the significant elements that distinguish ABS from other simulation methods is that every ABS model is unique and takes shape according to the research subject. When examining any ABS model, it becomes evident that each model possesses unique attributes, including agents, topology, and more. This uniqueness poses a challenge in developing a single software solution that caters to all requirements. However, it also serves as a crucial factor in enhancing the model's realism.

The software were developed with the Python programming language. Python interpreter language gives the possibility for developing complex programs in a short amount of time. The Python programming language is widely regarded for its flexible high-level nature and its concise and intuitive syntax, which is often seen as a significant advantage [53]. Without security attributes, programs become simpler and more understandable [54].

Simulation models need random numbers for many operations. The "random" library was used for this reason. The "math" library was used for mathematical operations. The software gives the model's output as an Excel spreadsheet. The "xlsxwrite" and the "openpyxl" libraries were used for this reason.

ABS software can be developed with methodologies of agent-oriented software engineering (AOSE). ADELFE, ELDAMeth, Gaia, Tropos, and PEABS are examples of AOSE methodologies [55–59]. Nevertheless, the literature presents varying viewpoints regarding the effectiveness of these methods [59, 60].

Although there are significant benefits to using software development methodologies, there is no "best" methodology in software engineering [61]. In the field of software engineering, there are two approaches to software development: either improving and transforming existing methodologies or following the guidance of specific needs. The second approach is called situational method engineering (SME). The underlying premise is that the identification of the appropriate design approach hinges on the information provided by the "situation" [62]. The SME method was used in the software development process in this study.

3.4 THE MODEL

3.4.1 Agents

3.4.1.1 Warehouses

Food and water are held at warehouses in the model. Distributor "aid trucks" must go to these places when their supplies diminish.

3.4.1.2 Aid Trucks

Aid trucks are one of the two agent types that can make their own decisions. This agent type represents humanitarian aid workers whose mission is to get food and water to people. These agents are responsible for deciding which gathering place to go to and determining the shortest path to reach it. They have the ability to find the shortest path to their destination. They randomly chose which gathering place to go to. They can interact with the earthquake victim agents.

3.4.1.3 Earthquake Victims

Earthquake victim agents are one of the two agent types that can make their own decisions. They represent the 2.5 million people who could be in need of emergency shelter after the earthquake. These agents have character traits and physical attributes which can change by food and water deliveries. The earthquake victim agents have calorie and thirst attributes which are determined by possibilities and have a panic value (which increases if aid does not reach in a certain amount of time). The goal of earthquake victim agents is reaching the nearest gathering place after the earthquake and staying there for 48 hours. If humanitarian aid reaches their destination, they can queue for supplies. They may use the supplies immediately or put them in their inventory for later use. These gathering places are their last destination; however, panic can initiate their mobility. If they are unable to obtain supplies and their panic level reaches a certain threshold, they may choose to relocate to another gathering place.

These agents enter the supply queues according to their character attributes and needs.

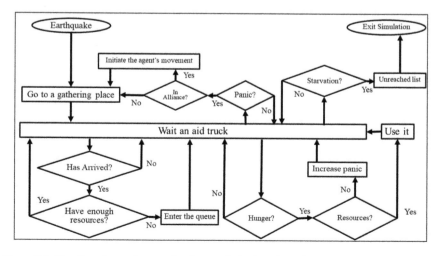

Figure 3.2 The flowchart of generalized agent behavior algorithm.

Character Attributes

Opportunist: The queue entry rule in the model dictates that an earthquake victim agent should join the supply queue if the inventory count for its supplies is 0. An exception to this rule is agents which have the opportunist character trait. These agents can enter the supply queue until the number of the supply reaches two in their inventory. The impact of individuals exhibiting a propensity to acquire more supplies than their allocated share on the humanitarian supply chain was analyzed using this character trait.

Child: Agents with this attribute represent people under 18 years old in the population. Agents with this attribute can't make their own location change decision. One parent agent is appointed to them by software. They can change their location according to their parent agent's decision. These agents can enter the supply queue; if their parent has supplies, a child agent can get them from their parent.

Parent: These agents are parents of the agents that have the child character trait. Every child agent has one parent agent. When these agents change their location, the child agent also changes its location. If a child agent requires supplies, they must fulfill this need using their inventory.

Mentally disabled: They represent people with mental disabilities. They can't make their own decisions. They get food and water supply through the guardian agent appointed by the software. They change their location with the guardian agent.

Guardian: They represent caregivers of mentally disabled persons. Every mentally disabled agent has one guardian agent. When these agents change their location, the mentally disabled agent also changes its location. The guardian agent is responsible for mentally disabled agents' supplies.

Panic-prone: These agents can make location change decisions earlier than others (they have the lowest panic threshold value). This character trait represents individuals who are psychologically unprepared for a disaster situation.

Physically disabled: This character attribute represents people with a physical disability. These agents have the lowest movement speed.

Demographic Attributes

Senior: This demographic attribute represents seniors. They have low movement speed.

Adult: This demographic attribute represents people who don't classify as seniors or children. Agents with this trait have the fastest movement speed. The panic threshold value of these agents is lower compared to others, resulting in a higher frequency of decision changes. This is because these agents aim to utilize their speed as an advantage.

3.4.2 System Description

Every agent enters the simulation in a certain distribution zone. Every distribution zone has two gathering places. Aid trucks of a warehouse go to their gathering

Table 3.1 The Summary of Agents Features

	Decisions and Inventory			
	Location Change	*Queue Entry*	*Inventory*	*Symbol*
Guardian	Yes	Yes	2	a
Mentally disabled	No	No	N/A	b
Parent	Yes	Yes	2	c
Child	No	Yes	1	d
Opportunist	Yes	Yes	2	e
	Behavioral Attributes			
	Movement Speed	*Panic Breakpoint*	*Available Traits*	
Senior	Moderate	High	a, b, c, e	
Adult	Very fast	Moderate	a, b, c, e	
Physically disabled	Very slow	High	a, c, d, e	
Panic-prone	N/A	Very low	a, c, e	

places to supply earthquake victims. None of the distribution teams can deliver supply to a zone of other distribution teams.

Earthquake victim agents start waiting for an aid truck after they reach the gathering place. They have calorie and thirst values which decrease over simulation time and have an inventory to store a supply for later use. Almost all agents can store only one supply. Supplies would be used when hunger or thirst values reach a specific value. The software creates queues for agents in need when an aid truck arrives at that gathering place. Agents that can store two supplies in their inventory are opportunist, parent, and guardian agent types. Guardians are responsible for taking supplies for the mentally disabled agent type they are caring for. Opportunist agents enter supply queues regardless of their needs.

Every agent's panic value increases as long as aid trucks haven't arrived at their location. If an aid truck arrives at their location and they can get their supplies, their panic value is set to 0. However, every agent develops a panic value while waiting for the aid truck, and when this value reaches a certain level, they would give up waiting and travel to another gathering place. It's not possible to help traveling agents until they arrive at the new gathering place. Their panic value is set to 0 when they reach their destination, and the loop starts again.

If an agent's calorie or thirst value reaches a certain point, they are classified as "unreached" and they exit the simulation.

The goal of aid trucks is to reach the maximum number of agents and minimize the number of agents in the unreached list. Every time an aid truck does not reach an agent in need is a risk for the humanitarian supply chain. Additionally, there are other factors that make it harder for aid trucks to reach their goals: agents are different from each other. For instance, failing to reach physically disabled agents in time may initiate these agents' location change decision. This is a risk for relief operations because agents cannot be supplied until they reach their destination.

When considering their lowered speed due to their disability, this may lead to failure. If a guardian of mentally disabled agents made a location change decision, this is a risk for two agents. Likewise, if a parent agent makes this decision, it is also a risk for two agents. The situation would be affected by whether the agent is an adult or a senior. Additionally, opportunist agents are one of the obstacles to the aid effort.

3.5 ANALYSIS

3.5.1 Scenario I

Agents started to make location change decisions due to panic after minute 1000. However, 80 percent of the agents didn't make this decision despite a spike at minute 1085 (163 instances of decision change). Their panic values started to decrease after minute 1230. The reaching capacity of aid trucks increased, and this caused a time increase between new location change decisions. In a strategic sense, considering the inability to supply agents that are on the move, the controllable panic

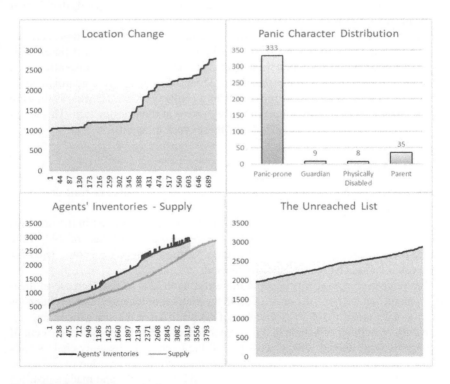

Figure 3.3 Results of scenario I.

level for aid efforts extends until minute 2153. Aid efforts become harder after this point due to agents making this decision too often. This situation's effect on aid efforts can be observed by examining character trait distribution among agents that made this decision.

The speed of taking supplies by agents increases after minute 1555. If agents need to use a supply from their inventory before aid reaches them, they will not save these supplies for future needs. It can be inferred that strategic supply usage decreases after minute 800. Increased supplies after minute 2150 allow earthquake victim agents to hold supplies in their inventory for future challenges, thus increasing strategic supply usage.

The number of agents listed in the unreached category is 510. This number started to increase after minute 1975 and reached its peak around minute 2043. In total, 49 percent of the agents received assistance. The success rate of the hypothetical supply chain in this scenario is 49 percent. Additionally, when examining the rate of increase in the unreached category, it can be inferred that the capacity of the supply chain was exceeded after minute 2502.

Thirty-three percent of agents that made the location change decision have the "panic-prone" character trait. It poses a risk to aid efforts when physically disabled agents make this decision. Considering their low movement speed, this further complicates aid efforts.

In the scenario, there were ten guardian agents. Some agents with this character trait made the decision to change their gathering place a total of nine times. This poses a risk to aid efforts when these agents are on the move, as it also affects the mentally disabled agents under their care. The presence of both a guardian and a mentally disabled agent on the move creates a challenge for aid trucks, as they are unable to supply both individuals until they arrive at their destination. This situation highlights a failure in aid efforts for these types of agents.

3.5.2 Scenario 2

In scenario 2, agents' change to have the panic-prone character trait decreased from 40 percent to 10 percent.

The number of location change decisions due to panic was 724 in the previous scenario. This number decreased to 673 in scenario 2. A decrease of 297 in the panic-prone character trait leads to 51 fewer location change decisions. The time between location change decisions increased.

Earthquake victim agents become more reachable due to the decrease in location change decisions. A decrease of 51 in the number of location change decisions leads to a decrease of 109 in the number of agents listed in the unreached category. The current number of agents in the unreached list is 401. In total, 59.9 percent of the agents were helped. The success rate of the hypothetical supply chain stands at 59.9 percent. By reducing the frequency of location changes due to panic, the agents improved their chances of being reached by aid trucks and made a positive contribution to the success rate of the aid efforts.

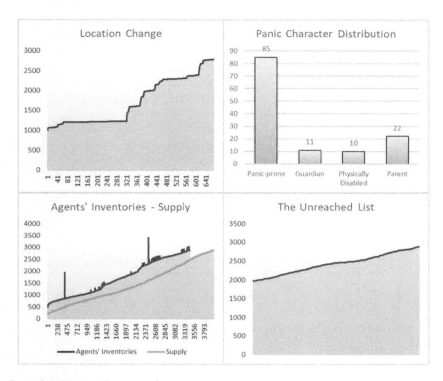

Figure 3.4 Results of scenario 2.

3.5.3 Scenario 3

In scenario 3, agents' change to have the mentally disabled character trait increased from 1.3 percent to 10 percent.

The behavior of taking more than one supply happened 506 times. Agents that have parent or guardian character traits take supplies for their child or mentally disabled agents, respectively. Agents that have the opportunist character trait also take more supplies whether they need them or not; this affected the success rate of the aid efforts. By taking more supply than their needs 204 times, opportunists took 40.3 percent of all supply.

The increase in agents' change of having the mentally disabled character trait increased the number of agents in the unreached list. The number of agents in the unreached list is 542. In total, 45.8 percent of agents were helped. The success rate of the hypothetical humanitarian supply chain is 45.8 percent. This result is caused by the fact that agents that have the mentally disabled character trait need the guardian agents for their supply needs, and aid trucks' inability to reach these guardian agents or reaching with insufficient supply (less than two units). This

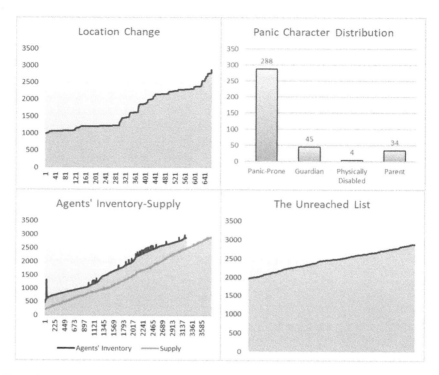

Figure 3.5 Results of scenario 3.

result also indicates at the planning stage of disaster relief operations, planners should consider individuals who have special needs. This is one of the significant elements for the success of entire relief operations.

3.6 DISCUSSION

The model's accuracy has been affected by limited data regarding the system despite efforts to obtain more data.

The model for representing the aftermath of the expected Istanbul earthquake was created using the ABS method. Scenario-based analysis was conducted. Agents' ability to change location because of panic is a significant feature of this study. Panic was associated with passing time while waiting for humanitarian aid in the model. Some studies show waiting has a cost and can increase the risk of anxiety [15]. The results indicated that the psychology of crowds has importance in disaster management. There is a similarity with studies analyzing crowd psychology in a disaster [14, 33].

3.7 CONCLUSIONS

Disasters are low-probability events. In most cases, it is impossible to predict exactly when and where they will occur and what will be the devastating effects. However, many improvements can be made in order to reduce losses.

The model for representing the aftermath of the expected Istanbul earthquake was created using the ABS method, and the following conclusions were drawn:

- The model's location change due to the panic feature is significant. Planners of disaster relief operations should always be prepared to address emotions such as panic, as it can negatively impact the success rate of aid efforts and disrupt the order of the humanitarian supply chain. Therefore, it is crucial to prioritize the psychological preparedness of individuals for disaster events.
- Agents with the mentally disabled and the physically disabled traits represent people with special needs. Relief operation plans which do not consider differences among people are more likely unsuccessful.
- Agents with the opportunist character trait represent people who don't follow the rules of distribution and jeopardize all aid efforts for their own benefit. The success rate of the humanitarian supply chain does not solely depend on getting supplies from one place to another; equal and right distribution among people is a crucial element. Therefore, relief operation planners should prioritize the establishment of an equitable and efficient distribution system.
- In the model, the random selection of gathering places as the distribution strategy has impacted the success rate of the hypothetical humanitarian supply chain. Strategists of a humanitarian supply chain would greatly benefit from knowing the number of people awaiting aid at each distribution point. If there is no information about the location where aid is expected, it is unlikely that distribution points will be selected randomly. A relief organization may rely entirely on the manager's instincts. However, this would not be enough. In a real situation, the supply of various goods poses a challenge due to the complexity involved. When supplies do not reach the intended destinations, it leads to a loss of time and increases the risk of failure for the humanitarian supply chain. The coordination of hundreds of individuals also should be considered, and technological infrastructures must be improved.

REFERENCES

[1] N. R. Britton, "What's a word—opening up the debate," in *What is a disaster: New answers to old questions*, R. W. Perry and E. L. Quarantelli, Eds. Philadelphia: Xlibris Publishers, 2005, pp. 60–78.

[2] P. Buckle, "Mandated definitions, local knowledge and complexity," in *What is a disaster? New answers to old questions*, R. W. Perry and E. L. Quarantelli, Eds. Philadelphia: Xlibris Publishers, 2005, pp. 173–200.

[3] A. P. L. Mayner, and P. P. Arbon, "Defining disaster: The need for harmonisation of terminology," *Australas. J. Disaster Trauma Stud.*, vol. 19, p. 6, 2015.

[4] K. J. Tierney, M. K. Lindell, and R. W. Perry, *Facing the unexpected: Disaster preparedness and response in the United States*. Washington, DC: Joseph Henry Press, 2001, p. 9834. doi: 10.17226/9834.

[5] J. H. Kruhl, R. Adhikari, and U. E. Dorka, Eds., *Living under the threat of earthquakes: short and long-term management of earthquake risks and damage prevention in Nepal* (Springer Natural Hazards). Cham: Springer International Publishing, 2018. doi: 10.1007/978-3-319-68044-6.

[6] D. McLoughlin, "A framework for integrated emergency management," *Public Adm. Rev.*, vol. 45, p. 165, 1985. doi: 10.2307/3135011.

[7] I. A. Rana, M. Asim, A. B. Aslam, and A. Jamshed, "Disaster management cycle and its application for flood risk reduction in urban areas of Pakistan," *Urban Clim.*, vol. 38, p. 100893, 2021. doi: 10.1016/j.uclim.2021.100893.

[8] C. Warfield, "The disaster management cycle," *Urban Environmental Management*, 2022. www.gdrc.org/uem/disasters/1-dm_cycle.html

[9] D. P. Coppola, *Introduction to international disaster management*, Third edition. Amsterdam: Elsevier/Butterworth-Hein, 2015.

[10] M. Bohnhoff, F. Bulut, G. Dresen, P. E. Malin, T. Eken, and M. Aktar, "An earthquake gap south of Istanbul," *Nat. Commun.*, vol. 4, no. 1, p. 1999, 2013. doi: 10.1038/ncomms2999.

[11] TBMM, "Deprem Riskinin Araştırılarak Deprem Yönetiminde Alınması Gereken Önlemlerin Belirlenmesi Amacıyla Kurulanmeclis Araştırması Komisyonu Raporu," *Türkiye Büyük Millet Meclisi*, 549, 2010.

[12] E. Kayaalp, and O. Arslan, "Earth in practice: Uncertainty, expertise and the expected Istanbul earthquake," *Environ. Plan. E Nat. Space*, vol. 5, no. 3, pp. 1579–1596, 2022. doi: 10.1177/25148486211022451.

[13] IBB, "İstanbul Deprem Master Planı," *İstanbul Büyükşehir Belediyesi Planlama Ve İmar Dairesi Zemin Ve Deprem İnceleme Müdürlüğü*. Istanbul: Master Plan, 2003.

[14] Z.-H. Hu, J.-B. Sheu, and L. Xiao, "Post-disaster evacuation and temporary resettlement considering panic and panic spread," *Transp. Res. Part B Methodol.*, vol. 69, pp. 112–132, 2014, doi: 10.1016/j.trb.2014.08.004.

[15] E. E. Osuna, "The psychological cost of waiting," *J. Math. Psychol.*, vol. 29, pp. 82–105, 1985.

[16] I. Kelman, and L. M. Stough, Eds., *Disability and disaster*. London: Palgrave Macmillan UK, 2015. doi: 10.1057/9781137486004.

[17] National Council on Disability, "Effective emergency management: Making improvements for communities and people with disabilities," in *National Council on Disability*. Washington, DC, 2009. http://files.eric.ed.gov/fulltext/ED507740.pdf

[18] B. Wisner, J. C. Gaillard, and I. Kelman, Eds., *The Routledge handbook of hazards and disaster risk reduction*. London: New York: Routledge, 2012.

[19] WHO, "Disability," 2011. www.who.int/health-topics/disability#tab=tab_1

[20] H. Rodríguez, W. Donner, and J. E. Trainor, Eds., "Handbook of disaster research," in *Handbooks of sociology and social research*. Cham: Springer International Publishing, 2018. doi: 10.1007/978-3-319-63254-4.

[21] L. Peek, and L. M. Stough, "Children with disabilities in the context of disaster: A social vulnerability perspective: Children with disabilities in disaster," *Child Dev.*, vol. 81, no. 4, pp. 1260–1270, 2010. doi: 10.1111/j.1467-8624.2010.01466.x.

[22] L. M. Stough, and C. B. Mayhorn, "Population segments with disabilities," *Int. J. Mass Emerg. Disasters*, vol. 31, no. 3, pp. 384–402, 2013.

[23] M. W. Brault, "Americans with disabilities: 2010," *Curr. Popul. Rep.*, p. 24, 2012.

[24] Office of the United Nations High Commissioner for Human Rights, *Convention on the rights of the child*, 1989. www.ohchr.org/en/professionalinterest/pages/crc.aspx

[25] B. D. Phillips, D. S. K. Thomas, W. E. Lovekamp, and A. Fothergill, Eds., *Social vulnerability to disasters*, Second edition. Boca Raton: CRC Press, 2013.

[26] G. Barbarosoğlu, and Y. Arda, "A two-stage stochastic programming framework for planning in disaster response," *J. Oper. Res. Soc.*, vol. 55, no. 1, pp. 43–53, 2004.

[27] Ç. U. Güler, "Afet Tedarik Zinciri Yönetiminde Stokastik, Çok Periyotlu, Çok-Modlu, Çok Malzemeli, İki-Seviyeli Yardım Malzemesi Dağıtım Modeli," PhD Thesis, Hava Harp Okulu Havacılık Ve Uzay Teknolojileri Enstitüsü, Istanbul, 2016.

[28] N. Görmez, M. Köksalan, and F. S. Salman, "Locating disaster response facilities in Istanbul," *J. Oper. Res. Soc.*, vol. 62, no. 7, pp. 1239–1252, 2011. doi: 10.1057/jors.2010.67.

[29] M. Gul, A. Fuat Guneri, and M. M. Gunal, "Emergency department network under disaster conditions: The case of possible major Istanbul earthquake," *J. Oper. Res. Soc.*, vol. 71, no. 5, pp. 733–747, 2020. doi: 10.1080/01605682.2019.1582588.

[30] M. Hashemi, and A. A. Alesheikh, "GIS: agent-based modeling and evaluation of an earthquake-stricken area with a case study in Tehran, Iran," *Nat. Hazards*, vol. 69, no. 3, pp. 1895–1917, 2013. doi: 10.1007/s11069-013-0784-x.

[31] C. Fikar, P. Hirsch, and P. C. Nolz, "Agent-based simulation optimization for dynamic disaster relief distribution," *Cent. Eur. J. Oper. Res.*, vol. 26, no. 2, pp. 423–442, 2018. doi: 10.1007/s10100-017-0518-3.

[32] J. Zang, H. Liu, and X. Ni, "Earthquake rescue mission modeling based on multi-agent," *TELKOMNIKA Indones. J. Electr. Eng.*, vol. 12, no. 4, pp. 2995–3000, 2014. doi: 10.11591/telkomnika.v12i4.4999.

[33] G. P. Cimellaro, F. Ozzello, A. Vallero, S. Mahin, and B. Shao, "Simulating earthquake evacuation using human behavior models: Simulating earthquake evacuation using human behavior models," *Earthq. Eng. Struct. Dyn.*, vol. 46, no. 6, pp. 985–1002, 2017. doi: 10.1002/eqe.2840.

[34] K. Paret, S. A. Rodriguez, M. E. Mayorga, L. Velotti, and E. J. Lodree, "Agent-based simulation of spontaneous volunteer convergence to improve disaster planning," *Nat. Hazards Rev.*, vol. 24, no. 2, p. 04023016, 2023. doi: 10.1061/NHREFO.NHENG-1659.

[35] Z. Wang, and J. Zhang, "Agent-based evaluation of humanitarian relief goods supply capability," *Int. J. Disaster Risk Reduct.*, vol. 36, p. 101105, 2019. doi: 10.1016/j.ijdrr.2019.101105.

[36] M. Lalith, W. Petprakob, M. Hori, T. Ichimura, and K. Fujita, "A non-signalized junction model for agent-based simulations of car–pedestrian mode mass evacuations," *GeoHazards*, vol. 3, no. 2, pp. 144–161, 2022. doi: 10.3390/geohazards3020008.

[37] A. Takahashi, "Evaluation of underground space for tsunami evacuation safety with route obstacles by agent-based simulation," *Int. J. Geomate*, vol. 22, no. 92, 2022. doi: 10.21660/2022.92.gxi245.

[38] S. Widiyanto, D. Adi, and R. V. Soans, "Agent-based simulation disaster evacuation awareness on night situation in Aceh," *IPTEK J. Eng.*, vol. 8, no. 1, p. 36, 2022. doi: 10.12962/j23378557.v8i1.a12799.

[39] W. Fitrianip, A. F. Edriani, R. Hardiansyah, R. Lestyanti, and L. Z. Mase, "Implementation of agent based modelling to observe the evacuating behavior at faculty of engineering building, University of Bengkulu, Indonesia," *J. Civ. Eng. Forum*, pp. 179–192, 2022, doi: 10.22146/jcef.3589.

[40] S. H. Putri, R. S. M. Haerdy, and A. Nurdini, "Evacuation access simulation during earthquake disaster in vertical public housing, rancacili bandung as a case study," *IOP Conf. Ser. Earth Environ. Sci.*, vol. 1058, no. 1, p. 012004, 2022. doi: 10.1088/1755-1315/1058/1/012004.

[41] I. Alisjahbana, A. Moura-Cook, R. Costa, and A. Kiremidjian, "An agent-based financing model for post-earthquake housing recovery: Quantifying recovery inequalities across income groups," *Earthq. Spectra*, vol. 38, no. 2, pp. 1254–1282, 2022. doi: 10.1177/87552930211064319.

[42] H. V. D. Parunak, "Social simulation for non-hackers," in *Multi-agent-based simulation XXII* (Lecture Notes in Computer Science), vol. 13128, K. H. Van Dam and N. Verstaevel, Eds. Cham: Springer International Publishing, 2022, pp. 1–15. doi: 10.1007/978-3-030-94548-0.

[43] C. Macal, and M. North, "Tutorial on agent-based modeling and simulation," in *Agent-based modeling and simulation* (OR Essentials), S. J. E. Taylor, Ed. Cham: Palgrave Macmillan, 2014, pp. 11–32. http://link.springer.com/10.1057/9781137453648

[44] T. T. Allen, *Introduction to discrete event simulation and agent-based modeling*. London: Springer London, 2011. doi: 10.1007/978-0-85729-139-4.

[45] S. J. E. Taylor, "Introducing agent-based modeling and simulation," in *Agent-based modeling and simulation* (OR Essentials), S. J. E. Taylor, Ed. London: Palgrave Macmillan, 2014, pp. 1–11. doi: 10.1057/9781137453648.

[46] D. Blanco-Fernández, S. Leitner, and A. Rausch, "Multi-level adaptation of distributed decision-making agents in complex task environments," in *Multi-agent-based simulation XXII* (Lecture Notes in Computer Science, vol. 13128), K. H. Van Dam and N. Verstaevel, Eds. Cham: Springer International Publishing, 2022, pp. 29–42. doi: 10.1007/978-3-030-94548-0.

[47] M. Wooldridge, *An introduction to multi agent systems*. West Sussex: Wiley, 2002.

[48] S. Janssen, A. Sharpanskykh, and S. S. M. Ziabari, "Using causal discovery to design agent-based models," in *Multi-agent-based simulation XXII* (Lecture Notes in Computer Science, vol. 13128), K. H. Van Dam and N. Verstaevel, Eds. Cham: Springer International Publishing, 2022, pp. 15–29. doi: 10.1007/978-3-030-94548-0.

[49] S. Russell, and P. Norvig, *Artificial intelligence: A modern approach*, International edition. Harlow: Pearson, 1998.

[50] TurkStat, "Turkey disability survey," 2002. https://data.tuik.gov.tr/Search/Search?text=engellilik%20oran%C4%B1

[51] TurkStat, "Yıllara göre il nüfusları 2000–2019," *Turkish Statistical Institute (TURKSTAT)—TÜİK*, 2019. https://biruni.tuik.gov.tr/medas/?kn=95&locale=tr

[52] IBB, "Şehir Haritası," *The Istanbul Metropolitan Municipality*, 2020. https://sehirharitasi.ibb.gov.tr

[53] J. Sundnes, *Introduction to scientific programming with Python*. Cham: Springer International Publishing, 2020. doi: 10.1007/978-3-030-50356-7.

[54] A. Bogdanchikov, M. Zhaparov, and R. Suliyev, "Python to learn programming," *J. Phys. Conf. Ser.*, vol. 423, p. 012027, 2013. doi: 10.1088/1742-6596/423/1/012027.

[55] N. Bonjean, W. Mefteh, M. P. Gleizes, and C. Maurel, "ADELFE 2.0," in *Handbook on agent-oriented design processes*, M. Cossentino, V. Hilaire, A. Molesini, and V. Seidita, Eds. Berlin Heidelberg: Springer-Verlag, 2014, pp. 19–64.

[56] G. Fortino, and W. Russo, "ELDAMeth: An agent-oriented methodology for simulation-based prototyping of distributed agent systems," *Inf. Softw. Technol.*, vol. 54, no. 6, pp. 608–624, 2012. doi: 10.1016/j.infsof.2011.08.006.

[57] M. Wooldridge, N. R. Jennings, and D. Kinny, "The Gaia methodology for agent-oriented analysis and design," *Auton. Agents Multi-Agent Syst.*, vol. 3, p. 28, 2000.

[58] P. Bresciani, A. Perini, P. Giorgini, F. Giunchiglia, and J. Mylopoulos, "Tropos: an agent-oriented software development methodology," *Auton. Agents Multi-Agent Syst.*, vol. 8, no. 3, pp. 203–236, 2004. doi: 10.1023/B:AGNT.0000018806.20944.ef.

[59] I. García-Magariño, A. Gómez-Rodríguez, J. C. González-Moreno, and G. Palacios-Navarro, "PEABS: a process for developing efficient agent-based simulators," *Eng. Appl. Artif. Intell.*, vol. 46, pp. 104–112, 2015. doi: 10.1016/j.engappai.2015.09.003.

[60] A. Molesini, M. Casadei, A. Omicini, and M. Viroli, "Simulation in agent-oriented software engineering: The SODA case study," *Sci. Comput. Program.*, vol. 78, no. 6, pp. 705–714, 2013. doi: 10.1016/j.scico.2011.09.007.

[61] I. Sommerville, *Software engineering* (International computer science series), Eighth edition. Harlow; New York: Addison-Wesley, 2007.

[62] M. Cossentino, V. Hilaire, A. Molesini, and V. Seidita, Eds., *Handbook on agent-oriented design processes*. Berlin, Heidelberg: Springer Berlin Heidelberg, 2014. doi: 10.1007/978-3-642-39975-6.

Chapter 4

Comprehensive Survey on Artificial Intelligence in Blockchain
A Futuristic Integration

Supriya M. S. and Mridula G. Narang

4.1 INTRODUCTION

When the Internet was made available for both personal and commercial usage in the 1990s, companies like Google, Amazon, Facebook, YouTube, and Instagram were born. The Internet of Information, the first generation of the Internet, made it possible to share any type of digital content. The first generation of the Internet has shown us that content creators do not receive a fair price for their work, and businesses that can profit from the digital information are taking all the value, leaving little to nothing for the content owners [1].

People have spent thousands of years trying to comprehend the way people think, how a small bit of substance may particularly observe, interpret, forecast, and govern a world that is much better and artificially far more sophisticated than itself. By striving to develop intelligent beings in addition to understanding those that already exist, the study of AI goes considerably further. AI is one of the most recent branches of science and engineering. After the Second World War, work really got going, but the name was not used until 1956. AI is frequently mentioned by scientists from a range of disciplines as the "area I would most like to be in," along with molecular biology. A physics student would naturally assume that Galileo, Newton, Einstein, and the rest had already developed the greatest theories. However, the field of AI still has a few full-time Einsteins and Edisons. AI today refers to a wide range of subfields, from the fundamental (learning and perception) to the specialised (playing chess, proving mathematical theorems, writing poetry, driving a car through a congested street, and detecting diseases). Because it may be utilised to enhance any intellectual job, AI is a genuinely global field [2].

The 2008 global financial crisis raised questions about the function of banks and other financial institutions as well as their ability to be regarded as reliable institutions. In order to address this problem at the time, the first cryptocurrency, Bitcoin, was developed. The first commercial implementation of Blockchain technology was Bitcoin, which uses it as its foundational technology. It was created to carry out Bitcoin transactions without the use of middlemen and central banks. Although Blockchain technology initially attracted interest for use in cryptocurrencies, it

DOI: 10.1201/9781003486244-7

has since been discovered that it can also be used in a variety of industries other than finance, allowing for the fair and trustless exchange of assets and value while reducing or completely eliminating the need for middlemen [1].

In the realm of AI, data serves as the lifeblood for various algorithms and unraveling pivotal insights. Yet, the internet hosts a vast expanse of dispersed data, often shrouded in ambiguity regarding ownership. This ambiguity complicates the task of authenticating and granting permission for its use in the intricate cyberspace landscape, fraught with diverse stakeholders harbouring mutual distrust. Enabling data sharing for actual vast data and actual powerful AI in cyberspace is therefore very difficult. To create a more safe cyberspace with real big data and, subsequently, improved AI with numerous data sources, it is important to integrate three essential components into an architecture that can support secure data storage, computation, and, in the context of the vast Internet, sharing. The use of Blockchain-based data sharing with ownership guarantees a trusted value-exchange method for paying for security services, as well as an AI-based secure computing platform to provide more intelligent security policies [3].

The development and widespread usage of technologies like AI, the Internet of Things (IoT), and Blockchain are fuelling the Fourth Industrial Revolution by improving the quality of human–machine interaction. The integration of smart technologies into nearly everything is bringing the physical and virtual worlds closer together than ever. Enabling digital technologies to achieve transformative speed and efficiency is the primary goal of the Fourth Industrial Revolution [4].

The combination of AI and Blockchain is covered in this chapter, along with how we may use both to address the shortcomings of the other and do away with their respective limits. Additionally, the chapter focuses on integrating Blockchain and AI with cloud technology.

4.2 ARTIFICIAL INTELLIGENCE

Orchestrating a machine that handles unpretentious everyday inconveniences done or accomplishes targets as well as humans do is the essence of AI. Where we humans use brain power to accomplish them, machines do so with the help of programs. The computational portion of the capacity to accomplish goals is insinuated as intelligence. AI entails determining elucidations which humans might have missed while determining them. Machine learning (ML), deep learning, natural language processing (NLP), fuzzy logic, expert systems, and genetic programming are some of the many branches of AI. Online shopping, marketing, social media, banks, healthcare, enhanced image, smart cars, surveillance, and gaming are some of its applications [4].

The author Nils Nilsson stipulates that the so-called intelligent machines being engineered by humans ought to carry out the thinking-related tasks that individuals can do. The initial pursuit for AI encompassed ascertaining explicit tasks which required intelligence and brainstorming on how machines can do them. In the 1950s and 1960s, conundrums such as puzzle solving, playing chess and checkers, theorem proving, finding answers to simple questions, and classification of visual images were undertaken by the pioneers. Alongside these laboratory-style problems, researchers were simultaneously working to solve real-world conundrums such as language translation and reading highly stylised magnetic characters on bank cheques automatically. AI as a bona fide and promising field of research was unveiled with three of the most eminent meetings in history which were conducted in 1955, 1956, and 1958. In 1955, a "Session on Learning Machines" and the Western Joint Computer Conference were held concurrently. At Dartmouth College, a "Summer Research Project on AI" was organised in 1956. And a conference on the "Mechanization of Thought Processes" was funded by the National Physical Laboratory in the United Kingdom in 1958 [5].

4.2.1 The Symbolic Artificial Intelligence Approach

There exist many approaches to AI. One of these is symbolic AI. The main hypotheses behind this strategy are:

- Clearly specifying a model for an intelligent system
- Symbolically representing knowledge in such a model
- Illustrating the cognitive operations in the form of formal operations using symbolic expressions and structures belonging to an existing model.

Symbolic AI can be classified into two subcategories. In the first subcategory, we try to define models encompassing a broad spectrum of knowledge and can perform intelligent operations. Cognitive simulation and logic-based reasoning are the core concepts of this subcategory. On the other hand, the second subcategory involves delineating models concerning distinct applications. Hence, these models are grounded on the exemplifications of domain knowledge. This subcategory includes approaches based on mathematical linguistics, structural knowledge representation, and rule-based knowledge representation [6].

The earliest approach to AI was cognitive simulation. Pioneered by Newell and Simon, this structure was used to develop General Problem Solver and Logic Theorist systems. The conceptualisation of cognitive simulation revolves around outlining heuristic algorithms with the intention of stimulating cognitive abilities resembling those of humans such as learning, problem-solving, object recognition, and reasoning. A set of rudimentary instructions akin to those carried out by humans is implemented by a computer during such a simulation. Designing such algorithms can prove to be a daunting task. Thus, we start off by identifying the sophisticated pattern of logic a human being uses to solve customary hitches. The fundamental concepts of cognitive simulation include state space, means-end analysis (MEA), problematic reduction, and problem-solving as examining state space [6].

4.2.2 State Space

The original idea of cognitive simulation is based on the state space. The preliminary state of a state space embodies the status quo where we begin solving the problem. Let us examine the game of chess in order to explain this concept. The opening position of the pieces represent the initial state. Goal state(s) are those which exemplify the problem at a point in time where we aim to find a solution. Thus, all those status quos wherein we can checkmate the opponent are examples of goal states. All the transitional states characterise the many ways to solve the problem. So, while keeping in mind the game's rules, we attempt to depict the game's numerous situations. A state space is essentially a graph, with the initial, interim, and goal states represented by the nodes and the edges denoting the transitions between them [6].

4.2.3 Solving Issues through State Space Search

The idea behind cognitive simulation is this. The philosophy is quite upfront: if the rubrics of formulating the algorithm are undetermined, we use the guess and check or trial and error method. For example, let us assume that we fail to recall the password of our computer. The methods we use to unlock the computer can either be blind or restricted to a small portion of the state space. Here we define a function called "heuristic function" which allows to realise how far or how close we are to the actual solution. There are three properties that a suitable method should possess in order to generate all the conceivable solutions:

1. It is essential that it needs to be complete; that is, it must come up with every conceivable answer.
2. It shouldn't repeatedly offer a potential answer.
3. It is supposed to utilise data which places a restriction the state space to its subarea in addition to gauging the worth of the possible solutions generated [6].

4.2.4 Means-End Analysis

MEA is the third fundamental idea. Assume for the moment that we have a function that allows us to evaluate how superior potential solutions are. Then, we employ the MEA approach to limit the generation of potential solutions. The distance between the current state and goal state is determined using this function, and we use a means (operator or procedure) to condense this difference. Commencing from the initial state, this method is carried out in an iterative fashion until the goal state is reached [6].

4.2.5 Problem Reduction

The fourth and final concept is problem reduction. Superseding a convoluted conundrum into straightforward subproblems is the core ideology of this method. It is important to note that the reduction of a problem to its subproblem is crucial because diverse state spaces, quality functions, and operators need to be outlined [6].

4.2.6 The Logic-Based Approach

Presented by John McCarthy, this approach claims that devising intelligent systems ought to be based on the solemnised models of logical reasoning in preference to simulations of empirical rubrics of human perceptual processes. At the end of 1950s, this ideology proved to be avant-garde due to the following principles. During the 1950s, the design and implementation of systems was based on the imperative paradigm. The imperative paradigm implies that the sequence of commands to be performed by a computer should be defined in a program. In order to achieve the required result, the developer had to decide "how" the computations should be carried out. In the interim, McCarthy was of the opinion that in order to implement an intelligent system, only the required properties of the solution need to be determined. To say simply, the programmer needs to specify "what" the solution is rather than specifying "how" to obtain it. A universal issue solver, or generic programme, is designed to be used to identify the solution. Such a methodology is said to be based on the declarative paradigm. The key approaches applied in AI using the declarative paradigm are logical programming and functional programming. Logic programming is the process of expressing a problem's key characteristics as a collection of formulas in a logical language, usually first-order logic. Therefore, in order to find a solution to a particular problem using such a solver, we devise a postulate. The verification of this postulate is done by the system utilising the specifics amassed in its database along with theorems. Functional programming's foundation is the lambda calculus, which Alonzo Church and Stephen C. Kleene first introduced. By using extremely structured formulations, lambda calculus, a type of mathematical logic, is utilised to specify computing functions. The oecumenical problem-solver will be able to interpret the expression and execute a valuation of the similar functions in accordance with the dogmas of lambda calculus because the solution's mandatory qualities will be delineated by such a complex function [6].

4.2.7 Knowledge Representation Based on Rules

Newell and Simon kept researching the cognitive process model after the premise of cognitive simulation was first put forward. They proposed the production system model in 1972. Production memory and working memory are the key aspects of this model. As per psychology, long-term memory is consistent with production memory, and short-term memory is consistent with working memory. The production memory knowledge bank is exemplified using productions/rules. The outline of a production is as follows: carry out a specific activity if and only if a particular condition holds true. The activity can either be a specific activity executed on the system or an inference drawn from the condition. Given that the productions are amassed in long-term memory, it is presumed that they are accessed consistently. The data contained in the working memory changes with time. The data vis-à-vis the environment of the system is usually hoarded in the working memory. In one system reasoning mode, information is continually compared to the conditional components of the rules. The application of a rule depends on whether or not the condition is met. The working memory holds the conclusion that results from the application of a rule. If the implementation of a rule requires acting out a definite action on the environment of the system, the action is started by the system, for instance by sending a command to the processor in charge of turning off a device or by sending a command to a robot to move the robot arm [6].

4.2.8 The Structural Model Approach

Structural models of representing erudition are used to circumscribe declarative knowledge. Hierarchical structures such as graphs are typically used to outline these models. Although it was primarily used for NLP, it became clear over time that it could also be used in other AI applications. The first model of its kind, named the conceptual dependency theory, was established by Schank in the late 1960s. In contrast to Chomsky's generative grammar, Schank thought that a language's syntax was essentially a set of indicators to important material which may potentially be the foundation for semantic analysis. In order to give useful structural formalisms for automatically concluding a semantic study, conceptual dependence theory was developed. In order to undertake an automated semantic analysis using sentences of a real language, Schank devised a canonical, normalised representation of the semantic connections between language structures such as phrases and sentences. Conceptual dependency graphs are used to define such a canonical representation. These graphs' labelled nodes are conceptual primitives that can be utilised to define semantic representations. One of the earliest graph models developed using the presumptions previously outlined is semantic networks, which were first published by Collins and Quillian. Their nodes serve as representations of items or ideas, and their edges describe the connections between them (classes of abstraction, categories). Two separate relations are identified for signalling that an object goes to a specific class, as in "John Smith is a human being" and "triangle is subclass of polygon" [6].

4.2.9 What Can Artificial Intelligence Do Today? [2]

1. *Automated cars*: In 2005, STANLEY, the industry's first automated car, won the DARPA Grand Challenge. It was the first autonomous vehicle to finish the 132-mile Mojave Desert route at 22 mph. The Volkswagen Touareg is equipped with cameras, radar, and laser rangefinders to observe its surroundings. Onboard software was added to manage steering, braking, and acceleration.

2. *Speech recognition*: An automated speech recognition and dialogue management system can handle the entire call from a customer calling United Airlines to book a flight.

3. *Space exploration*: The first on-board autonomous planning programme to oversee the scheduling of activities for a spaceship was NASA's Remote Agent programme, which was launched from Earth 100 million miles away. A replacement programme called MAPGEN oversees daily operations for NASA's Mars Exploration Rovers, whereas MEXA prepared the 2008 European Space Agency Mars Express mission, including logistical and science preparation. Plans were created using high-level objectives established from the ground up, and remote agents watched as those plans were carried out, spotting flaws, diagnosing them, and correcting them.

4. *Playing the game*: In an exhibition match against Garry Kasparov, IBM's Deep Blue defeated the world champion with a mark of 3.5 to 2.5, becoming the first computer programme to do so. The competition was termed "The Brain's Last Fight" by *Newsweek* magazine, and according to Kasparov, everyone surrounding him showed a "new form of intellect." Human champions were able to draw a few games in the years that followed after reflecting on Kasparov's defeat, but in the most recent contests between humans and computers, the machine has easily won.

5. *Fighting spam*: Every day, more than a billion communications are flagged as spam by learning algorithms, preventing the recipient from having to spend time deleting what, for many users, may make up as much as 80 or 90 percent of all communications if not filtered out by algorithms. A static programmed approach would struggle to keep up with spammers' regular updating of their strategies, therefore learning algorithms perform best.

6. *Automating transportation logistics planning and scheduling*: US forces used the Dynamic Analysis and Replanning Tool (DART) during the 1991 Persian Gulf Crisis. It was necessary to simultaneously assess the starting sites, destinations, routes, and potential conflict resolution strategies for up to 50,000 vehicles (cars, trucks, and people). A plan that would have previously taken weeks to prepare using more traditional approaches might now be developed quickly thanks to AI planning tools. The 30-year investment in AI made by the Defence Advanced Research Project Agency (DARPA) is said to have more than been repaid by this one application.

7. *Robotics*: More than 2 million residential Roomba robot vacuum cleaners are available and have been marketed by the iRobot Corporation. The business also sends the more powerful PackBot to Afghanistan and Iraq to handle hazardous materials, disarm explosives, and locate snipers.

8. *Machine translation*: An automatic translation from Arabic to English allows a speaker of English to understand the headline "Erdogan Confirms That Turkey Would Not Accept any Pressure, Urging Them to Recognize Cyprus." The software created a statistical model from two trillion words

of English text samples and Arabic to English translation examples. Despite not speaking Arabic, the team's computer scientists are all skilled in ML and statistics.

4.2.10 Decentralised Artificial Intelligence Applications [7]

AI applications use a variety of planning, search, optimisation, learning, information discovery, and knowledge management methodologies to work independently and make intelligent judgments. Decentralising AI processes is a difficult and complex task, though.

1. *Autonomic computing*: One of the fundamental goals of AI applications is to enable a large number of intelligent agents—that is, little computer programs—to observe their separate environments, maintain their internal states, and take appropriate actions as necessary. In order to operate independently, in all domains—data sources, devices, data processing systems, data storage systems, and application interfaces, to mention a few—modern computing systems must manage tremendous heterogeneity. Enabling multiagent systems across all verticals facilitates the development of inter- and interlayer operability throughout entire systems, in addition to making heterogeneity easier to manage. The Blockchain architecture can aid in the creation of fully decentralised autonomous systems by enabling operational decentralisation and upholding durable traces of interactions between users, data, apps, devices, and systems [7].

2. *Optimisation*: The identification of a set of optimum answers from among all viable possibilities is one of the essential features of AI-enabled applications and systems. Modern AI applications and systems operate in a variety of environments, including ubiquitous and pervasive environments (e.g., edge computing systems), resource-constrained environments (e.g., mobile devices/systems), geographically bounded systems (e.g., personal area networks, wireless local area networks), and centralised massively parallel and distributed computing environments (e.g., cloud computing systems). Depending on the application-level and system-level objectives, the optimisation approaches can be used effectively in limited or unconstrained environments. With the aid of these methods, it is simpler to find the best solutions, such as selecting the most relevant data sources for pervasive systems, the best edge or cloud servers for processing data and applications, or enabling resource-efficient data management in massive distributed computing environments. The processing of unneeded and irrelevant data as well as poor system and application performance result from the execution of current optimisation strategies under centrally controlled supervision while taking into account system- and application-wide optimisation objectives. The use of Blockchain to enable

decentralised optimisation algorithms creates new options for research and development. The decentralised optimisation processes highly pertinent data to improve system performance. When several techniques with various optimisation goals must be used simultaneously across applications and systems, decentralised optimisation is also advantageous [7].

3. *Planning*: Planning approaches are used by AI applications and systems to collaborate with other applications and systems to address complex problems in unique contexts. Planning strategies improve the operational effectiveness and resilience of AI applications and systems by utilising the current input state and executing various logic and rule-based algorithms to complete predefined goals. Decentralised AI planning solutions based on Blockchain are necessary to deliver more effective strategies with ongoing tracking and provenance history, while centralised planning is currently a challenging and time-consuming endeavour. The Blockchain can be used to build an essential and immutable blueprint for strategic applications and mission-critical systems [7].

4. *Knowledge discovery and knowledge management*: Because they handle enormous amounts of data streams, modern AI applications must enable centralised big data processing systems. The centralisation of information discovery and knowledge management promotes the provision of application- and system-wide intelligence, but the applications enable customised knowledge patterns for specific user groups, applications, devices, and systems. Decentralised knowledge management and knowledge discovery methods are intended to deliver tailored knowledge patterns that take into account the needs of all system stakeholders. Additionally, the Blockchain technology can help diverse AI application and system stakeholders transmit knowledge in a traceable and safe manner [7].

5. *Perception*: Intelligent agents and bots systems are used by AI applications to continuously collect, analyse, choose, and organise ambient environment data, which results in monolithic data collection. The collecting of information from various points of view can be made easier by decentralised perception systems. Decentralisation based on Blockchain technology makes it easier to track perception trajectories, transfer collected data securely, and store data in an immutable way. Because successful and high-quality perceptions do not require recurrent data collection by applications and systems, decentralised perception solutions are advantageous. Because of its permanent nature, Blockchain should only be used to record the traces of successful perceptions [7].

6. *Learning*: The core of AI applications continues to be learning algorithms, which allow automation and knowledge discovery processes. Different learning algorithms include supervised, unsupervised, semi-supervised, ensemble, reinforcement, transfer, and deep learning models. These learning models deal with a range of ML concerns, such as mining for regular patterns, clustering, and regression analysis. Traditional learning models are trained and deployed using centralised infrastructure in order to achieve

global intelligence. Decentralised learning models can be used to create the highly distributed and autonomous learning systems that support fully coordinated local intelligence across all domains in modern AI systems. The Blockchain also enables the immutable and extremely secure modification of learning models by keeping the origin and history of data. However, due to the irreversible nature of smart contracts, learning models must be fully trained and assessed before being implemented on Blockchain [7].

7. *Search*: Due to the fact that AI applications must function in extremely large and sparse search areas, effective search algorithms are at the heart of AI technology (big datasets or multivariable high-dimensional data streams). Completeness, complexity, and optimality are only a few of the factors that are taken into consideration when designing the search algorithms. The algorithms used by these techniques often operate on nonlinear data structures like trees and graphs, where they begin small and progressively get larger until they find the required variable or complete traversing the full search space. In order to enhance operational efficiency, search strategies are typically executed employing large-scale centralised and distributed infrastructure. However, their utilisation of a decentralised infrastructure requires critical examination. It is suggested that Blockchain and decentralised structure be utilised to permanently and securely retain successful search traces and traversal paths that can provide the best search solutions for comparable activities in the upcoming instead of building fundamental search algorithms [7].

8. *Rationalisation*: A crucial element of AI applications is logic programming, which enables the creation of rules for inductive or deductive reasoning. In AI applications, centralised reasoning results in generalised global behaviour across all application components. Blockchain-based distributed reasoning techniques are projected to make it easier to construct individualised reasoning strategies that could be more advantageous when it comes to perception, learning, and model application. Additionally, imprintable reasoning processes are made available by Blockchain-based decentralised distributed reasoning powered by smart contracts, which may facilitate the execution of comparable reasoning techniques in the future [7].

4.2.11 Challenges for Artificial Intelligence [1]

Some of the challenges for AI are:

1. Inconvenient to explain results
2. Possibility of bias in algorithms and data
3. Procuring vast and all-inclusive datasets for training
4. Manual labelling of training data
5. Generalisation of learning
6. Privacy concerns.

4.3 BLOCKCHAIN TECHNOLOGY

Blockchain is a record-keeping tool that was created so that hacking the system or forging the data stored on it is out of the question, thereby protecting it and validating its immutability. The category of distributed ledger technology (DLT) includes Blockchain. The DLT is a technological tool for simultaneously logging transactions and linked data across many different places. Each computer in a Blockchain network maintains a replica of the ledger that is instantly updated and validated in order to prevent having a single point of failure. Although it varies from conventional databases in instead of rows, columns, tables, and files, it stores data in blocks that are digitally connected together, Blockchain is also recognised as a sort of database. Because it is run by computers connected to a peer-to-peer network relatively than the central computer network of conventional databases, it is a decentralised database [8]. Decentralisation, persistency, anonymity, and auditability are the fundamental characteristics of a Blockchain. It is potential for Blockchain to function in a decentralised environment since it integrates several key technologies like cryptographic hash, asymmetric cryptography, and distributed consensus mechanism. With the use of Blockchain, transactions take place in a decentralised manner, proving to be efficient and cost-effective [9].

Due to its decentralisation feature, a third-party trusted authority does not exist. Hence a consensus mechanism is adopted to assure consistency and steadiness of data, along with the transactions undertaken by each distributed node. Proof of Stake (PoS) and Proof of Work (PoW) are the two primary consensus processes used by current Blockchain systems (PoW). Other consensus mechanisms under operation include Proof of Bandwidth and Proof of Elapsed Time. The PoW mechanism is used by the most common applications, including Bitcoin and Ethereum. The PoS method is included in Ethereum as well. The PoS technique is also used by cryptocurrencies like PeerCoin and ShadowCash. Ascertaining the credibility of the data by solving a series of puzzles is referred to as a PoW mechanism. Though the puzzle is computationally gruelling, its verification is effortless. Each time a block or transaction is initiated by a node, it must unscramble a PoW puzzle. Once the PoW has been unscrambled, it is transmitted to erstwhile nodes, thus accomplishing the purpose of consensus [9]. Figure 4.1 depicts the difference between a legitimate block and a malicious block.

The three chief components of a block are PrevHash, Nonce, and Transaction (T). The block's distinguishing information is provided by PrevHash. Nonce is acquired by unscrambling the PoW puzzle. T is the transaction carried out. Finding a Nonce is the primary goal of solving the PoW problem. Once the Nonce is obtained, the miner hashes some other information along with the Nonce; the result of this hashing must be lower than a target value. The intricacy of the PoW puzzle can be modified by varying the target value. The PoS mechanism works on the basis of validating the authority of the data by proving the ownership of cryptocurrency. Ethereum's money, known as Ethers, must be paid in a predetermined quantity by the miners in order to create a block. The Ether is returned to the original

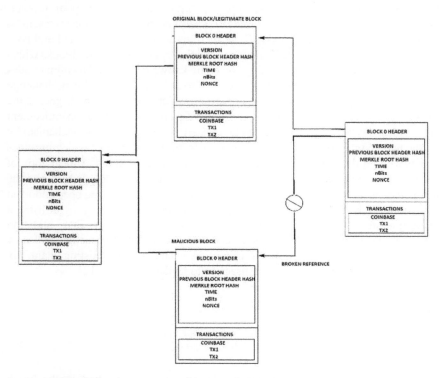

Figure 4.1 Representation of a legitimate block and a malicious block [10].

node if the block can be validated in due time; otherwise, it is fined. The PoW mechanism requires lots of calculations, leading to a wastage of computational capability. However, PoS technology greatly reduces the computations, increasing the throughput of the Blockchain system [11]. The financial sector is the key user of Blockchain technology. The usage of Blockchain extends beyond money, even if Bitcoin is the most well-known application. Blockchain can be used in many monetary services, including digital assets, remittance, and online payments; subsequently it allows the completion of payments without the participation of a bank or new middleman. Blockchain is one of the most promising technologies for the IoT, security, reputation, smart contracts, and public services [9].

4.3.1 Blockchain Architecture

A transaction is initiated in a decentralised network by a node. The node uses a private key cryptography technique for digital signatures. A transaction can be thought of as a specific kind of data structure that represents the exchange of digital assets between peers on a Blockchain network. A flooding protocol named Gossip is used to propagate the unendorsed transactions hoarded in the transaction pool throughout the network. The peers are required to choose and authenticate the transactions using pre-established benchmarks. Once the transaction has been tested and confirmed by the miners, the node is added to a block. Peers who mine for blocks with a significant portion of their processing power are known as miners. The miner nodes must expend enough of their CPU resources to solve a computational challenge before they may publish a block. The opportunity of creating a new node goes to the miner who solves the puzzle first. Upon successful creation of block, an enticement is provided. The new block is then authenticated using a consensus mechanism by all the peers in the network. Consensus mechanism is a technique which provides assistance to a decentralised network to agree on specific affairs. A local copy of the newly added block is then sent to each peer in the immutable ledger, and the fresh block is then added to the chain. The deal is regarded as having been endorsed at this point. The following block connects to the most recent block by utilising a cryptographic hash pointer. This results in the block receiving its first validation while the transaction receives its second confirmation. The transaction will now need to be reconfirmed each time a fresh block is added to the existing chain. Six confirmations are necessary for a transaction to be deemed final [12].

Components of a Block

Block body and block header are the two primary parts.
   The following are the parts of the block header:

1. The set of appropriate block validation rules is described in the block version.
2. The block before it is referenced by this 256-bit hash value is called the parent block hash.
3. The sum of all the transactions in the block is shown by the Merkle tree root hash.
4. The timestamp, as of 1970–01–01T00:00 UTC, is displayed.
5. nBits give a compressed version of the hash value of the current target.
6. When a hash calculation is made, a 4-byte field called a nonce is created [9].

A Distributed Ledger System's Characteristics [13]

1. *Programmable*: Smart contract usage suggests that Blockchain technology can be programmed.
2. *Safeguarded*: Each record is encrypted individually.
3. *Anonymity*: The participant's identity is either unheard of or pseudonymous.
4. *Unanimous*: All participants in the network authenticate each other's records.
5. *Timestamped*: A block records the timestamp at which a transaction has occurred.

6. *Immutable*: Authenticated records cannot be changed.
7. *Distributed*: A copy of the ledger is provided to the participants to ensure transparency.

Blockchain Characteristics [14]

1. *Decentralisation*: With regard to traditional centralised transaction systems, every transaction is authenticated via a reliable central organisation. Keeping this in mind, decentralisation requires trust—the primary concern—accompanied by lift resilience, availability, and fail over. The Blockchain architecture, consisting of a decentralised peer-to-peer network, is proven to solve most of the issues. A transaction in the Blockchain network is conducted without the validation of a central agency amid any two peers in contrast to the traditional centralised systems. Thus, the primary concern of reliability is mitigated by utilising the plethora of consensus mechanisms available. Additionally, it reduces the server costs and also helps to abate the performance bottlenecks occurring at the central server. On the other hand, Blockchain has several tradeoffs. For instance, the server and energy costs of Bitcoin and Ethereum are rather high, with the performance being somewhat lower.

2. *Persistence*: An infrastructure that can measure the truthfulness of data is provided by Blockchain. This empowers producers and consumers alike to prove that their data is genuine and that their data has not been modified. Every transaction is connected to the previous one. For instance, let us consider that a Blockchain comprises 30 blocks, and the 30th block contains the hash value of the preceding block. In order to create a new block, the knowledge of the current block is used. Thus, all blocks are interlinked and interconnected to each other throughout the chain. At this point, if any transaction is revised elementarily, the hash of the entire block is transformed appreciably. Consequently, in order to alter any info, an individual needs to modify the entire preceding block's hash data. Considering the amount of rework that needs to be done, it is a daunting and exorbitantly arduous task. In addition, after a miner creates a block, the network as a whole verifies it. As a result, any data tampering or fabrication will be discovered right away. Blockchain is regarded as an immutable distributed ledger because it can't be easily altered for the aforementioned reasons.

3. *Anonymity*: With a randomly created address, communication with the network of Blockchain is possible. With a randomly created address, communication with the Blockchain network is possible. A Blockchain user can have numerous addresses on a Blockchain network to conceal his or her identity. The system is decentralised, thus there is not a centralised body that keeps track of or logs user data. Thus to a certain extent, anonymity is offered by Blockchain owing to its trustless environment.

4. *Auditability*: A digital timestamp and distributed ledger serve as the record and verification, respectively, of every transaction that takes place within a Blockchain network. As a result, by gaining access to any network node, it is feasible to audit and trace earlier records. For instance, Bitcoin allows for the iterative tracing of all transactions, facilitating the auditability and transparency of the data state in the Blockchain. However, it becomes extremely difficult to track the source of the money when it is spread across numerous accounts.

Blockchain Taxonomy [9]

Public Blockchain, private Blockchain, and consortium Blockchain are the three broad categories currently used to describe Blockchain systems. They are evaluated based these three varieties of Blockchain from various angles.

1. *Establishing consensus*: In a public Blockchain, any node may partake in the consensus process. Additionally, in association of Blockchain, only a specific group of nodes are in responsible of validating blocks. Private chains are totally governed by a single organisation, which has the power to select the ultimate consensus.
2. *Read permission*: A private Blockchain or consortium Blockchain is necessary for read permission, even though anybody can access transactions on a public Blockchain. Whether or not the stored information is open to the public can be decided by the consortium or the organisation.
3. *Immutability*: It is nearly impossible to alter the public Blockchain because transactions are kept across multiple nodes in the distributed network. The dominant organisation or the majority of the consortium, however, may decide to meddle in or reverse the private or consortium Blockchain.
4. *Efficiency*: Blocks and transactions spread slowly on the public Blockchain network because of the enormous number of nodes. If network security were taken into consideration, public Blockchain laws would be far tougher. High latency and limited transaction throughput are the results. Both consortium Blockchain and private Blockchain might operate more effectively with fewer validators.
5. *Centralised*: Because a single entity controls private Blockchains, they are completely centralised, whereas consortium Blockchains are partially centralised and public Blockchains are decentralised. This is where the three different types of Blockchains diverge most.
6. *Process of consensus*: The consensus procedure on the public Blockchain is open to everybody on the planet. Private and consortium Blockchains, in contrast to public Blockchains, both require authorisation to function. One node must be certified in order to participate in the consensus process in a consortium or private Blockchain.

4.3.2 Applications [15]

Applications for Financing

1. *Cryptocurrency*: A system of interconnected networks and a medium of exchange that guarantees secure exchanges. Bitcoin, Litecoin, Ripple, and Monero are examples.
2. *Trading, settlement, and securities settlement*: Businesses only provide a bank syndicate with public shares. On a market powered by the Blockchain, private shares may be traded. Examples include Medici, Blockstream, Coinsetter, and NASDAQ private equity.
3. *Insurance*: A Blockchain can be used to register real estate. The transaction history is available to insurers for monitoring. Example: Everledger.

Non-financial Applications

1. *Public Notary*: Central notary authorisation will no longer be obligatory. Examples: Stampery, Viacoin, and Ascribe.
2. *Music industry*: Managing ownership rights. Example: Imogen Heap.
3. *Proof of documents*: Storing and authenticating a document's signature and timestamp using Blockchain.
4. *Storage*: A peer-to-peer distributed cloud storing technique can be used to transfer the documents without the aid of a third party.
5. *IoT*: Blockchain-based storage of smart device communication within the IoT. Filament ADEPT is an example (developed by IBM and Samsung).
6. *Anti-forgery applications*: A Blockchain network made up of market participants can be used to verify the commodities' legitimacy. Example: Blockverify.
7. *Internet applications*: Domain name servers are co-ordinated by the users rather than governments and corporations. Example: Namecoin.

4.3.3 Limitations

There are a number of technological challenges to overcome even if the Blockchain technology has a lot of potential for developing the next generation of Internet infrastructure. Scalability is the primary problem, and it is a big one. Bitcoin blocks can only be 1 MB in size and are mined every 10 minutes or so. High-frequency trading is not possible since the Bitcoin network can only process seven transactions per second. Greater blocks, however, require more storage space and propagate more slowly over the network. Users will want to maintain a large Blockchain, which will gradually lead to centralisation. Consequently, it has become difficult to balance security and block size. Second, it has been demonstrated that selfish mining tactics can let miners earn more money than is fair to them. To generate more money in the future, miners conceal their extracted blocks. Because of the possibility of frequent branching, Blockchain development is hampered. Therefore, some remedies must be proposed in order to resolve this issue. Additionally, it has been established that Blockchain users still experience privacy leakage even when they utilise their public key and private key solely for transactions. Even the actual IP address of the user can be known. Additionally, there are a number of significant issues with current consensus mechanisms like PoW and PoS. For example, PoW consumes excessive amounts of electricity, and the PoS consensus process may result in a situation where the wealthy continue to get richer [9]. The financial crisis also showed that it is not always simple to determine who is the right current owner of an asset, especially in the financial services industry. For international financial transaction services, tracing ownership over a longer chain of shifting consumers presents a more difficult challenge [15].

4.4 INTEGRATING ARTIFICIAL INTELLIGENCE AND BLOCKCHAIN

Blockchain and AI are two disruptive technologies that have the power to alter corporate practises and have an impact on society. Their fusion may result in decentralised AI, which permits analysis, judgments, and self-learning using shared, trusted data kept on the Blockchain. In a multi-agent environment, autonomous agents are able to work together, take action, and make decisions. Decentralised AI can enhance system performance by digesting pertinent data and doing parallel computations across nodes depending on various goals [1]. Organisations and consortiums are able to communicate data across organisational boundaries using Blockchain while maintaining confidence in the shared data. It will be feasible for AI systems to offer more valuable insights by giving them access to this common data, which would not otherwise be available [1].

On one hand, Blockchain has flaws including security, scalability, and effectiveness. However, AI also has its fair share of privacy, explainability, and trustworthiness problems. The union of these two technologies seems inevitable; they might enhance one another and transform the upcoming digital generation. Blockchain's trustlessness, anonymity, and explain ability will be advantageous to AI; in exchange, AI can assist in the development of an ML system on the Blockchain for greater security, scalability, and more effective personalisation and governance. For a variety of AI components, including data, algorithms, and processing power, Blockchain can enable decentralised marketplaces and coordination platforms. These will encourage AI innovation and adoption at a never-before-seen pace. Additionally, Blockchain will make AI judgments more transparent, comprehensible, and reliable. AI is necessary for protecting user security and privacy because all data on Blockchain is open to the public. A Blockchain's design and operation entail tens of thousands of variables and trade-offs among security, speed, decentralisation, and other factors. AI can simplify these decisions and automate and optimise Blockchain for better performance and governance. Additionally, AI is necessary for maintaining users' security and privacy because all data on Blockchain is open to the public [16].

Transforming AI Using Blockchain

1. *Advanced information security*: The storage of data on Blockchains is incredibly secure. Blockchains are renowned for securely storing private and sensitive data in a diskless environment. Since digitally signed data is stored in Blockchain databases, the "respective private keys" need to be kept protected. Results of decision-making are made more dependable and believable by allowing AI algorithms to operate on protected data.

2. *Enhancing trust in robotic decisions*. When an AI agent makes a decision that is hard for users or customers to comprehend and believe, the AI agent becomes dysfunctional. Blockchain is well-known for documenting transactions in decentralised ledgers point by point, in addition to making it easier to accept and trust the judgments made. This makes it simpler to accept and have faith in the decisions made because it guarantees that the records have not been altered during the human-involved auditing process. If an AI system's decision-making process were documented on a Blockchain, which would encourage openness, the public would be more willing to believe robotic results. The requirement for a third-party auditor can be avoided in a swarm robotic ecosystem where the swarm's consensus can be obtained through an entirely decentralised method.

3. *Collective decision-making*: All agents in a robotic swarm environment must cooperate in order to accomplish the swarm goal. Many robotic applications use decentralised and distributed decision-making algorithms, since they do not require a central authority. Robots vote on issues, with the decision being decided by the majority. Since Blockchain is available to all robots and allows for the submission of transactions, it can be used to verify election results. Each robot can cast a vote. All robots participate in this procedure repeatedly until the swarm comes to a finish.

4. *Decentralised intelligence*: When making intelligent high-level decisions that require multiple agents performing different subtasks while having access to the same training data, scheduling issues can be overcome and various individual cybersecurity AI agents can be combined to provide fully coordinated security across the underlying networks.

5. *High effectiveness*: Because so many parties must approve business transactions, multiuser business procedures including individual users, corporate corporations, and governmental organisations are inherently inefficient. Intelligent decentralised autonomous agents (or DAOs) can be used for automatic and quick validation of data, value, and asset transfers across various stakeholders thanks to the integration of Blockchain and AI technology [7].

Due to the deficiency of trust among multiple data stakeholders, the data utilised for AI training or analysis is limited in quantity and incomplete in diversity, which significantly restricts data sharing throughout the entire Internet. Since actual large data acquired from numerous sources is the fuel for AI, the rise of Blockchain technology has happily created a viable, efficient, and real way to enable trust data interchange in a trustless environment. This could aid AI in making better judgement calls. The efficiency of AI algorithms can be considerably increased if data can be efficiently networked and merged. By allowing data sharing among many service providers, it might be possible to maximise the use of distributed data across numerous companies with potential conflicts of interest, which might lead to a more useful AI. It is not surprising that AI can become one of the most efficient technologies and methods to increase cybersecurity-assumed sufficient data and Blockchain-based smart contracts for secure data sharing. In order to save time, AI can evaluate massive amounts of data more quickly, identify dangers more quickly, and help decision-makers make more accurate predictions about the security measures that a PDC should take. Additionally, as AI is built with ML inside, it is constantly able to recognise patterns in both real-world data and fictional data produced by generative adversarial network (GAN). This allows AI to continuously refine its tactics and strengthen its capacity for doing so on a 24/7/365 basis [3].

Blockchain in AI [7]

Blockchain applications can be classified as permissioned or permission-less systems.

1. *Public*: It is well-known that users of public Blockchain s have the ability to download the Blockchain code onto their own computers, alter it, and practice it any way they see fit. Additionally easy to use, read-only public Blockchains are accessible to all network users for both read and write operations. These Blockchains manage user identities and transactional privacy by using anonymous and pseudonymous data on the network due to their openness. These open Blockchains also use advanced security and consensus protocols. To move assets and data, these Blockchains require native tokens, which are sometimes referred to as cryptocurrencies or value pointers for each public Blockchain. Because of their high decentralisation and transparency, public Blockchains are widely used; yet, the users and validators on these Blockchains are never identified. These Blockchains are therefore constantly vulnerable to malicious security attacks, which may lead to data theft and the loss of priceless things. In order to crack security codes on public Blockchains, it takes a lot of work and consensus from at least 51 percent of validators. If invaders manage to seize 51 percent of the validators on the network, they are also exposed to attack.

2. *Private*: A single business controls a private Blockchain. In contrast to public Blockchains, where users and participants must be pre-approved for read/write activities and are known to the network every time, private Blockchains are designed as permissioned systems. Private Blockchains are comparable faster because validators and network members have established identities, necessitating less intricate mathematical procedures to validate network transactions. Additionally, private Blockchains can move any ways of local information, assets, and values throughout the network. Algorithms for voting or multiparty consensus are used to approve transactions and asset transfers since they are low energy and enable rapid transactions. On private Blockchains, the sanction time for a transaction typically falls under a second.

3. *Consortium*: Federated Blockchains, also known as consortium Blockchains, are managed by a variety of organisations. The foundation of the individuals typically comprises the shared interests of the participating organisations. Various federated Blockchain models are offered by various entities, including banks, governmental organisations, and private Blockchain companies. Although only a small number of users have read and write access to the Blockchain, consortium Blockchains operate as permissioned systems similarly to private Blockchains. All network users can normally access data on the Blockchain, but only a select group of verified and authorised users are permitted to write data to the Blockchain. They are substantially faster than public Blockchains since consortium members are each time pre-approved and have established identities. Energy utilisation is also reduced as a result of the voting-based or multiparty approval-based consensus mechanisms utilised by these Blockchains. A transaction is often authorised on federated Blockchains in one second.

4. *Blockchain-as-a-Service (BaaS)*: Due to their extensive adoption and endorsement by major corporations and governments, Blockchain technologies are attracting a lot of interest from cloud service providers. Major cloud providers including Microsoft, Amazon, and IBM are developing and testing Blockchain services for users in their environments. Both private and consortium Blockchain firms stand to benefit from the creation of BaaS as long as their primary focus is on value addition through application development, testing, and deployment rather than taking into account underlying network, storage, and compute infrastructure. BaaS enablement supports the exploitation of new business opportunities, company-customer engagement models, and cross-industry public-private consortiums. Developers have the option to set up BaaS services with a single click in order to generate smart contracts. Given that the major cloud providers already provide a variety of cloud services for AI applications, the marriage of BaaS and AI services is opening up an entirely new universe of opportunities for application developers.

4.4.1 Applications of Decentralised Frameworks in Artificial Intelligence and Blockchain

4.4.1.1 Nonlinear Architecture

In addition to continuous execution, the multichain designs may support a wide range of business situations and cross-chain value transfers. Blockchain geographies are employed in multichain topologies that execute nonlinear Blockchain models as principal side chains, parent–child chains, and equal chains. In a multichain design, at least one chain serves as the fundamental chain and stores information about other chains. The remaining chains serve as equal, side, or child chains. Equal chains can function apart from other chains. Both child chains and side chains normally work in a similar way; however, although side chains can unquestionably exist independently from basic chains, commercial issues in child chains are tightly tied to parent chains. The pegging approach, which is employed to carry out the worth exchange between several chains, uses a two-way peg measure for bidirectional worth exchange at a fixed swapping scale. Local coins or tokens speak to the value of trading in the Blockchain. Nonlinear Blockchains for AI applications promote the execution of multiple connected or autonomous AI processes in the decentralised apps. The AI management for environment production is sent on the parent chain, whereas the preparation and testing applications are provided on test nets or side chains. Additionally, the adaptability features allow for equal execution of AI applications during both the planning and event phases. For this situation, learning models are created on side chains and sent on major chains. Applications that employ support and flexible learning calculations, for example, have an advantage over those that do not use nonlinear designs since the main applications must regularly update their presentation by retraining the learning models [6].

4.4.1.2 Linear Structure

Single chains are used by early decentralised systems, although these frameworks have a number of drawbacks. As they compete with the ongoing exhibition of decentralised applications, single chains expand slowly. In Blockchain designs based on single chains, which are generated linearly, current blocks are attached at the end of the chain. Every business scenario involving this type of data also requires different single chains, and resource exchange in several chains is confusing. Single chain–based Blockchains may be more advantageous when only the presentation history needs to be permanently maintained reasonably rather than operating the AI applications employing smart contracts. For a single AI application to conduct search, augmentation, and learning, or to function independently in consistent surroundings, a single Blockchain can be employed. Consider how a powerful learning model is used in radiology apps to analyse liver cancer and produce accurate results. A full AI application segment on Blockchain is not a possibility because AI apps often function in unconstrained settings. The efficient hunt impressions of far-off mechanical robots could serve as another paradigm [6].

4.5 INTEGRATING THE CLOUD

Here, we demonstrate how Blockchain and AI may use the cloud to enhance AI applications' security, dependability, trustworthiness, transparency, information management, and computation. The importance and aspects of integrating Blockchain technology and AI with cloud infrastructure are described next.

With regard to Blockchain as a cloud service, cloud computing is not replaced by a Blockchain foundation. Consequently, it isolates and democratises a few parts of it. The cloud computing architecture is imitated by the Blockchain foundation as well. Blockchain can be used to run new kinds of thin apps, also known as smart agreements, because it is a thin cloud when compared to an effective standard cloud computing base. These are the grounds for adopting Blockchain virtual computers for business transactions. It now pays to execute a company plan on the Blockchain that runs with genuine employees, which represents a development in terms of the cost of the virtual machine. One need not bother about setting them up because they are managed by further clients who are funded to run the framework [17].

4.6 OPEN RESEARCH CONTROVERSIES

The current difficulties with fusing Blockchain and AI technology are covered in this section. The following is a list of potential obstacles to combining both technologies:

1. *Privacy*: While public Blockchain ledgers provide secure and authentic data processing, all readers have open access to the information that has been gathered. This could lead to concerns about privacy infringement. Additionally, IoT's ubiquitous sensing devices continuously collect the private and sensitive information of users, and posting that information to open ledgers may cause privacy concerns. Private Blockchain ledgers could protect data privacy by enabling encryption and allowing only certain users to access the ledgers. However, such private Blockchain systems would be limiting in terms of access and exposure the large amount of data that may be needed for AI to ingest and execute decision-making and analytics that are precise and accurate.
2. *Scalability*: This is one of the main problems with the current Blockchain platform. Side chains are another problem. In terms of cryptocurrency Blockchain platforms, the Ethereum Blockchain can process 12 transactions per

second compared to the Bitcoin Blockchain's average processing speed of 4 transactions per second. Comparatively speaking, Facebook, which does millions of transactions per second, including likes, posts, and comments, such performance is just awful. Blockchains that allow for speedy settlement of transactions between parties outside of the main chain and just one settlement per day on the main chain are known as side chains (also known as side channels). The consensus methods used by mining nodes are greatly improved by several new emerging types of Blockchains. As an illustration, systems like Algorand and IoTA can deliver performance that is noticeably superior to Ethereum and Hyperledger Blockchains. However, additional work needs to be done to increase the scalability so that it can compete with Facebook and similar services.

3. *Deterministic execution and vulnerabilities in smart contracts*: The implementation of a smart contract must be ensured to be secure from attacks and be bug-free. The network's code and data need to be protected since they could be targets for assaults. For instance, a severe programming weakness led to the hacking of the DAO's Ethereum-based smart contract in 2016. As a result 3.6 million Ether were lost. Undoubtedly, to address the issue raised by smart contract programming and other Blockchain-based applications, Blockchain engineering is necessary. Poor and careless programming methods in the languages used to construct the smart contracts code are to blame for the vulnerability issues (e.g., Solidity and Chaincode). It is now essential to test smart contracts for vulnerabilities, and a number of tools have been developed to assess the code's security. Additionally, smart contract execution results are currently entirely deterministic and cannot be probabilistic. Decentralised AI that uses ML and AI decision-making algorithms that are executed as smart contracts by mining nodes may find this to be a significant difficulty. Smart contracts are often deterministic, but more unexpected, erratic, and frequently approximate. This calls for a cutting-edge approach to handle approximation in computation and to design consensus protocols for mining nodes to agree on outcomes with a certain level of certainty, accuracy, or precision, as well as with data input that may be highly erratic, like that of IoT and sensory readings.

4. *Trusted oracles*: Smart contracts are planned to be triggered through uncontrollable external events or uncontrollable uninterruptible external operations by Blockchain participants. Triggering of events or the self-starting data retrieval are not features of smart contracts. In other words, data from the outside world cannot be retrieved by the contracts. To the contracts, data and events must be pushed. The usage of trustworthy oracles, which are essentially trusted third parties or nodes, as an option to push events and data to smart contracts, is being suggested as a way to address these drawbacks. When using oracles, a truly decentralised system becomes concentrated around a collection of oracles that must be trusted, which adds a layer

of complexity and insecurity to establishing and managing trust. To obtain agreement, voting among reliable oracles is frequently employed.

5. *New consensus protocols tailored for AI*: By permitting various proof-of-X protocols, existing consensus algorithms take into account the network and middleware layers of Blockchain systems. Future researchers have a wide range of chances to investigate whether application-level consensus protocols may be created taking into account proofs based on the quality of learning models, effective search techniques, quality and provenance of data, and quality of optimisation.

6. *Fog computing concept*: A recently created paradigm for computing known as "fog computing" enables localised processing and data storage near the sources of data being produced by consumers or IoT devices. Fog nodes are frequently utilised to improve the significant delay that cloud computing and storage experience. Fog nodes can be compared to a nearby little cloud. In order to manage, access, and govern data locally, future fog nodes must have access to AI and ML capabilities as well as a Blockchain interface. This is necessary in the context of Blockchain and AI.

7. *Inadequate standards, interoperability, and rules*: Blockchain technology standards have not yet been developed. Standards are now being developed for Blockchain interoperability, governance, integration, and architecture by organisations like IEEE, NIST, ITU, and many more standards groups. Additionally, institutional and governmental guidelines, rules, laws, and regulations must be established at the local, national, and international levels for Blockchain deployment, arbitration, and dispute resolution in the context of AI applications, particularly for open Blockchain transactions involving financing and automated payments using cryptocurrencies. In order to define the right set of technical standards for Blockchain architectural models, services, deployment, and interoperability, research must be directed towards creating models and proof of concepts.

8. *Quantum computing*: It is anticipated that in the upcoming, this technology will be able to breakdown public key encryption, exposing the private key. The current state of Blockchain relies on digital signatures that use public key encryption. According to some researchers, quantum computing will weaken Blockchain's core security by 2027. In order to guarantee high performance and scalability while enduring such breakability, this necessitates considerable study on quantum-safe and secure Blockchain. This also calls for reliable migration strategies and compatibility with quantum-resistant Blockchain platforms.

9. *Governance*: A Blockchain platform with many users and stakeholders requires a lot of work to set up, develop, and manage. There are many important issues to consider, including the type of Blockchain to deploy (e.g., Hyperledger or Ethereum); who will manage and troubleshoot the Blockchain; where the Blockchain nodes will be deployed; who will develop the

smart contracts; how to handle disputes; how to choose trustworthy oracles; how to deploy side channels; and rules and standards to adhere to. This calls for study aimed at developing effective governance models [7].

4.7 CONCLUSIONS

Blockchain integration has the ability to destroy current business models and have a long-lasting impact on technology, hence it might be viewed as disruptive. Since its birth in the late 1950s, AI has grown manifold today. Almost all of the current Internet services utilise AI to enhance the user's experience and provide accurate results. Blockchain proved to be a revolutionary technology since the financial crisis of 2008. Today the application of Blockchain goes beyond cryptocurrency. However, each technology comes with its own inadequacies. When it comes to AI privacy, explainability and trustworthiness are the major concerns. On the other hand, Blockchain's flaws include security, scalability, and effectiveness. Integrating the two technologies would transform the upcoming digital generation. If we integrate the two technologies, the two would complement each other and help in building a better technology for the future.

REFERENCES

[1] Chavali, B., Khatri, S.K. and Hossain, S.A., 2020, June. AI and Blockchain Integration. In *2020 8th International Conference on Reliability, Infocom Technologies and Optimization (Trends and Future Directions)(ICRITO)* (pp. 548–552). IEEE.

[2] Russell, S.J. and Norvig, P., 2010. *Artificial intelligence a modern approach.* Prentice Hall.

[3] Jeon, H.J., Youn, H.C., Ko, S.M. and Kim, T.H., 2022. Blockchain and AI meet in the metaverse. In *Advances in the convergence of blockchain and artificial intelligence*, Vol. 73. IntechOpen Limited, United Kingdom. doi: 10.5772/intechopen.99114

[4] Norris, D.J., 2017. *Beginning AI with the Raspberry Pi* (pp. 1–369). Apress.

[5] Nilsson, N.J., 2009. *The quest for AI.* Cambridge University Press.

[6] Flasiński, M., 2016. *Introduction to AI.* Springer International Publishing.

[7] Salah, K., Rehman, M.H.U., Nizamuddin, N. and Al-Fuqaha, A., 2019. Blockchain for AI: Review and open research challenges. *IEEE Access*, 7, pp. 10127–10149.

[8] Online Source. Available at: www.techtarget.com/searchcio/definition/Blockchain #:~:text=Blockchain %20is%20a%20record%2Dkeeping,places%20at%20the%20 same%20time.

[9] Zheng, Z., Xie, S., Dai, H.N., Chen, X. and Wang, H., 2018. Blockchain challenges and opportunities: A survey. *International Journal of Web and Grid Services*, 14(4), pp. 352–375.

[10] Online Source. Available at: https://academy.horizen.io/technology/advanced/ Blockchain -as-a-data-structure/.

[11] Li, X., Jiang, P., Chen, T., Luo, X. and Wen, Q., 2020. A survey on the security of Blockchain systems. *Future Generation Computer Systems*, 107, pp. 841–853.

[12] Monrat, A.A., Schelén, O. and Andersson, K., 2019. A survey of Blockchain from the perspectives of applications, challenges, and opportunities. *IEEE Access*, 7, pp. 117134–117151.

[13] Online Source. Available at: www.euromoney.com/learning/Blockchain-explained/what-is-Blockchain

[14] Monrat, A.A., Schelén, O. and Andersson, K., 2019. A survey of Blockchain from the perspectives of applications, challenges, and opportunities. *IEEE Access*, 7, pp. 117134–117151.

[15] Nofer, M., Gomber, P., Hinz, O. and Schiereck, D., 2017. Blockchain. *Business & Information Systems Engineering*, 59(3), pp. 183–187.

[16] Dinh, T.N. and Thai, M.T., 2018. AI and blockchain: A disruptive integration. *Computer*, 51(9), pp. 48–53.

[17] Hussain, A.A. and Al-Turjman, F., 2021. AI and Blockchain: A review. *Transactions on Emerging Telecommunications Technologies*, 32(9), p. e4268.

Chapter 5

Impact of Renewable Energy Resources and Industry 4.0 on Growth of Economics and Policy for Developing Nations

Dheeraj Kumar, Rakesh Kumar, Nagendra Kumar, Amit Kumar, Gopi Kannan K., and Ashish Kumar

5.1 INTRODUCTION

The industrial revolution, which introduces progress, change, and disparities across nations, is the use of new methods and procedures for manufacturing and associated activities [1]. It causes rapid, profound changes that have an impact on all society levels for a very long time.

Coal and the steam engine were originally introduced during the First Industrial Revolution [2]. The Second Industrial Revolution, which was defined by the era of science and electricity, followed this [3]. The emergence of the Internet, micro-electronics, renewable resources, cleaner technology, and recycling are examples of the Third Industrial Revolution, which was an improvement over the second in the early 1990s [4]. The mass manufacturing age, renewable energy (RE), and the Internet of Things (IoT) are the forerunners of Industry 4.0 [5]. The gap between industrialized and developing nations widened as a result of this transition [6]. Developing countries lagged despite having a large population and an abundance of natural resources because they lacked the reliable electricity and energy required to operate batch systems and other mass-production equipment. Industry 4.0, the current industrial revolution, began in the last ten years. Several nations, such as China, have implemented and used different aspects of this technology [7].

Developing nations continue to lag behind, despite the fact that they seem to be leading the deployment of technology for Industry 4.0 [8]. The Third Industrial Revolution depended on energy, and it seems that the Fourth Industrial Revolution is now succeeding in the same way.

Energy is a fundamental component of both human and mechanical presence. A safe, adequate, and open supply of energy is an essential prerequisite for the maintainability of present-day social orders and its economic prosperity. This is independent of the degree of economic development achieved. Economic development and output might be mutually decided on the grounds that financial development is firmly identified with energy utilization. What is more, higher financial improvement requires more RE utilization. Subsequently, increasingly proficient energy use needs a more significant level of financial advancement. Therefore,

DOI: 10.1201/9781003486244-8

increasingly productive energy use needs a more significant level of economic development [9].

The introduction is followed by a discussion on Industry 4.0, which is followed by a discussion on the necessity for emerging countries to incorporate RE sources. The full study of RE and its impact to national GDP development is provided in this chapter. It also includes the difficulties in implementing Industry 4.0 in developing countries and suggests solutions. This chapter also focuses on the governance of policies and the implementation challenges they face. On the strategies for policy governance, a debate has been added to the Indian scene.

5.1.1 Industry 4.0

The Fourth Industrial Revolution (4IR), sometimes referred to as Industry 4.0, is the current industrial revolution. In 2011 a phrase was coined to characterize the blending of information, communication, and associated technologies into production and industry [10].

Four separate revolutions have occurred. During the First Industrial Revolution, the use of animals of burden declined as the steam engine replaced them in both industrial and domestic settings. This led to the building of railroads, the production of steel, and the transportation of raw materials and completed commodities, all of which enhanced the quality of life for those impacted and accelerated urbanization. During the 1880s until the 1950s, there was a Second Industrial Revolution. It was distinguished by the discovery of electricity, which enhanced productivity and improved communication and other aspects of life. The Third Industrial Revolution, which lasted from the 1950s to 2000, was made possible by the invention of the computer in the early 1950s and the Internet around the year 2000. The use of computers in the sector facilitated substantial advancements in the creation of new technologies. With the help of this processing power, humans were able to carry out very complicated sets of instructions and even go to the Moon's surface. In the 1980s, businesses like IBM and Apple introduced personal computers, which quickly improved the quality of life for commercial enterprises [11].

The 4IR is spreading through all industries in various regions of the globe, from businesses to research institutions. The 4IR is a topic that is brought up at every gathering and conference in Europe and other developed continents [12]. The 4IR is the era of global interconnectedness of technology in daily life, such as biological processes, physical infrastructure, and digital architecture. Governments in those continents have incorporated it into their nations' main developmental goals. These technologies include centralized digital control, such as the IoT, intelligent systems, smart machinery, gene sequencing, smart energy, and nanotechnology [13].

Accelerating digitalization, artificial intelligence (AI), cloud computing, robots, and 3D printing are the major technologies of the 4IR, and they have significant and evident effects on employment, education, and the nature of work in the future [14]. For governments in developing nations, this is particularly true. The main innovations that define the stages of the 4IR are shown in Figure 5.1.

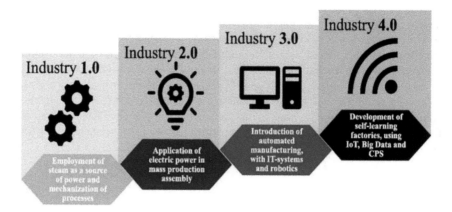

Figure 5.1 Stages of the Fourth Industrial Revolution.

AI is the mechanical equivalent of human thinking. In particular, when it comes to problem-solving, reasoning, and learning, machines reproduce and behave like people [15]. By analyzing spending patterns, AI is used in everyday life to detect and stop bank card fraud. The technology can interpret handwriting and speech in addition to other characteristics that reflect buying habits. It has previously been used in large data, construction, and medical. By the use of sensors, software, and primarily Wi-Fi to transfer data over the Internet, the IoT connects physical objects. While not all IoT devices need the Internet to work, they all need to connect to other devices. They are used in linked products, biometric scanners, smart factories, and smart residences [16].

5.2 SOME DEVELOPING ECONOMIES PROACTIVELY QUICKEN THE APPROPRIATION OF RENEWABLE ENERGY. WHY?

Conventional fuels like oil, coal, and gases boost the growth of the country's economy through carbon dioxide (CO_2) to the environment, which is the main culprit for climatic changes and the driving agent for global warming [17]. Overcome the problems, and to enhance energy security, it is suggested that a more reliable source of RE is required in the future. Furthermore, due to the continuous increase in the price of energy, the exploration of RE sources has attracted more focus as a free energy source to fossil fuel. Therefore, across the globe, more numbers of research from academic industries and other institutions have been started for sustainable development of the world through RE [18]. The growth of the RE sector is moving quickly across the world. Global investment for RE during the Global Financial Crisis of 2008, has increased from $104 to $120 billion. The RE global status report gives a grading to the rising economies countries according to their expenditure and size in RE [19]. Countries like Brazil, China, India, Indonesia, the Philippines, and Turkey are funding considerably high in different renewable sources.

Burning of conventional fuel should be allowed to the evolved countries in a minimal quantity for industrialization, as many evolved economies have already begun to use renewable sources. It is stated that an increase in the real GDP per capita and carbon dioxide per capita is the principal driving agent for non-fossil fuel utilization per capita. Furthermore, there is a relation between two developing nations' 20-year income and RE utilization. The conclusion derived from the study is small but rapid utilization of RE in undeveloped countries. Therefore, renewable technology that enhances the use of RE is required for developing nations [20].

Evolving economies are rising rapidly and trying to evolve further in the future until the environmentally friendly energy sources obtained by these countries will raise continuous incremental emissions. To increase the energy mix and to reduce the environmental pollutions, these evolving countries need to raise their renewable power capacity soon. Furthermore, financing in the RE sector from an evolving economy is increasing rapidly according to the annual report of RE networks. The majority of funding done in RE is from Indonesia, Brazil, India, the Philippines, China and Turkey. With funding of 33.7 billion USD, China is the leading investor in this sector. Whereas the fifth and eighth positions are secured by Brazil and India with total funding of $10.5 billion in the world. Investment by Indonesia and the Philippines is $300 million and $200 million in RE, respectively. Moreover, Turkey's capacity of renewable sources is still unused. Few of the driving agents of RE are explored today, whereas fossil fuel driving agents are studied thoroughly. Studies recognize the driving agents for alternative energy in G7 nations [21]. The same technique (co-integration) is applied for both studies, and their conclusion is almost the same.

There is a requirement of replacing fossil fuel consumption by renewable sources to get the maximum benefits of the economy and global climate change by the world. Some of the sufficient initiatives have been already taken by developing countries like China, Brazil, India, Indonesia, the Philippines, and Turkey to redesign/reconstruct energy utilization and funding in RE sources [22].

5.3 RENEWABLE ENERGY: A RESOURCEFUL WAY TO INCREASE GDP

There are various attempts taken by the United Nations Framework on Climate Change and its impact on climate change time to time like the Kyoto Protocol (2006) and other summits (Paris, 2008 and 2015) and is considered as sufficient at this time. Even now there are numerous effective paths heading for climate change, like enhancing environmentally friendly sustainable technology, enhancing renewable power, planting of trees, reducing deforestation, and increasing the efficiency of the present systems, thus saving energy [23]. RE acceptance and enhancement are the most effective ways of doing all these practices; this renewable power enhances macroeconomic efficiency, necessary for energy mix, and to achieve maximum reduction of emissions through the power industry.

Expanding the use of renewable power has already been evaluated in many countries and it is forecasted that RE has an appreciable future to overcome energy scarcity and climate change problems. For example, almost 50 percent of China's greenhouse gas (GHG) emission by 2020 is from its electricity sector, which is solved by the use of non–fossil fuels like solar, wind, and thermal power. Many of the policies written to get RE in the present energy mix are made by several economies. For the utilization of public investment and the promotion of RE, efficient energy use, and subsidy procedure, a group of policies was made [24]. Furthermore, it is observed that only 0.5 percent of material is other than construction material required for a new RE system. Though many of the countries are treating renewables as the solution to the current climate change problem and promoting it via lots of policies, how renewable promotes GDP is unknown. There is not any single such direct relation proven between GDP and renewables, but many of the agents of renewables affect GDP simultaneously. Hypotheses forecast that there are pondering variables in the likely possible ways, and use of structural equation modeling (SEM) to check all the ways in between. SEM can compute how renewables improve GDP [25].

5.3.1 Macroeconomics Hypothesis of the Effect of Renewables on GDP

Sustainable energy consumption has been the focus of many countries recently. Environmental, economic point of view, and regional evolutions are focused on renewables and are explored [26]. The process by which RE improves the GDP is through (1) employment generation and business expansion and (2) trade balancing and import substitution of energy by fossil fuels, which improve the economy. Since RE is locally generated, it generates local employment and economy rather than energy imported from other states [27].

5.3.2 The Pathway Analysis of the Impact on GDP

GDP is calculated by investment approaches as shown in Figure 5.2, and it can be estimated by

$$GDP = C + I + G + (X - M), \qquad (5.1)$$

where C = finalized household consumption, I = gross domestic capitalized formation; G = general government final consumption; X = export, M = import, and (X − M) = Trade balance.

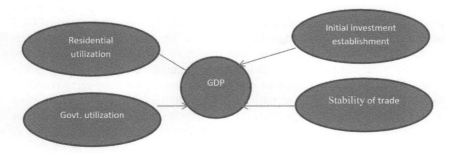

Figure 5.2 Framework of GDP constitution.

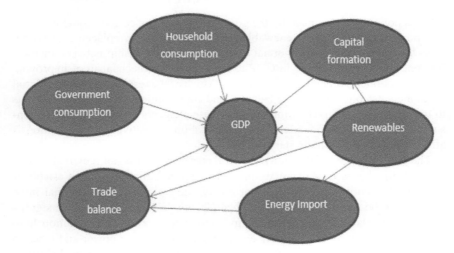

Figure 5.3 Conceptual framework of the influences of renewables on GDP.

Value-added approaches calculate GDP by

$$GDP = w + r + I + \pi + \delta, \tag{5.2}$$

where w = wage, r = rent, i = interest, π = revenue, and δ = depreciation.

Here we will go for expenditure approaches for the impact of renewables on GDP since the impact on the trade balance is affected by the renewables. Economic product within the national boundary is GDP, whereas GNP stands for the market value of goods and services produced by all citizens of a country—both domestically and abroad [28].

Figure 5.3 shows that the consumption of renewables affects GDP in two ways: (1) there is an increase in the capital formation by emerging RE business and

(2) RE generates power locally and reduces the import from traditional power plants, which directly and indirectly affects the trade balance. The growth of GDP depends on capital formation and trade balance; hence as these two parameters increase, GDP also grows. The most recognizable thing for policymakers is to select from various policy tools and first to recognize the most important tool, a renewable mechanism to make an economic impact. Since developing countries have an abundant available quantity of biomass, so RE is more in the energy mix as compared to the developed countries. In contrast, developed countries have more power from geothermal, solar, tidal, and wind fuels in the energy mix as compared to developing countries [29].

5.3.3 Concluding Remarks and Policy Implications

Various policies can be made by the government to enhance and promote renewable power like research on renewable enhancement and the replacement of fossil fuels by renewables. It is important to explore the relationship between increasing renewables and increase in GDP to understand the mechanism of improving macroeconomics by renewable increments. Much of the research shows that initial investment establishment, trade balance, and consumption are the basic elements to improve GDP positively. Moreover, all these elements depend on RE and consumption. Energy import affects the trade stability negatively. Consumption is affected negatively by trade stability.

The path between GDP, renewables, and energy import is not remarkable. It is probable that because GDP is the sum of utilization, initial investment establishment, trade stability, and government outlay, the weightage of the initial three elements is the variation of GDP. Taichen Chien's (2008) result shows a significant positive relationship between energy import and renewables. In addition, high demand of energy by an economy explores more renewable power and takes in more power, such that two power sources try to hike GDP simultaneously [30].

5.4 FINANCIAL AND ENVIRONMENTAL VALUATION FOR CHOOSING THE OPTIMAL NEW RENEWABLE ENERGY STRUCTURE FOR AN ENLIGHTENING FACILITY IN DEVELOPING COUNTRIES

The United Nations Framework Convention on Climate Change provides worldwide action for the enhancement of renewable and sustainable development to deploy climate change. The aims of this research are to enlighten the utilization of selecting optimum new renewable systems for educational purpose and their impact on the economy and environment. The globe is now struggling with the challenges posed by global warming, and much research is being conducted to find innovative and effective solutions that address this issue utilizing renewable energy resources [31].

In 2000 the goal of replacing its half of the supply from RE by 2050 was the act named the Renewable Energy Source Act. Several schemes were running by the South Korean government to increase the production and supply from new and renewable energies like subsidy, tax incentives loans, and a scheme for 1 million green homes; not only this, but they made it mandatory to install RE. Furthermore, South Korea established plan of action for the enhancement of the learning environment and the formation of eco-schools and green schools. The effect of new renewable energy (NRE) on learning facilities is forecasted to be higher as the floor area is smaller compared to other facilities like commercial buildings, offices, and apartments. Precursory research conducted on NRE is on the diversity of the viewpoint, like life cycle cost (LCC) and life cycle CO_2 emissions (LCCO$_2$) analysis of renewable setup. Rooftop application of solar energy aims for the reduction in LCCO$_2$ emissions by 13–21 percent [32].

5.4.1 The Challenges of Defining the Employment Attributes of Renewable Energy

Climate change mitigation, job creation, and energy security are socially and globally expected benefits of RE. Except for job creation, the other two are generally accepted, too, but job creation through renewables is still doubtful. A wide variety of research based on different parameters was done and showed a boost in the economy through a large number of new jobs created by the use of RE. There is frequently an excessive positive and superficial assumption that drives the results [33].

Rosebud Jasmine Lambert et al. (2012) examined several factors that can affect the analysis of RE and ways to create employment, and briefly discussed factors that are ignored while elaborating the effects of RE on job creation. Some of the countries became the focus of the analysis and reports that RE and employments are interconnected; this can be drawn from the previous research. Due to the increasing penetration of RE in the energy mix and achieving the target of renewable installation and employment, Germany and Spain in Europe have consistently been cited for their growing reliance on renewable energy sources, partially driven by the adoption of objectives to achieve the European 2020 renewable energy goal [34].

5.4.2 Challenges Facing Industry 4.0 Actualization and Proposed Remedies

Considering that the 4IR will place a greater emphasis on enhancing manufacturing, data analysis, and communication, it is important to keep in mind that many developing nations lack these three capabilities. In light of this, could 4IR be used as a grassroots tool to assist poor nations in their development, and must the same be done to establish an energy economy? International financial institutions are now providing governments in developing nations with large sums of money to support the development of RE production.

Yet, the need of crucial energy economy components continues to be unmet. This indicates that the funds are not utilized or that a power plant is constructed and commissioned but never used [35].

Consequently, the emphasis has to be on smaller, decentralized facilities to improve education and innovation in rural areas before implementing large-scale RE facilities. The growing requirements of the populations in these places might generate demand. 4IR is really beneficial in this situation. The need for efficient distribution networks and a sustainable supply have already been mentioned as the main problems with the use of RE technologies [36]. 4IR can do the same to drive the smaller-scale elements needed to actualize this objective. Productivity will be increased by small energy systems that permit illumination and the use of necessary building equipment. A community may be educated about the benefits of technology like 3D printers by using communication technologies like mobile phones and tablets, which can provide access to other individuals and information. A localized economy might be built around 3D printers as the foundation for a commodity that can be sold for a profit, opening up access to more potent manufacturing tools like CNC machinery and more complicated, large-scale 3D printing techniques like laser sintering and resin-based systems [37].

5.4.3 The Future of Developing Countries' Participation in Industry 4.0

RE sources provide a developing country considerable possibility for implementing its Industry 4.0 strategy. Because of their connection to the Indian or Atlantic Oceans—whether directly or indirectly—almost all developing nations are able to produce hydropower. In addition, several nations in the developing world have some extremely tall waterfalls that could be used to produce hydropower.

Collaboration between the business sector, civil society, and the communities in developing countries and throughout the globe should be practiced while working on digital innovation and policy. Strong digital strategies, strengthened innovation and entrepreneurial ecosystems, upgraded key digital infrastructure, enhanced digital skills, and suitable transportation infrastructure are all necessary for the 4IR.

Modernizing agriculture is also a crucial transition path for the implementation of Industry 4.0 in developing countries. Yet, this is in jeopardy due to the catastrophic effects of climate change. By promoting resilience, climate-smart agriculture may help increase farmer productivity. Developing countries have to apply technology breakthroughs throughout the whole agricultural value chain in order to turn climate worries into opportunities. This will diversify their economies, improve their capacity to compete on a global basis, and enable Industry 4.0.

Solar energy has enormous potential for use in developing countries, clean, universally accessible, and able to produce more energy than is required. Yet, because the initial cost of solar energy farms is out of reach for the typical home in a developing country, the government or corporate organizations should be prepared to fund it for its rural population. The establishment of solar energy harvesting equipment manufacturing plants in developing countries would be a great approach to reduce expenses [38].

5.5 RENEWABLE ENERGY POLICIES AND BARRIERS

The policies that boost the utilization of RE or are used to promote renewables frequently encounter roadblocks that displace the investments coming to this sector. Moreover, there is a requirement of some policies or programs to resolve these barriers like economic, regulatory, and other disadvantages. The most critical and effective barrier categories are described next [39].

5.5.1 Costs and Pricing

To initiate or set up a RE plant, the cost is very high (capital) as compared to the other energy resource, which results in the cost-regulated decision and policies that neglect RE. There are several cost factors responsible for the high cost. Various policies were made and announced to compensate the cost related issues/barrier by providing the subsidies in the terms of tax benefits, encouragement special pricing and power purchase agreements and by dropping down the transaction cost.

5.5.1.1 Subsidies for Competing Fuels

A considerable amount of subsidies are started for every form of energy, which can compensate for the costs associated with it. The subsidies can be in the form of tax depreciation, budgetary transfer, insurance, and others. Providing huge subsidies to the fossil fuel industry results in reduced capital cost; hence RE should also be provided equally large subsidies to enjoy these enhancements.

5.5.1.2 High Initial Capital Costs

Although the cost of operations and management (O&M) of RE is making it cheaper in the means of life cycle assessment (LCA), the high capital cost results in lowering the installation of RE plants. RE is also increased by the import and export taxes and dumping duties. The taxes and duties should be providing some rebates to the field so that the capital cost can be reduced.

5.5.1.3 The Difficulty of Fuel Price Risk Assessment

Almost negligible or no fuel is required for a RE system, so this risk is not present. However, this advantage of risk reduction premiums is still not included in the economic comparison since fossil fuel future prices cannot be forecasted, and till the date is assumed to be constant in the future too.

5.5.1.4 Unfavorable Power Pricing Rules

Since RE is generally distributed, it may be possible that it will not get full benefit while sending the power to the central grid. However, it will be more beneficial if projected near to the end-user location, and the end-user is directly paying for the power purchased. So, the power pricing depends on the location of the system. Furthermore, based on the location, the potential varies and compensates the output, and because of this the power price is also affected.

5.5.1.5 Transaction Costs

RE requires more time, attention, and financing because of the mismatch in technology and uncertainty over performance and because this transaction cost may increase. At the same time, transaction costs may be high because of some irrelevant factors like troublesome grid interconnection and heavy grid fees for testing and examination.

5.5.1.6 Environmental Externalities

RE sources are either eco-friendly or have a negligible amount of pollutants, which results in the saving of the economy in terms of human health, emission reduction, reduction in GHGs, and climate change. The environmental cost is computed in dollars, and a project developer always evaluates the environmental impact and associated cost in the bottom line [40].

5.6 RENEWABLE ENERGY IN INDIA: CURRENT ENERGY POLICIES

This topic of interest will cover the following policies in India [41]. Few of them are discussed next:

- The Electricity Act 2003
- National Electricity Policy, 2005
- National Rural Electrification Policies, 2006

5.6.1 The Electricity Act 2003

The Electricity Act 2003 is a combination of several codifications and policies on electricity operating in India. This Act refuses to have a single buyer model and allows free entry to production and captive power production by the inclusion of consumer association and reproduction of captive power, which results in the replacement of cross-subsidies from consumers to distribution companies. Loss of cross-subsidizing consumers would result in open access to specific classes of consumers and perhaps entry to independent power production in a generation. Since there is no restriction in the Act, there may be some integration of generation and distribution.

The regulatory framework predicts that the Act meets the requirement of a credible system. Funding for commissions and strict provision arrangements for subsidy by the government should confirm better independence. Tariff calculation has made more flexible and can be used for a multiyear tariff forecast and tariff principles. The absence of proper distribution business is expected to suffer and also supply chain [42].

5.6.2 National Electricity Policy, 2005

In February 2005, the government of India had announced the National Electricity Policy, 2005. With the wish list of everything desired in the Indian power sector, how to achieve it was still a Question. [43]

The objectives of this policy are:

- In the next five years, provide access to electricity for all households;
- By 2012, fully meet the demands of power and the supply of reliable and quality standards in efficient ways at an affordable cost;
- The availability of electricity per capita will be increased 1,000 times by 2012;
- For lower community and BPL (below poverty line) households, a minimal lifeline of consumptions of 1 unit per household per day by 2012;
- Commercial viability and financial turnaround of the electricity sector.

5.6.3 National Rural Electrification Policies, 2006

Till 2003, the village electrification programs were screened by definition: "a town is accepted as jolted if power is being utilized inside its income territory for any reason what-so-ever." Accordingly, 512,153 out of the 587,556 towns in India were pronounced electric as in March 2002, speaking to 87 percent of the aggregate; yet in excess of 60 percent of the rustic family units had no entrance to power. This meaning of town jolt was properly altered in the new rustic zap approaches, which specify that a town is considered electric if at any rate 10 percent of the family units are energized, one circulation transformer exists in the town, and open spots like schools, emergency clinics, and so on are zapped and bring down network's areas approach power [44].

This policy was initialized with following aims for rural electrification:

1. Creation of the Rural Electrification Distribution Backbone (REDB) with at any rate one 33/11 kV (or 66/11 kV) substation in each square associated with state transmission framework;
2. At least one dissemination transformer in each town settlement;

3. Decentralized conveyed age offices along with the nearby dispersion organize any place where augmentation of the network is not possible.
4. Particular consideration for family unit charge of lower networks, inborn regions, and other more vulnerable segments.

5.7 CONCLUSION

The present study investigated the interdependency between economic growth and RE consumption along with applicable policies. The results indicate that economic growth rises more frequently with the consumption of RE. For domestic production, labor and capital provide an essential place for the economic growth of the nation. The detailed, comprehensive analysis for the policymakers helps a lot in the formulation of RE for the sustainable growth of a country's economy. For the generation of higher quality green patents, policies governing the environmental standards are more crucial, but competitions in the global market enhance the low-quality green patents generation.

The aftereffects of this examination have significant implications for the execution of future approaches on advancing sustainable energy sources together with macroeconomic policies. The consequences of the Pedroni cointegration test reveal that there is a long-running balance connection between real GDP or real GDP per capita, free sustainable energy source use or portion of complete RE source utilization, real gross fixed capital arrangement, work, and the R&D uses of the countries. These discoveries bolster the upsides of government strategies advancing the utilization of RE source by building up sustainable energy source markets, RE source portfolio norms not exclusively to improve the natural conditions yet additionally from a macroeconomic perspective. By no means does this investigation propose another macroeconomic approach; it just advances the thought that strategies for sustainable power sources will in any event not hurt the financial government assistance of the nations.

Similarly, as there is no single strategy for deciding the effect of an inexhaustible source of energy on work, there is no single clear outcome about whether sustainable energy sources emphatically or contrarily impact business. Advancement of a sustainable power source in one area of a nation may deliver a net increase in employment, marginally decrease work on a national scale, or welcome a slight net advantage on a global scale. It is additionally critical to recognize that regardless of whether an investigation exhibits that sustainable energy sources diminish net business, there might be other potential advantages; for example, a decrease in CO_2 emissions or an expansion in energy security. In summary, re-establishing capable energy ought not be done exclusively as a result of an apparent advantage to the business, nor should it be dismissed without thought of other possible advantages.

The way that RE has been conveyed appears to have a monetarily counterproductive impact, bringing about wasteful aspects in total and a significant expense of energy. It is proposed that better approaches to create renewables ought to be investigated by open arrangements. From one perspective, the center ought to be moved to the advancement of research and development, licensing, and motivations for the fare of innovation. This assessment intends to demonstrate how developing nations might benefit from the potential and promises of 4IR. The sluggish adoption of the 4IR was historically the main issue facing developing countries. RE may be produced using a variety of methods, each of which has benefits and drawbacks. Analyzing each technology reveals a pattern that speaks to the two main problems with using RE as a first-line energy option in developing nations: energy storage, or more broadly, the viability of the energy supply; and the efficient transmission and distribution of energy. In order to achieve these goals, it is necessary for countries to have the political will, greater regional integration, road and digital infrastructure, well-informed decision-making, and attempt to introduce policies that are suggested to help implement the 4IR in developing nations. The curriculum for schools in developing countries should contain new skill sets including big data management, cognitive abilities, social media management, processing, and problem-solving.

REFERENCES

[1] Stern, D.I. and Kander, A., 2012. The role of energy in the industrial revolution and modern economic growth. *Energy J.*, *33*, pp. 125–152.

[2] Deane, P.M., 1979. *The first industrial revolution*. Cambridge University Press.

[3] Mohajan, H., 2019. The second industrial revolution has brought modern social and economic developments. *Journal of Social Sciences and Humanities*, *6*, pp. 1–14.

[4] Cooper, C. and Kaplinsky, R. eds., 2005. *Technology and development in the third industrial revolution*. Routledge—Business & Economics.

[5] Popkova, E.G., Ragulina, Y.V. and Bogoviz, A.V. eds., 2019. *Industry 4.0: Industrial revolution of the 21st century* (Vol. 169, p. 249). Springer.

[6] Kumar, D., Singh, R.K. and Layek, A., 2020. Block chain and its application. *Supply Chain Intelligence: Application and Optimization*, pp. 113–127.

[7] Dogaru, L., 2020. The main goals of the fourth industrial revolution. Renewable energy perspectives. *Procedia Manufacturing*, *46*, pp. 397–401.

[8] Kumar, D., Kumar, A., Kumar, N., Sharma, A., Choudhury, R., Faisal, N., Singh, R.K. and Mane, B.K., 2023. Current trends, regulations, challenges, and management strategies of e-waste in India. In *Sustainable approaches and strategies for e-waste management and utilization* (pp. 1–25). IGI Global.

[9] Cheng, Y., Awan, U., Ahmad, S. and Tan, Z., 2021. How do technological innovation and fiscal decentralization affect the environment? A story of the fourth industrial revolution and sustainable growth. *Technological Forecasting and Social Change*, *162*, p. 120398.

[10] Kumar, D., Faisal, N., Choudhury, R. and Deshmukh, S.S., 2022. Experimental investigation of the mechanical and thermal properties of natural green fibres. In *Recent developments in nanofibers research*. IntechOpen. doi: 10.5772/intechopen.102453

[11] Kumar, N., Kumar, D., Layek, A. and Yadav, S., 2022. Renewable energy and sustainable development: A global approach towards artificial intelligence. In *Artificial intelligence for renewable energy systems* (pp. 305–328). Woodhead Publishing.

[12] Stăncioiu, A., 2017. The fourth industrial revolution 'Industry 4.0'. *Fiabilitate Şi Durabilitate, 1*(19), pp. 74–78.

[13] Bradu, P., Biswas, A., Nair, C., Sreevalsakumar, S., Patil, M., Kannampuzha, S., Mukherjee, A.G., Wanjari, U.R., Renu, K., Vellingiri, B. and Gopalakrishnan, A.V., 2022. Recent advances in green technology and Industrial Revolution 4.0 for a sustainable future. *Environmental Science and Pollution Research*, pp. 1–32.

[14] Kumar, A., Kumar, D., Choudhury, R., Goyal, A., Oza, A.D., Patel, A., Joshi, A. and Kumar, D., 2022. Application of 3D printing for engineering and bio-medicals: Recent trends and development. *International Journal on Interactive Design and Manufacturing (IJIDeM)*, pp. 1–10.

[15] Kumar, D., Faisal, N., Layek, A. and Priyadarshi, G., 2021, May. Enhancement of mechanical properties of carbon and flax fibre hybrid composites for engineering applications. In *AIP conference proceedings* (Vol. 2341, No. 1, p. 040032). AIP Publishing LLC.

[16] Scharl, S. and Praktiknjo, A., 2019. The role of a digital industry 4.0 in a renewable energy system. *International Journal of Energy Research, 43*(8), pp. 3891–3904.

[17] Kumar, D. and Layek, A., 2023. Experimental assessment of thermohydraulic performance of a rectangular solar air heater duct using twisted v-shaped staggered ribs. *Journal of Thermal Science and Engineering Applications, 15*(4), p. 041009.

[18] Kumar, D. and Layek, A., 2023. Heat Transfer augmentation of a solar air heater using a twisted v-shaped staggered rib over the absorber plate. *Journal of Solar Energy Engineering, 145*(2), p. 021013.

[19] Popović, A., 2020. Implications of the fourth industrial revolution on sustainable development. *Economics of Sustainable Development, 4*(1), pp. 45–60.

[20] Kumar, D. and Layek, A., 2022. Heat transfer enhancement of solar air heater having twisted v-shaped staggered roughness over absorber plate. *Arabian Journal for Science and Engineering*, pp. 1–16.

[21] Arcelay, I., Goti, A., Oyarbide-Zubillaga, A., Akyazi, T., Alberdi, E. and Garcia-Bringas, P., 2021. Definition of the future skills needs of job profiles in the renewable energy sector. *Energies, 14*(9), p. 2609.

[22] Delera, M., Pietrobelli, C., Calza, E. and Lavopa, A., 2022. Does value chain participation facilitate the adoption of industry 4.0 technologies in developing countries? *World Development, 152*, p. 105788.

[23] Chien, T. and Hu, J.L., 2008. Renewable energy: An efficient mechanism to improve GDP. *Energy Policy, 36*(8), pp. 3045–3052.

[24] Saidi, K. and Omri, A., 2020. Reducing CO2 emissions in OECD countries: Do renewable and nuclear energy matter? *Progress in Nuclear Energy, 126*, p. 103425.

[25] Alam, T.F., Sultana, N. and Rayhan, M.I., 2019. Structural equation modeling: An application of broadband penetration and GDP growth in Asia. *Journal of Economic Structures, 8*, pp. 1–11.

[26] Chien, T. and Hu, J.L., 2007. Renewable energy and macroeconomic efficiency of OECD and non-OECD economies. *Energy Policy, 35*(7), pp. 3606–3615.

[27] Kumar, D., Layek, A. and Kumar, A., 2020, November. Performance enhancement of single slope solar still integrated with flat plate collector for different basin water depth. In *AIP conference proceedings* (Vol. 2273, No. 1, p. 050007). AIP Publishing LLC.

[28] Anghelache, C. and Anghel, M.G., 2017. Econometric methods and models used in the analysis of the factorial influence of the gross domestic product growth. *Network Intelligence Studies*, *9*(1), pp. 67–78.

[29] Ohler, A. and Fetters, I., 2014. The causal relationship between renewable electricity generation and GDP growth: A study of energy sources. *Energy Economics*, *43*, pp. 125–139.

[30] Sahlian, D.N., Popa, A.F. and Crețu, R.F., 2021. Does the increase in renewable energy influence GDP growth? An EU-28 analysis. *Energies*, *14*(16), p. 4762.

[31] Wüstenhagen, R. and Menichetti, E., 2012. Strategic choices for renewable energy investment: Conceptual framework and opportunities for further research. *Energy Policy*, *40*, pp. 1–10.

[32] Kumar, D., Choudhury, R. and Layek, A., 2022. Application of liquid crystal thermography for temperature measurement of the absorber plate of solar air heater. *Materials Today: Proceedings*, *59*, pp. 605–611.

[33] Wüstenhagen, R., Wolsink, M. and Bürer, M.J., 2007. Social acceptance of renewable energy innovation: An introduction to the concept. *Energy Policy*, *35*(5), pp. 2683–2691.

[34] Lambert, R.J. and Silva, P.P., 2012. The challenges of determining the employment effects of renewable energy. *Renewable and Sustainable Energy Reviews*, *16*(7), pp. 4667–4674.

[35] Ukoba, K., Kunene, T.J., Harmse, P., Lukong, V.T. and Chien Jen, T., 2023. The role of renewable energy sources and industry 4.0 focus for Africa: A review. *Applied Sciences*, *13*(2), p. 1074.

[36] Kumar, R.R., Singh, A., Kumar, A., Ansu, A.K., Kumar, A., Kumar, S., Kumar, D., Goyal, A., Oza, A.D. and Singh, D., 2022. Enhancement of friction stir welding characteristics of alloy AA6061 by design of experiment methodology. *International Journal on Interactive Design and Manufacturing (IJIDeM)*, pp. 1–13.

[37] Mehrpouya, M., Dehghanghadikolaei, A., Fotovvati, B., Vosooghnia, A., Emamian, S.S. and Gisario, A., 2019. The potential of additive manufacturing in the smart factory industrial 4.0: A review. *Applied Sciences*, *9*(18), p. 3865.

[38] Kumar, D., Singh, R.K. and Layek, A., 2020. Cold chain and its application. In *Supply chain intelligence: Application and optimization* (pp. 63–80). Springer

[39] Raina, G. and Sinha, S., 2019. Outlook on the Indian scenario of solar energy strategies: Policies and challenges. *Energy Strategy Reviews*, *24*, pp. 331–341.

[40] Tripathi, L., Mishra, A.K., Dubey, A.K., Tripathi, C.B. and Baredar, P., 2016. Renewable energy: An overview on its contribution in current energy scenario of India. *Renewable and Sustainable Energy Reviews*, *60*, pp. 226–233.

[41] Kumar, A., Kumar, K., Kaushik, N., Sharma, S. and Mishra, S., 2010. Renewable energy in India: Current status and future potentials. *Renewable and Sustainable Energy Reviews*, *14*(8), pp. 2434–2442.

[42] Ranganathan, V., 2004. Electricity Act 2003: Moving to a competitive environment. *Economic and Political Weekly*, pp. 2001–2005.

[43] Rejikumar, R., 2005. National electricity policy and plan: A critical examination. *Economic and Political Weekly*, pp. 2028–2032.

[44] Haanyika, C.M., 2006. Rural electrification policy and institutional linkages. *Energy Policy*, *34*(17), pp. 2977–2993.

Additive Manufacturing and Industry 4.0

Chapter 6

Revolutionizing Industrial Engineering
Exploring Additive Manufacturing Technologies in the Era of Industry 4.0

Chikesh Ranjan and Kaushik Kumar

6.1 INTRODUCTION

The realm of additive manufacturing (AM) thrives on a diverse array of cutting-edge technologies as categorized by ASTM International into seven distinct groups. These methodologies encompass material extrusion exemplified by fused deposition modeling (FDM), which involves layering materials through extrusion mechanisms [1]. Powder bed fusion represents another category, where particles are selectively fused layer by layer, showcasing techniques like selective laser sintering (SLS). Vat photo polymerization, seen in stereolithography (SLA), utilizes light to solidify liquid resin, crafting intricate structures layer upon layer. Material jetting, such as the PolyJet system, deposits materials droplet by droplet to construct high-resolution models. Sheet lamination, as observed in laminated object manufacturing (LOM), builds objects layer by layer through cutting and bonding sheets of material. Directed energy deposition focuses on adding materials via focused energy beams, while binder jetting involves selectively depositing binding agents onto powder beds, forming intricate shapes [2]. This diversity of AM technologies underscores a rich landscape of additive processes, each with distinct mechanisms and applications, collectively reshaping the possibilities in modern manufacturing [3].

The majority of published review articles predominantly focus on experimental investigations concerning selective laser melting (SLM), delving into technical considerations and findings. An inherent challenge arises from the multitude of influential parameters affecting part quality, process repeatability, and consistency [4]. Given that SLM operates as a heat transfer process involving repeated phase changes, synthesizing conducted studies into numerical simulations becomes imperative [5]. This approach aids in comprehensively analyzing SLM's aspects, including heat transfer, melt pool dynamics, microstructure evolution, and induced residual stress. Consequently, this review chapter is structured in two sections: the first offers an overview of AM processes and their technical nuances, while the second section meticulously examines studies that have endeavored to numerically simulate the intricate dynamics of heat transfer, melt pool behavior, microstructure evolution, and residual stress induction during SLM operations.

DOI: 10.1201/9781003486244-10

6.2 ADDITIVE MANUFACTURING

AM comprises various types, each employing distinct processes to create 3D objects from digital models. Here are some key types:

Material Extrusion: This method, exemplified by FDM, involves melting and extruding material through a nozzle to create layers. It is cost-effective and versatile, using thermoplastics or other materials.

Powder Bed Fusion: Techniques like SLS and direct metal laser sintering (DMLS) use lasers to fuse powdered materials, layer by layer, to build objects. It is popular for creating complex and durable parts in metals or polymers.

Vat Photo Polymerization: Methods such as SLA use ultraviolet (UV) light to solidify liquid resin layer by layer, producing high-resolution models with smooth finishes. It is commonly used in prototyping and intricate designs.

Material Jetting: Utilizing techniques like PolyJet, this method deposits droplets of material onto a build platform, layer by layer, to create multi-material and high-resolution models.

Sheet Lamination: LOM involves bonding and cutting sheets of material, like paper or plastic, layer by layer, to form objects. It is suitable for larger parts and cost-effective production.

Directed Energy Deposition: This method involves focusing energy (usually a laser or electron beam) to melt and deposit material onto a substrate, primarily used for metalworking and repair applications.

Binder Jetting: It selectively deposits binding agents onto powdered materials, layer by layer, to form objects, often used for creating sand molds or metal parts.

These diverse AM types cater to different industries and applications, offering unique advantages such as precision, material diversity, speed, and scalability. They collectively represent a revolution in manufacturing by enabling the creation of complex geometries, customization, and rapid prototyping while reducing waste and production time [6].

AM offers a range of advantages across various industries and applications:

Advantages

Design Flexibility: AM enables the creation of complex geometries that are difficult or impossible to achieve with traditional manufacturing methods. This allows for innovative designs and customized products.

Reduced Material Waste: By adding material layer by layer, AM significantly reduces material wastage compared to subtractive manufacturing methods, where excess material is removed.

Rapid Prototyping: It allows for quick and cost-effective prototyping, facilitating iterative design improvements and faster product development cycles.

Customization and Personalization: AM allows for on-demand and customizable production, catering to individual preferences and specific customer needs without incurring additional costs.

Supply Chain Efficiency: It can minimize supply chain complexities by enabling localized manufacturing, reducing inventory, and allowing for on-demand production.

Applications

Aerospace and Automotive: AM is used to produce lightweight and complex parts, reducing overall weight while maintaining strength. It is employed in aircraft components, engine parts, prototypes, and customized automotive parts.

Healthcare and Biomedical: In healthcare, AM is used for producing prosthetics, dental implants, orthopedic implants, and patient-specific medical devices. Bioprinting is also advancing for tissue engineering and drug development.

Engineering and Manufacturing: AM aids in the production of tooling, jigs, fixtures, and manufacturing aids. It is also utilized in creating one-off or low-volume parts for machinery and equipment.

Consumer Goods: AM is increasingly used in the production of consumer products, jewelry, fashion accessories, and home goods, allowing for unique designs and limited production runs.

Architecture and Construction: It is employed for creating architectural models, intricate designs, and prototypes in construction, enabling rapid iterations and showcasing design concepts.

Education and Research: AM serves as an educational tool in universities and research institutions, allowing students and researchers to experiment, prototype, and explore new concepts in various fields.

Overall, AM's versatility, efficiency, and ability to create highly customized, intricate designs have broadened its applications across diverse industries, transforming production methodologies and product development processes.

The following is a brief explanation of AM technologies and their types [7].

6.2.1 Stereolithography

SLA is one of the earliest and most widely used rapid prototyping or 3D printing technologies. It involves the creation of three-dimensional objects by selectively curing (solidifying) layers of a liquid photopolymer resin using a UV laser.

Stereolithography Process

3D Model Preparation: The process begins with a 3D digital model of the object you want to create. This model is usually designed using computer-aided design (CAD) software.

Slicing: The 3D model is sliced into thin, horizontal layers or cross-sections using specialized software. These slices are used to guide the SLA machine in creating the object layer by layer.

Resin Tank: The SLA machine has a resin tank containing liquid photopolymer resin. The resin is typically a transparent or translucent material that can be solidified by UV light.

Build Platform: A build platform, connected to a vertical elevator or z-axis, is submerged in the resin tank just below the surface of the liquid resin.

Laser Curing: The SLA machine uses a UV laser to trace the first layer of the object's cross-section on the surface of the liquid resin. Wherever the laser beam touches the resin, it solidifies, adhering to the build platform.

Layer by Layer: After curing the first layer, the build platform is slightly lowered to immerse it in the resin again, and the laser traces the next layer on top of the previous one. This process is repeated, with each layer bonding to the layer below it.

Solidification and Support Structures: In addition to the main object, SLA machines can also generate support structures if needed. These supports help hold the object in place during the printing process and are later removed after the print is complete.

Completion: The SLA machine continues this layer-by-layer process until the entire 3D object is built, with each layer being precisely cured and stacked on top of the previous one.

Post-Processing: Once the printing is finished, the object is carefully removed from the build platform. It may require additional post-processing steps, such as cleaning to remove excess resin and, if support structures were used, their removal and any necessary surface finishing.

Schematic of Stereolithography Device

A basic schematic of a stereolithography device typically includes the following components:

Resin Tank: A transparent or translucent tank containing the liquid photopolymer resin.

Build Platform: A platform that can be precisely raised and lowered within the resin tank.

UV Laser: A UV laser that is used to selectively cure the resin and create each layer of the object.

Scanning System: A scanning system that directs the laser beam to trace the shape of each layer according to the 3D model's instructions.

Control System: A control system that coordinates the movement of the build platform, the firing of the laser, and the overall printing process.

Support Structure Generation (optional): If support structures are needed for the object being printed, there may be additional components or mechanisms for generating and placing these supports.

User Interface: A user interface that allows the operator to load the 3D model, control printing parameters, and monitor the progress of the print.

Extraction and Cleaning System (post-processing): Equipment or processes for safely removing the printed object from the build platform and cleaning it of excess resin.

6.2.2 Selective Laser Sintering

SLS is an additive manufacturing technology that uses a high-power laser to selectively fuse powdered materials, typically polymers or metals, layer by layer to create 3D objects.

Selective Laser Sintering Process

Powder Bed: The process starts with a bed of powdered material, such as nylon, metal, or ceramics. This powder serves as the raw material for building the object.

Layer Application: A thin layer of the powdered material is evenly spread across the build platform using a roller or similar mechanism.

Laser Sintering: A high-powered laser scans the cross-section of the object's current layer according to the 3D model's instructions. When the laser comes into contact with the powder, it heats and fuses the particles together, solidifying the material.

Layer-by-Layer: After completing one layer, the build platform is lowered slightly, and a new layer of powder is spread on top of the previous one. The laser then scans the new layer to sinter it to the layer below. This process is repeated iteratively, with each layer fusing to the one beneath it.

Cooling: As the laser sinters each layer, the surrounding powder helps dissipate heat, allowing the material to cool and solidify.

Support Structures (optional): If the object being printed has overhangs or complex geometries that require support, additional unsintered powder can be used to create temporary support structures.

Completion: Once all layers are sintered, the build platform is raised to expose the completed 3D object, which is still surrounded by unsintered powder.

Recovery and Cleaning: The printed object is carefully removed from the powder bed. Excess unsintered powder can be brushed or blown away and sieved for reuse in future prints.

Post-Processing: Depending on the application and material, post-processing steps may be required, such as surface finishing, heat treatment, or additional machining.

Schematic of Selective Laser Sintering Device

A basic schematic of a selective laser sintering device includes the following components:

Powder Bed: The build platform with a layer of powdered material spread evenly across it.

Recoater: A mechanism that spreads a new layer of powder over the build platform after each sintering cycle.

High-Powered Laser: A powerful laser, often a CO_2 or fiber laser, capable of selectively sintering the powdered material. This laser is directed by a scanning system.

Scanning System: A system that controls the movement and direction of the laser beam, ensuring it follows the shape of each layer according to the 3D model's instructions.

Control System: The brains of the SLS machine that coordinates the laser, build platform movement, and overall printing process. Operators input parameters and monitor progress through this system.

Build Platform: The platform that holds the object being printed. It can be lowered incrementally to accommodate each new layer.

Heating System (optional): Some SLS machines have a heating system to preheat the powder bed, which can improve sintering quality.

Powder Handling System: Mechanisms for powder recovery, recycling, and distribution. This includes removing excess unsintered powder and ensuring it is available for future prints.

Safety Measures: SLS machines often have safety features such as fume extraction, fire suppression systems, and interlocks to protect operators and the equipment.

User Interface: A user interface for loading 3D models, configuring printing parameters, and monitoring the print process.

6.2.3 Fused Deposition Modeling

FDM is an additive manufacturing technology used in 3D printing [7]. It operates by melting and extruding thermoplastic materials layer by layer to create three-dimensional objects.

Here is how FDM works:

Material Filament: FDM printers utilize a filament made of thermoplastic materials like acrylonitrile butadiene styrene (ABS), polylactic acid (PLA), polyethylene terephthalate glycol (PETG), and others. This filament is loaded into the printer's extrusion system.

Melting and Extrusion: The filament is fed into a heated nozzle, where it is melted at high temperatures. The printer's nozzle moves along predefined paths, depositing the melted material onto the build platform in thin layers.

Layer-by-Layer Building: The nozzle moves in the *x*-, *y*-, and *z*-axes, depositing material layer upon layer, following the pattern dictated by the 3D model. As each layer cools and solidifies, it bonds to the previous layer, gradually building up the object.

Support Structures (if needed): For overhanging or complex geometries, FDM printers can create temporary support structures using a different material or a soluble support material. These supports provide stability during printing and are removed or dissolved after printing is complete.

Post-Processing: Once printing finishes, the object may require post-processing steps like removing supports, surface finishing, or additional treatments to achieve the desired final appearance and functionality.

FDM is widely used in various industries due to its relatively low cost, ease of use, and versatility. It is employed in prototyping, manufacturing tooling, custom part production, and even in the production of end-use parts in industries such as automotive, aerospace, healthcare, and consumer goods.

6.2.4 Laminated Object Manufacturing

LOM is an AM technique that involves layering and bonding sheets of material to create 3D objects [8]. Here is a schematic explanation of the LOM process:

Layer Preparation: The process begins with a stack of thin sheets of material, typically paper or plastic, arranged in a feeder. These sheets are pre-coated with an adhesive on one side.

Laser Cutting: A computer-controlled laser or blade cuts the shape of the object's cross-section onto each sheet according to the digital design. The laser traces the outline of the object, cutting through the material but leaving the bottom layer intact.

Layer Bonding: Once a layer is cut, it is bonded to the layer below using heat or pressure. The adhesive present on the sheets helps in sticking the layers together, forming the 3D object's shape.

Layer Addition: The process repeats, layer by layer, cutting and bonding sheets until the entire object is formed. Each layer represents a cross-sectional slice of the final object, gradually building up its structure.

Finalizing the Object: Once all layers are cut, bonded, and stacked, excess material around the object might be removed, leaving behind the finished 3D model. Post-processing steps, such as smoothing or sealing, may be applied for a desired finish.

This process results in objects with visible layer lines due to the stacked sheets. LOM is advantageous for creating larger-scale parts or prototypes economically, although it might have slightly lower resolution compared to other AM methods. It is often used in applications where cost-effectiveness and feasibility for larger parts outweigh the need for high surface detail.

6.2.5 Solid Ground Curing

Solid ground curing (SGC) is an AM technique similar to SLA that utilizes light to solidify liquid resin into 3D objects. Here is an overview of the SGC process and its schematic:

Liquid Resin: SGC starts with a tank filled with liquid resin, often a photopolymer, which hardens when exposed to a specific wavelength of light, typically UV light.

Platform Preparation: A platform is submerged in the liquid resin at the bottom of the tank. The platform gradually moves upwards, layer by layer, as the object is constructed.

Light Projection: A UV light source, such as a laser or a projector, is directed onto the surface of the resin tank. The light is precisely controlled by mirrors or lenses to trace the shape of the object's cross-section onto the surface of the liquid resin.

Solidification: Wherever the UV light hits the liquid resin, it causes the material to solidify or cure, forming a thin layer corresponding to the object's shape. This layer adheres to the platform at the bottom of the tank.

Layer-by-Layer Building: After solidifying one layer, the platform incrementally rises or the resin vat lowers to immerse the cured layer and expose a fresh layer of liquid resin. The process repeats, with the light tracing the next layer's pattern, solidifying it atop the previous layer.

Completion: Layer by layer, the object gradually emerges from the resin tank until the entire 3D structure is formed. Once finished, excess resin is drained or removed, and the object may undergo additional curing or post-processing steps for surface finishing.

SGC produces high-resolution models with smooth surface finishes, similar to SLA, but with the key difference of the solidification occurring on a solid platform rather than within a vat. This method minimizes resin wastage and allows for increased accuracy in the final object. SGC is beneficial for creating intricate, detailed parts or prototypes in various industries like engineering, design, and prototyping.

6.2.6 Laser-Engineered Net Shaping

Laser-engineered net shaping (LENS) is an AM technique that utilizes a high-power laser to melt and fuse metallic powders or wires onto a substrate, enabling the creation of complex metal parts. Here is an overview of the LENS process and its schematic:

Powder or Wire Feedstock: LENS starts with metallic powder or wire feedstock, which is precisely deposited onto a substrate, often a metal base or previously deposited layer.

Focused Laser Beam: A high-power laser beam, guided by a computer-controlled system, precisely melts the metal powder or wire at specific points on the substrate. The laser's heat source creates a small molten pool on the substrate's surface.

Layer-by-Layer Building: As the laser melts the material, the substrate or the deposition head, which holds the material feedstock, moves along the programmed path. Layer upon layer of molten metal is deposited, allowing the material to solidify and fuse with the previous layers.

Real-Time Monitoring: During the process, various sensors and monitoring systems ensure precise control of parameters like temperature, laser power, and material deposition rates. This control ensures accurate layer formation and quality.

Complex Shapes Formation: The computer-controlled deposition of molten metal allows for the creation of complex geometries and near-net-shape parts without the need for extensive post-machining.

Finalization and Finishing: Once the desired object or part is fully built layer by layer, any excess material or support structures are removed. The part may undergo additional finishing processes such as machining or surface treatments for precise dimensions and surface quality.

LENS is widely used in industries like aerospace, automotive, and biomedical for producing functional metal parts, repairing components, or adding features to existing parts. It offers advantages in creating fully dense, high-quality metal parts with reduced material waste and production time compared to traditional manufacturing methods.

6.2.7 Rapid Prototyping

Rapid prototyping is a crucial phase in product development, where CAD plays a pivotal role. It involves the quick and cost-effective creation of physical prototypes or models directly from digital CAD designs. Here is a brief discussion of CAD rapid prototyping [6]:

Key Components

CAD Software: CAD software is the foundation of rapid prototyping. Designers and engineers use CAD tools to create 3D digital models of the product or component they want to prototype.

Prototyping Technology: Various rapid prototyping technologies, such as 3D printing, CNC machining, laser cutting, and additive manufacturing, are used to transform CAD designs into physical prototypes.

The Rapid Prototyping Process

CAD Design: The process begins with the creation of a detailed 3D CAD model of the product or component. This digital representation serves as the blueprint for the prototype.

Material Selection: Depending on the prototyping technology chosen, an appropriate material or combination of materials is selected. These can include plastics, metals, ceramics, or composites.

Prototype Generation: The CAD model is fed into the chosen rapid prototyping machine or equipment. The machine follows the digital design instructions to build the physical prototype layer by layer (in the case of 3D printing) or through subtractive processes like CNC machining.

Post-Processing: After prototype generation, some post-processing steps may be necessary, such as removing support structures, sanding, painting, or assembling multiple parts into a complete prototype.

Testing and Evaluation: The prototype is thoroughly tested and evaluated to assess its form, fit, function, and performance. This step allows for design refinement and verification.

Iterative Process: If necessary, the CAD design is modified based on the prototype's test results, and the rapid prototyping process is repeated to create an improved prototype.

Advantages

Speed: Rapid prototyping significantly accelerates the product development process by quickly producing physical prototypes for testing and validation.

Cost Savings: It reduces costs associated with traditional prototype manufacturing, such as tooling and molding expenses, and minimizes the risk of costly design errors.

Design Flexibility: CAD allows for easy design modifications, enabling designers to iterate rapidly and explore multiple design alternatives.

Customization: Rapid prototyping is ideal for producing customized or one-off prototypes tailored to specific requirements.

Applications

Product Design: Rapid prototyping is widely used in product design and development to visualize and test concepts before full-scale production.

Engineering Prototypes: Engineers use rapid prototypes to validate and refine mechanical and structural designs.

Medical Models: In the medical field, it is used to create anatomical models for surgical planning and medical device development.

Aerospace: Prototypes of aircraft components and aerospace parts are created to test their performance and fit.

Automotive: Car manufacturers employ rapid prototyping to develop and test vehicle components and interiors.

Consumer Electronics: Prototyping is used to design and evaluate electronic devices, casings, and user interfaces.

Rapid prototyping is a critical step in modern product development processes. It bridges the gap between digital design and physical prototypes, enabling designers and engineers to quickly validate and refine their ideas before committing to full-scale production. This approach enhances innovation, reduces time to market, and minimizes development costs.

6.2.8 Bioprinting

Bioprinting is an innovative subset of 3D printing that specializes in creating biological constructs by layering living cells, biomaterials, and biological molecules to form tissue-like structures or functional living tissues [8]. Here is an overview of bioprinters:

Technology: Bioprinters work similarly to traditional 3D printers but use bio-inks containing living cells and biomaterials instead of plastics or metals. These printers deposit these bio-inks layer by layer according to a digital model, creating complex biological structures.

Bio-inks: These inks consist of living cells, such as stem cells or specialized cells like skin cells, along with supportive biomaterials like hydrogels or scaffolds that provide structural support for cell growth and organization.

Precision: Bioprinters require high precision to place cells accurately and maintain their viability throughout the printing process. Temperature and environmental conditions are controlled to ensure the cells remain viable and functional.

Applications

Bioprinting finds applications in tissue engineering, regenerative medicine, drug development, and disease modeling. It enables the creation of tissues and organs for transplantation, pharmaceutical testing on bioprinted tissues, and personalized medical treatments.

Challenges

Challenges in bioprinting include ensuring cell viability and functionality, mimicking complex biological structures, vascularization to supply nutrients to printed tissues, and integrating different cell types to form functional tissues.

Advancements

Ongoing advancements in bioprinting focus on improving printing resolution, enhancing bio-ink formulations, and developing techniques to print larger and more complex tissues or organ-like structures.

Bioprinting holds immense potential for revolutionizing healthcare by enabling the creation of patient-specific tissues and organs, reducing the need for organ transplantation waiting lists, and advancing the understanding and treatment of various diseases. Despite being a relatively nascent field, bioprinting shows promising avenues for future medical applications.

6.3 3D PRINTING

3D printing, a core element of AM, refers to the process of creating three-dimensional objects by adding material layer by layer, based on a digital model [8]. This technology allows for the production of intricate and complex structures with high precision, offering numerous advantages in various industries.

Process Overview

Digital Design: The process begins with a digital 3D model created using CAD software or obtained from 3D scanning technologies.

Slicing: The digital model is sliced into thin horizontal layers using specialized software. These layers serve as instructions for the 3D printer.

Printing: The 3D printer interprets these layers and deposits material (plastic, metal, resin, etc.) layer by layer according to the sliced model. Each layer fuses or solidifies to form the final 3D object.

Applications

Prototyping: It is extensively used for rapid prototyping, allowing quick iterations and design validation.

Customization: 3D printing enables the production of customized or personalized products, such as prosthetics, dental implants, or bespoke components.

Manufacturing: Industries like aerospace and automotive use 3D printing for producing lightweight and complex parts, optimizing design and functionality.

Advantages

Design Flexibility: Allows for the creation of complex geometries and intricate designs not feasible with traditional manufacturing methods.

Rapid Prototyping: Accelerates the product development cycle, reducing time to market for new designs.

Cost-Efficiency: Reduces material wastage by building parts only where needed, minimizing production costs.

Customization: Enables personalized products tailored to individual needs or specifications.

6.3.1 3D Printing Digital Design

Digital design in 3D printing involves creating computer-generated 3D models using specialized software known as CAD. These digital models serve as the blueprint for the physical objects to be manufactured using 3D printing technology. The design process allows for the creation and customization of intricate and complex geometries, offering flexibility in shaping the final product.

Advantages

Design Flexibility: Digital design allows for the creation of complex, customized, and intricate geometries that are challenging or impossible to achieve through traditional manufacturing methods.

Rapid Prototyping: It facilitates quick iterations and modifications in designs, enabling faster product development cycles and reducing time to market.

Cost-Efficiency: Digital design reduces material wastage as it enables precise control over the amount of material used for printing, optimizing resource utilization.

Customization: It allows for personalized and tailored products, catering to specific individual or industry needs.

Applications and Examples

Prototyping: In industries like automotive and aerospace, 3D printing digital design is extensively used for rapid prototyping of parts and components for testing and validation before mass production.

Healthcare: Customized prosthetics, implants, and medical devices are designed using 3D printing digital design, tailored to fit the specific anatomical requirements of patients.

Architecture and Construction: Architects and builders use digital design for creating complex architectural models, prototypes, or even functional components like detailed building parts.

Consumer Products: From fashion accessories to household items, companies leverage digital design in 3D printing to produce customized and unique consumer products.

6.3.2 3D Printing Slicing

3D printing slicing is a crucial process that prepares a digital model for printing by breaking it down into layers, much like slicing a loaf of bread. This technique involves using specialized software to translate a 3D model (created using CAD software) into a series of thin horizontal layers, generating instructions (G-code) for the 3D printer. Each layer's parameters, including thickness and print settings, are defined during slicing [9]. This method determines how the printer deposits material layer by layer, ensuring precise replication of the digital model in the physical object. Slicing allows for customization of layer thickness, infill patterns, and other settings, optimizing print quality, time, and material usage. It is a fundamental step in 3D printing, ensuring accuracy and enabling the creation of intricate and complex geometries and structures.

Steps in 3D Printing Slicing

Digital Model Preparation: Begin with a digital 3D model designed using CAD software.

Slicing Software: Utilize specialized slicing software that translates the 3D model into a series of thin horizontal layers, generating a set of instructions (G-code) for the 3D printer.

Layer Division: The software divides the digital model into numerous horizontal layers, determining the thickness and parameters for each layer.

Support Structures and Settings: Determine support structures and print settings such as layer height, infill density, print speed, and temperature.

Advantages of 3D Printing Slicing

Precision and Customization: Allows for precise control over layer thickness and settings, ensuring accurate replication of the digital model.

Time and Material Efficiency: Optimizes printing time and minimizes material wastage by strategically layering the object for efficient printing.

Complex Geometries: Enables printing of intricate geometries and structures that might be challenging using other manufacturing methods.

Ease of Modification: Facilitates adjustments in print settings or structures without altering the original 3D model.

Applications and Examples

Prototyping: Enables rapid prototyping of mechanical parts, architectural models, or prototypes with specific layer settings.

Art and Sculptures: Artists leverage slicing to create detailed sculptures or artistic pieces with precise layering and textures.

Functional Components: Industries like aerospace and automotive utilize slicing for manufacturing intricate parts and components with customized layer structures for enhanced functionality.

Medical Models: In healthcare, precise layering is used to create detailed anatomical models or prosthetics, ensuring accurate replication of complex structures.

6.3.3 3D Printing Process

In the context of 3D printing, the process involves the 3D printer interpreting the sliced digital model by depositing material layer by layer to construct the physical object. The slicing software divides the digital model into thin horizontal layers, and the 3D printer follows these instructions, adding material (e.g., plastic, metal, resin) one layer at a time, in accordance with the sliced model [10]. Each layer of material is precisely deposited and fuses or solidifies, depending on the specific printing technology being used. This layer-by-layer deposition and fusion process continues until all the layers are added, eventually forming the complete and final 3D object. This method allows for the creation of intricate and complex shapes, offering precision and customization in manufacturing objects across various industries.

In the realm of 3D printing, various materials are used to create objects, including plastics, metals, composites, and resins. These materials come in different types and forms, offering diverse properties suitable for specific applications:

Plastics: This category includes various types of thermoplastics (such as ABS, PLA, PETG) and thermosetting plastics (like nylon and polycarbonate) that can be melted and solidified repeatedly, making them commonly used in filament-based 3D printing technologies.

Metals: Metals like stainless steel, titanium, aluminum, and cobalt-chrome alloys are used in metal additive manufacturing methods such as DMLS or electron beam melting, where metal powders are selectively fused layer by layer using a laser or electron beam.

Composites: Composite materials combine different elements to enhance properties such as strength, flexibility, or conductivity. Carbon fiber–reinforced polymers or glass fiber composites are used in 3D printing to create lightweight, strong, and durable parts.

Resins: Resin-based 3D printing, such as SLA or digital light processing, uses liquid photopolymer resins that solidify when exposed to light. These resins vary in properties, including rigidity, flexibility, transparency, or biocompatibility, suitable for applications in industries like healthcare, engineering, or prototyping.

6.4 4D PRINTING

4D printing is an extension of 3D printing that involves creating dynamic, self-transforming structures that change shape or function over time when subjected to external stimuli like heat, water, light, or other environmental factors. Here is an overview:

Process: 4D printing utilizes materials similar to those used in 3D printing but includes smart materials or programmable materials capable of responding to specific stimuli. These materials are layered using 3D printing techniques, and the resulting structure can transform or self-assemble when activated by the external trigger.

Advantages

Adaptability: 4D-printed structures can adapt to changing conditions, making them ideal for applications where dynamic responses are necessary.

Complexity: It allows for the creation of complex structures that can self-assemble or change shape, enabling intricate designs without complex assembly processes.

Sustainability: It has the potential to reduce material waste by creating structures that adapt or reconfigure themselves rather than being discarded.

Applications

Biomedical Devices: 4D printing holds promise in creating self-assembling medical devices, such as stents or implants that adapt to the body's conditions.

Construction: Self-assembling structures could be used in construction for adaptive buildings or structures that respond to environmental changes.

Aerospace: Smart materials that change shape in response to external stimuli can be valuable in aerospace for adaptive components or morphing aircraft wings.

Consumer Goods: Applications in consumer products include adaptive clothing, shoes, or household items that adjust to temperature or other conditions.

Challenges: Challenges in 4D printing include refining materials to achieve precise and predictable responses, controlling the transformation process, and scaling the technology for practical applications.

4D printing represents an innovative approach to manufacturing by introducing materials that can respond dynamically to external stimuli, opening up possibilities for adaptive structures and products across various industries. While still in the early stages of development, ongoing research and advancements in materials science aim to unlock its full potential.

6.5 ADDITIVE MANUFACTURING FOR SMART STRUCTURES

AM for smart structures involves the integration of sensors, actuators, and responsive materials into 3D-printed components to create intelligent and adaptive structures [10]. These structures can sense changes in their environment, respond to stimuli, and adapt their behavior or shape accordingly. Here is an overview:

Sensor Integration: AM allows for the incorporation of sensors directly into the structure during the printing process. These sensors can detect various parameters such as temperature, strain, pressure, or other environmental factors.

Actuator Integration: Similarly, actuators—components that enable movement or mechanical action—can be integrated into AM-produced structures. These actuators can respond to sensor data or external triggers to initiate specific actions or shape changes.

Responsive Materials: Smart structures often utilize materials with unique properties that can respond to external stimuli, such as shape memory alloys or polymers. These materials can change shape, stiffness, or conductivity based on environmental changes.

Advantages

Adaptability: Smart structures created via AM can adapt their shape, mechanical properties, or functionality in response to changing conditions or user inputs.
Customization: AM allows for the creation of highly customized smart structures tailored to specific applications or requirements.
Complexity: With the layer-by-layer printing process, intricate designs and complex geometries can be achieved, enabling sophisticated smart structures.

Applications

Aerospace: Smart structures in aerospace can monitor structural health, adjust aerodynamics, or change wing configurations in response to varying flight conditions.
Civil Engineering: In civil engineering, smart structures can monitor stress levels in buildings, bridges, or infrastructure and adapt to minimize damage or enhance stability.
Biomedical: AM-enabled smart structures can be used in medical implants or devices that respond to biological signals for improved functionality.
Consumer Goods: Applications in consumer products include adaptive clothing, footwear, or accessories that adjust to environmental conditions or user preferences.

The integration of additive manufacturing techniques with smart materials, sensors, and actuators opens up possibilities for creating intelligent structures that can adapt, respond, and enhance performance across various industries and applications.

6.6 INDUSTRIAL CASE STUDY

Industrial case study showcasing the implementation and benefits of AM.

Case Study: GE Aviation's Fuel Nozzle Redesign
Industry: Aerospace
Challenge: GE Aviation faced challenges in traditional manufacturing of fuel nozzles for jet engines. These nozzles comprised 20 parts assembled together, requiring intricate machining processes and creating design limitations.

Implementation of AM: GE Aviation adopted AM to redesign these fuel nozzles. Instead of assembling multiple parts, they 3D printed the nozzle in one piece using a process called direct metal laser melting (DMLM) with advanced alloys like cobalt-chrome and nickel super alloys.

Benefits and Results

Weight Reduction: The AM redesign reduced the weight of the fuel nozzle by 25 percent compared to the conventionally manufactured version. Lighter components contribute to improved fuel efficiency and aircraft performance.

Consolidation and Complexity: By 3D printing the nozzle in a single piece, the need for assembling multiple parts was eliminated, simplifying the design and reducing production complexities.

Improved Durability and Performance: The AM process allowed for complex internal geometries and cooling channels that enhanced the nozzle's efficiency and performance.

Lead Time and Cost Savings: AM enabled quicker prototyping and production. Despite initial higher costs for AM equipment and materials, the overall production costs were reduced due to streamlined manufacturing processes and reduced assembly requirements.

Quality and Reliability: The new design improved part reliability and minimized potential failure points inherent in assemblies of multiple parts.

Impact: GE Aviation's adoption of AM for fuel nozzles showcased significant advancements in the aerospace industry. It demonstrated the potential of AM to revolutionize part design, manufacturing processes, and performance, leading to more efficient and reliable aircraft components.

This case study illustrates how AM's capabilities in design complexity, material efficiency, and performance enhancements can be leveraged to overcome challenges in traditional manufacturing processes, leading to tangible benefits and advancements in various industries.

6.7 CONCLUSIONS

In the midst of Industry 4.0, the profound impact of AM technologies on industrial engineering emerges as a transformative force reshaping the manufacturing landscape. The exploration of these cutting-edge methodologies reveals a paradigm shift in the way components are conceptualized, designed, and produced. The intricate fusion of AM with Industry 4.0 unleashes a realm of possibilities, revolutionizing traditional manufacturing approaches. As we conclude this exploration, it becomes evident that AM technologies offer unparalleled advantages, from design flexibility to rapid prototyping and customized production. The marriage of digitalization, agility, and innovation within industrial engineering amplifies the potential for efficient, cost-effective, and tailored manufacturing solutions.

6.8 FUTURE SCOPE

The future scope of AM technologies within the realm of industrial engineering during Industry 4.0 holds immense potential for continued innovation and transformative advancements. Some key future prospects and areas of exploration include:

Materials Development and Integration: Further research into advanced materials compatible with AM processes, such as new alloys, composites, and biomaterials, to expand the range of applications across industries. This includes enhancing material properties, such as strength, conductivity, and biocompatibility, tailored for specific manufacturing needs.

Multi-Material and Multi-Functional Printing: Advancing capabilities for simultaneous printing of multiple materials or functionalities within a single component, allowing for the creation of integrated, multi-functional parts with diverse properties.

Scaling for Mass Production: Overcoming challenges related to speed, scalability, and cost-effectiveness to enable AM technologies to compete with traditional manufacturing methods for large-scale production. This involves optimizing production rates, reducing printing times, and minimizing material waste.

In-Situ Monitoring and Quality Control: Developing real-time monitoring systems and feedback mechanisms during the printing process to ensure quality control, detect defects, and adjust parameters dynamically. This includes implementing artificial intelligence–driven predictive analytics for process optimization and quality assurance.

Sustainability and Circular Economy: Exploring environmentally sustainable practices by focusing on recyclable materials, reducing energy consumption, and implementing closed-loop manufacturing processes to minimize waste and carbon footprint.

Regulatory Standards and Certification: Establishing industry-wide standards and certifications for AM technologies to ensure compliance with safety, reliability, and quality requirements, enabling broader adoption in critical sectors such as aerospace and healthcare.

Digital Twin Integration: Introducing digital twin concepts to synchronize physical and digital representations of AM-produced components, facilitating ongoing optimization, performance monitoring, and predictive maintenance throughout their life cycle.

Education and Workforce Development: Strengthening educational programs and skill development initiatives to equip engineers and technicians with the necessary expertise in AM technologies, ensuring a skilled workforce capable of harnessing the full potential of these innovations.

The future of AM within industrial engineering in the era of Industry 4.0 is poised for significant strides, offering avenues for continual advancements, innovation, and integration across diverse industries, paving the way for a more agile, customizable, and efficient manufacturing landscape.

REFERENCES

[1] Frazier, W.E. Metal additive manufacturing: A review. *J. Mater. Eng. Perform.* 2014, 23, 1917–1928.

[2] Uriondo, A.; Esperon-Miguez, M.; Perinpanayagam, S. The present and future of additive manufacturing in the aerospace sector: A review of important aspects. *J. Aerosp. Eng.* 2015, 229, 2132–2147.

[3] Leal, R.; Barreiros, F.M.; Alves, L.; Romeiro, F.; Vasco, J.C.; Santos, M.; Marto, C. Additive manufacturing tooling for the automotive industry. *Int. J. Adv. Manuf. Technol.* 2017, 92, 1671–1676.

[4] Horn, T.J.; Harrysson, O.L. Overview of current additive manufacturing technologies and selected applications. *Sci. Prog.* 2012, 95, 255–282.

[5] Galati, M.; Iuliano, L. A literature review of powder-based electron beam melting focusing on numerical simulations. *Addit. Manuf.* 2018, 19, 1–20.

[6] Thomas, D.S.; Gilbert, S.W. Costs and cost effectiveness of additive manufacturing. *NIST Spec. Publ.* 2014, 1176, 12.

[7] Bikas, H.; Stavropoulos, P.; Chryssolouris, G. Additive manufacturing methods and modelling approaches: A critical review. *Int. J. Adv. Manuf. Technol.* 2016, 83, 389–405.

[8] Turner, B.N.; Strong, R.; Gold, S.A. A review of melt extrusion additive manufacturing processes: I. Process design and modeling. *Rapid Prototyp. J.* 2014, 20, 192–204.

[9] Turner, B.N.; Gold, S.A. A review of melt extrusion additive manufacturing processes: II. Materials, dimensional accuracy. *Rapid Prototyp. J.* 2015, 21, 250–261.

[10] Wong, K.V.; Hernandez, A. A review of additive manufacturing. *Int. Sch. Res. Not.* 2012, doi:10.5402/2012/208760.

Chapter 7

Additive Manufacturing Technologies for On-Demand Production of Customised Goods in the Era of the 4th Industrial Revolution

Kamardeen O. Abdulrahman
and Rabiu Abdulkarim Baba

7.1 INTRODUCTION

The Fourth Industrial Revolution emergence is triggered by the demands for 3D manufacturing processes that are suitable to produce machine and material components which are highly cost-effective, high precision, interchangeable, and customised products (Dilberoglu et al., 2017). The revolution precedes the sequence of industrial transformation, which includes mechanical-driven machines (Industry 1.0), electrically powered machines (Industry 2.0), and computerised machines (Industry 3.0). Industry 3.0 was basically attributed with the evolution of programmable computer system (Lemu, 2019). The evolution has led us to the Fourth Industrial Revolution (Industry 4.0) in anticipation of better manufacturing and machining operations. This era is a combination of smart and intelligent systems, which are otherwise termed as physical and digital technologies. It mainly involves the association of artificial intelligence (AI), high-performance computing, additive manufacturing (AM), advanced materials, robotics, cloud computing, natural language processing, cognitive technologies, horizontal and vertical system integration, and so forth (Chen, 2017). This process is aided by a smart supply chain, a dedicated information system, and automated life cycle management system. A typical example of the Industry 4.0 is AM technologies, which involve the intelligent interpretation of digital data in 3D format into a 3D physical object using different AM techniques and processes. Among the transformation technologies within the context of the 4th Industrial Revolution, AM appears to be the only one that is connected with a manufacturing operation. Figure 7.1 illustrates key enabler technologies that are employed to interact and execute different functions in an autonomous way in Industry 4.0 concept. AM is a vital enabler in Industry 4.0 which is focused to convert the digital information to physical form through the use of different scanning tools with the aim to carry out smart manufacturing process in its fineness and cost-effective state.

DOI: 10.1201/9781003486244-11

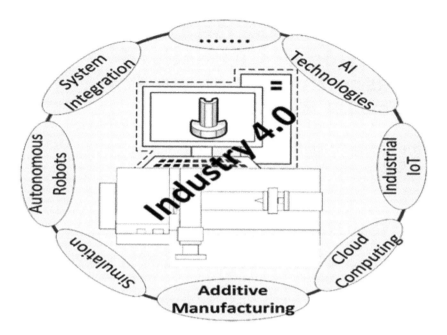

Figure 7.1 Emergence technologies in the Industry 4.0 concept.

Source: Lemu (2019).

In biomedical material development, Industry 4.0 has been significantly making an excellent impact in the production of customised implants and high-precision medical tools per patient requirements (Yang & Gu, 2021). The specification for personal solutions and demands has largely been achieved, which includes determination of the level of glucose and electronic-based digital testing equipment. This revolution allows biomedical engineers and medical doctors to conceptualise and study all the implications of their decision-making during the designing of customised medical prototypes before final development. The Fourth Industrial Revolution manufacturing processes are smart technologies that promote interconnectivity among the production systems with flexibility and a high-precision standard. Industry 4.0 technologies can accommodate high level of automation and computerisation such that permit varying degree of environmental parameters during manufacturing process. In the aerospace industry, Industry 4.0 has been used to develop lightweight aerospace parts with high-precision quality and excellent surface finishing (Awasthi et al., 2021). It is rapidly presenting new industrial paradigm towards changing the face of manufacturing processes to promote customisation demands in the printing and food industries, which includes printing of customised pizzas, burgers, confectionery, and coffee, among others.

One of the most significant breakthroughs in the printing industry in the last century is AM or 3D printing. This manufacturing process came into the limelight later in the 20th century and was patented by an American inventor, Charles Hull in 1984 (Hull, 2015). He is recognised as the inventor of a solid imaging process, which he later coined the term stereolithography (SLA), otherwise known as the 3D printing system. The technology uses UV lasers to cure liquid polymer resin deposited in layers by the SLA to form 3D geometries of intricate shapes and forms (Jandyal et al., 2022). The entire operation is digitalised where a 3D CAD file that is used to convey design information to a computer-aided package that involves slicing hardware capable to pile material in layer-by-layer cross-sections to form specific 3D shapes.

The most widely known CAD format is SLA, which has been helpful to design different geometries since its inception (Jiang et al., 2018). However, another new format known as the 3D manufacturing format (3MF) is coming up for usage, which has the tendencies to permit design applications to accurately transmit 3D models to connect with other applications, printers, platforms, and services. The innovation of this new format is introduced for two distinct reasons: there is a need to establish a universal standardised format for AM technology, to surmount the limitation of STL format that basically describes a raw, unstructured, and triangular geometry. The 3MF consortium was first developed in 2015, and its research on the XML file format is still under review (Lee et al., 2019). As at 2019, attempt to incorporate material colours into 3MF files was also established (Pei & Loh, 2019). The main objective for all these incorporations is to allow this new format to handle more information such as data of more objects in variable layer height settings, printer profile, and manually created supports. This format has started gaining relevance in the operations of some big industrial manufacturers like Ultimaker, 3D Systems, and Materialise (Jandyal et al., 2022). Another notable feature of AM that promotes its usage by manufacturers is the ability to work on different materials to produce a homogeneous and heterogeneous products with highly complicated geometries at a time-effective and more cost-effective ways.

The advent of AM draws some notable advantages over the earlier manufacturing processes, probably the most important one is its tendency to fabricate intricate geometries which are difficult to manufacture or impossible by other means. Personalisation and customisation are also benefits associated with the AM technologies making it an outstanding manufacturing process in Industry 4.0. There are seven established groups of AM including powder bed fusion, material extrusion, binder jetting, material jetting, vat photopolymerisation, sheet lamination, and direct energy decomposition (Tan et al., 2020). Despite the recent adoption of AM in the manufacturing industry, there are still some daunting limitations associated with this technology. These include building scalability, skills shortage, standardisation challenges, material heterogeneity, structural reliability, and intellectual property. For these limitations, some roadmaps have been set and reports developed, which include the NIST roadmap, the America Makes roadmap, the CSC report, and Wohler's report, among others (Butt, 2020). These are developed to enhance industry and business perspectives over the adoption of AM technologies. At the moment, researchers are clamoring for a better synergy among the research community, industry, and government to overcome the limitations hindering the universal of AM technologies. It is important to improve the research relationship between the industry and university community, thus enhancing the understanding and transferring of information on the fundamentals of AM processes in Industry 4.0. These recommendations have the potential to fill the knowledge gaps holding back the adoption of AM technologies as significant processes in Industry 4.0 as well as complementing the end-to-end digital implementation of the AM technologies.

7.1.1 Significance and Relevance of Additive Manufacturing to Industry 4.0

The global demands in manufacturing industries require more sophisticated technologies that are more flexible in operations, capable of handling complicated shapes, and with cost- and time-effective in-service delivery. AM technique has significantly been seen as a potential game changer in the Industry 4.0, even by big companies in the automobile and aerospace industries. Over the few decades, lots of researches and study have been invested on the AM technologies due to exponential increments in the number of low-cost 3D printers and awareness of 3D printing operations among small and medium business owners. This technology is rapidly changing the paradigm in the manufacturing industry with major impact on local and international markets. There are signs that AM is dominating manufacturing business perspectives in the near future beyond engineering uses. Home appliances and fashion accessories such as food printing, customised goods and services, among others are all going to be part of beneficiaries of the AM technologies.

The current manufacturing phase, Industry 4.0, is multi-technological and endowed with digitisation of manufacturing parameters, parallel with automation, cloud computing, the Internet of Things (IoT), simulation, among others, of which AM is considered as most significant because it is the only one that addresses manufacturing processes. Some countries have demonstrated it as part of their national goal, for instance, Norway in 2017 established a top Industry Center (Toppindustrisenteret), which focuses on AM as one of its vital areas to digitise the economy referred to as Norway 6.0 (Lemu, 2019). Researchers have also argued that digitisation of manufacturing process through AM technology has the potential to revolutionise engineering operations. AM in particular, being an important enabler of Industry 4.0, is capable of producing high-value components with limited resources, complex and customised goods in a time-effective manner, and enhances some operations such as maintenance, repair, and overhauling activities. It is also established that AM has the tendency to create sustainable manufacturing process in better environmentally friendly areas and to simplify the supply chain and market operations.

7.1.2 Principles of Additive Manufacturing Technologies

The discovery of AM technologies has tremendously shifted the paradigm of the manufacturing process. It has dynamically widened the types of printers that can be used to fabricate different materials including plastics, fibers, bio-composites, and metals. The AM technologies create 3D physical objects from a 3D CAD file created by design software or output scanners (Javaid & Haleem, 2019). It appears that all the AM technologies have similar characteristics as they all build in 3D layer by layer, depositing material in sequences, and fusing the material together. In categorising AM technologies, the types of material and the method of fusing the materials together are majorly considered. The types of AM technologies include direct metal laser sintering (DMLS), stereolithography (SLA), multi-jet printing (MJP), laminated object manufacturing (LOM), PolyJet 3D printing (PJP), selective laser sintering (SLS), fused deposition modeling (FDM), inkjet 3D printing (IJP), electron beam melting (EBM), and colour-jet printing (CJP) (Javaid & Haleem, 2019).

Customised products become easily designed with AM technologies as per customers' requirement and specifications in reduced time and cost. The principle of AM makes it easy to launch new products without much stress and to determine the functionality and performance characteristics of the prototypes before reaching end users. Due to the layer-by-layer deposition of the material, there exists little or no wastage during this manufacturing process. The AM process begins with a software model which describes the external geometry of the object that is developed in a CAD modeling environment (Gibson et al., 2021). The geometry information usually in 3D solid representation is then allowed to pass through the CAD software to the AM hardware in standard tessellation language (STL) or object file format (OBJ). Most of these file formats have been embedded into the solid modeling tools, which are majorly employed in the interface format with AM machines available in today's manufacturing industries (Lemu, 2019). The STL file format is presently mostly employed in industry as a standard format to send geometric data to 3D printers. The final output of the AM process is the extreme description of the 3D object that is corresponding by mesh of triangles, where the SLA file can be obtained as binary or ASCII format. Recently, additive manufacturing file (AMF), which is a new file format, is introduced to replace the standard STL file format, which has been in service as a common file format to relate the geometry and composition of any 3D component meant to be produced on any AM printer. Unlike SLA file format, AMF is equipped with the ability to support the transfer of data with information about colours, material, and lattices, among others.

7.1.3 Types of Additive Manufacturing Technologies

The mode of operations for AM machines are almost similar, as typical steps followed by all AM machines are to create a 3D solid model through layer-by-layer build-up via information transmitted from the CAD model. The model is usually generated by designing a software package or 3D scanner, computed tomography, or magnetic resonance imaging. The different types of AM technologies based on the methods of production of the physical model are discussed as follows.

7.1.3.1 Stereolithography

This system is built by the application of UV laser in a vat of resin, and the UV light is used to cure the photosensitivity material. Figure 7.2 shows a typical stereolithography system with laser scanner. The materials are built layer by layer as a 3D physical object through the CAD file package. The process starts with a STL file recognised as standard for AM technologies. Slicing the STL file, the 3D model is converted into 2D slices, which contain the data of cross-sectional coordinates of the design. Then the physical model is developed layer by layer through the information of the 2D slices. The 3D model of the STL format is expressed by many small triangular facets, with each facet describing by the coordinates of the three vertices and a unit vector pointing at a normal direction.

The fundamentals of the curing reactions of resins in the STL system, referred to as exothermic polymerisation, are typified by chemical cross-linking reactions. The reactions are initiated by supplying the energy UV light into the system, resulting in two transition curing processes: the gelation and vitrification. The gelation is characterised by liquid-to-rubber transition resulting in a rapid increase in viscosity, resulting in both sol phase and gel phase co-existing in the system. However, the vitrification transition is an unhurried, thermoreversible process that results in the transition from rubber resin or liquid to glassy solid resin. This system allows limited usage of material because of application of the light-sensitive polymers leading better surface finishing and lesser material wastage.

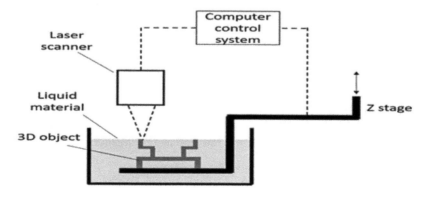

Figure 7.2 Schematic diagram of a stereolithography system.

Source: Huang et al. (2020).

7.1.3.2 Selective Laser Sintering

This type of AM technology achieves sintering through the use of a laser beam system. The material used is usually in powder form, and the laser sinters the powder. It is an industrial 3D printing technology, which uses powdered material to build up the 3D physical object. A typical SLS layout is shown in Figure 7.3. SLS technology uses the application of a laser to bind the powdered particles together (Fina et al., 2017). The peculiar working principle associated with SLS is the binding process, whereby the laser is controlled to draw a specific pattern on the surface of the powder bed. Once the first layer is finished, a roller is set to follow the first pattern and build up another layer on the pattern, resulting in a 3D object of the desired geometry.

This type of AM technology is a solvent-free process; common materials for this operation include powder plastic, ceramic, and metal alloys that require high temperature and energy input laser sintering.

7.1.3.3 Fused Deposition Modeling

The FDM system uses the extrusion method, in which a heated thermoplastic material is added layer by layer to fabricate a 3D object of specific coordinates. This

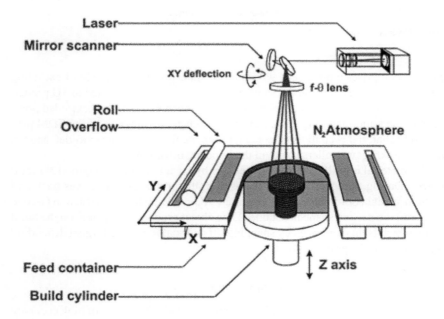

Figure 7.3 A typical selective laser sintering machine layout.

Source: Kruth et al. (2005).

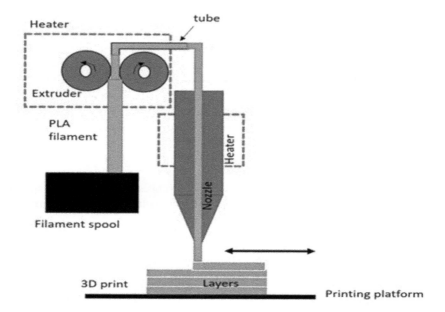

Figure 7.4 Principle of operation of fused deposition modeling.

Source: Mwema & Akinlabi (2020).

process comprises a print head with multiple nozzles that is capable of extruding jets of different materials at the same time. The nozzles are attached to 3D printer, capable to move in three degrees of freedom to deposit the molten extruded polymer on the build plate. Figure 7.4 shows the schematic diagram of the FDM process. The material is continuously fed through the filament of the extruder, and the nozzles linking two rollers rotate in the opposite direction.

The material is built on the bed plate layer by layer to form the required 3D solid object. During the layer-by-layer deposition, the printer nozzle moves back and forth in spatial coordinates of the original CAD model, which is written in G-code file, until the desired shape is obtained. The object produced is layered on the build plate, which is then removed by snapping off and soaking in a detergent depending on the type of the polymer used.

7.1.3.4 Direct Metal Laser Sintering

This type of AM technology is utilised to create metal 3D printing of high accuracy and better mechanical strength. Figure 7.5 shows a schematic diagram showing the typical setup of the DMLS process. This process involves metal powder of about 20 μm diameter in size, which is completely melted by the scanner of a high-power

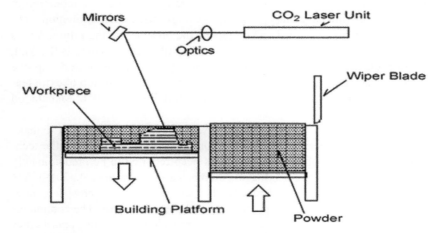

Figure 7.5 Schematic diagram of direct metal laser sintering setup.

Source: Khaing et al. (2001).

laser beam. The metal material is added in layer by layer without binder or fluxing agent, resulting in the production of 95 percent denser steel parts when compared to roughly 70 percent in SLS-produced products (Martinho, 2021).

The metallic materials commonly used for this production are alloy steel, cobalt-chrome, aluminum, bronze, stainless steel, and titanium. DMLS is commonly used to fabricate medical implants, aerospace parts, and rapid tooling.

7.1.3.5 Colour-Jet Printing (CJP)

The CJP technology uses material in powder form and resin as a binder during the formation of 3D solid profile by spreading the core material in layers over the build bed using rollers. The CAD software provides the design instruction to the printing jets, which spray binder on the powder layer at a particular point on the bed. This technology offers high flexibility through a controllable printing process to obtain products of intricate shapes, geometries, and function. The CJP technology has been extensively used in construction companies, machinery industry, aerospace, medicine, among others. The CJP technology is usually employ to develop colourful products, which have extensive applications in medical drug development.

7.2 APPLICATIONS OF ADDITIVE MANUFACTURING

From aerospace to automotive and oil and gas, AM is becoming highly acceptable and employed across a wide range of industries including medicine and biomedicals. AM advantages of design and geometric flexibility, near-net-shape production capability, parts fabrication from a range of materials, reduction in production cycle time and energy, and cost savings, makes the production technology a unique and advanced technology of the present and the future. AM is currently being applied in the building of functionally graded materials (FGMs), repair of broken or cracked parts, surface coating to tackle wear and improve corrosion resistance, printing of functional prototypes, and addition of extra features on existing parts (Abdulrahman et al., 2022; Balla et al., 2016; Mahamood et al., 2018).

The significant improvements currently witnessed in the field of AM make researchers and engineers continually explore possible application of the technology different fields of endeavor. AM has been reported to be predominantly employed in the field of engineering and biomedicals (Kosaraju et al., 2019). AM is now widely employed in different fields such as medicine, aerospace, automotive, electronic, defense, energy, mining, and petrochemicals. The continuous research and development in the field of AM is revealing numerous opportunities in the production of customised lightweight components and repair of other broken or worn-out components.

7.2.1 Medical Field

The application of AM has tremendously improved in the field of orthopaedics. AM now finds applications in the production of anatomic models, surgical tool and instruments design, implants, splints, and prostheses (Javaid & Haleem, 2018). AM provides desirable results in this area, as customised implants (based on required size and shape) can be produced. AM gives an exact fit implant needed for a particular patient. AM application in the medical field have been reported by researchers especially the application of 3D printing in areas such as prosthesis and implant modification, cell printing, organ and tissue bio-printing, drug discovery and delivery, and creation of anatomical models (Barua et al., 2019; Gibson et al., 2010). 3D printing of some medical parts (e.g., lumbar-support car seat, defective skull and personalised implant, spine, ankle joint and foot, implants, 3D model of part of human head both in hard and soft tissue form) for teaching and research are shown in Figure 7.6.

The application of AM can help surgeons and physicians in areas of planning, monitoring, diagnostics, and analysis. AM's ability in the provision of accurate physical model has been highly useful for surgical planning, training, and medical education (Kosaraju et al., 2019).

The development of rapid prototyping, otherwise known as the AM technique for clinical purposes, had been possible through three fundamental stages highlighted in Figure 7.7. The development of anatomical and biological models is a valuable factor that has assisted in the introduction of AM technique into the biomedical space (Ameddah & Mazouz, 2019).

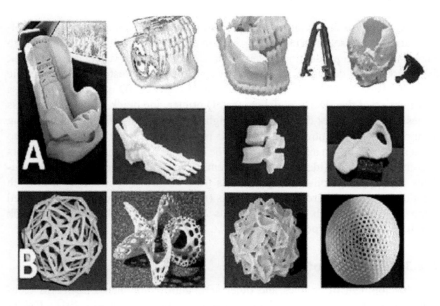

Figure 7.6 Representative images of application of additive manufacturing in the production of anatomical parts A. Solid Filled Components; B. Sparsh Filled Components.

Source: Sharma & Goel (2019).

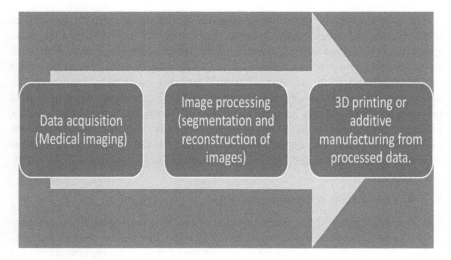

Figure 7.7 Clinical setting additive manufacturing stages.

Source: Rengier et al. (2010).

7.2.2 Educational Field

AM technology is an advanced and interesting educative manufacturing technology currently utilised, as it uses 3D printers in the fabrication of 3D objects through a layer-upon-layer production process from CAD model data. Using the computer, CAD models are designed, redesigned or controlled, and customised for specific product design requirements. The fast production of the 3D model, the seamless transmission of the 3D model data to the 3D printer, and quick production process of desired parts makes the technology highly flexible and effective. 3D printing technology has been introduced in schools in the fabrication of physical models to assist students (Bull et al., 2014, 2015). The advanced AM technology helps tutors to communicate their ideas better to students. Likewise, the technology helps students in the conversion of design models from 2D drawings to 3D models with the aid of CAD software. The 3D models (design prototype) can then be printed using 3D printer, which gives the students the opportunity of having a close look at a 3D printed prototype.

7.2.3 The Field of Aerospace

The development of engines and other aeronautic components from AM techniques have been documented by researchers (Baudana et al., 2016; Gebler et al., 2014; Kim & Kim, 2018; Kobryn et al., 2006; Peters et al., 2003). Gamma titanium aluminide alloys are seen as the most appropriate material for aerospace application owning to their high strength at higher temperatures and low-density attributes (Ranjana Kumari, 2015).

The components developed through the AM technique are currently applied for both military and commercial airplanes. The introduction of AM into the aerospace industry has led to the continuous development of major components such as fuel nozzles, compressors, turbine blades, and piping systems. The ultimate use of AM technology in the aerospace industry has been in operable launch vehicles and hypersonic airplanes (Ranjana Kumari, 2015). The notable merit of AM in the aerospace industry has been the capability of fabricating lightweight complex geometry components with the use of mixed materials. The outcome of AM technology in the production of aerospace components is the production of sustainable, high-performance, and fuel-efficient components (Singamneni et al., 2019).

7.2.4 The Field of Automobiles

The sustainability of AM in the production of machine parts is highly commendable. The traditional method of production like the subtractive production technique comes with the generation of waste in form of chips that consume additional energy to recycle or dispose as environmental waste. AM is characterised for proper management of raw material, and unused material in the part production process can be stored and reused without requiring additional energy and cost to recycle.

AM technology's contribution in the field of automobile has been highly positive, especially in the fabrication of lightweight FGM. Notable AM applications in this field include the fabrication of valves and pistons Carlota (2021) expressed that the SmarTech Analysis report indicated that 3D automotive printing of end-use parts will generate close to $9 billion by 2029 as against $1.39 billion generated in 2019. Volkswagen has been investing and collaborating with 3D printing technologies to further strengthen 3D activities and design process. Figure 7.8 shows the image of Audi W12 engine water connectors 3D printed from a metal material.

The recent developments in materials technology encourages the fabrication of automobile component components through the AM process. Most automotive components are produced from high-performance metals, polymers, and

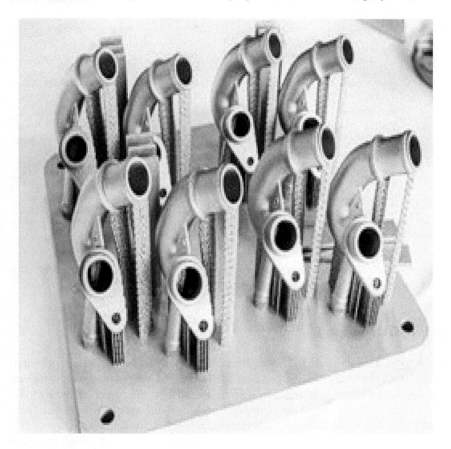

Figure 7.8 Image of 3D-printed water connectors for the Audi W12 engine.

Photo credits: Volkswagen AG.

Source: Carlota (2021).

Table 7.1 Trends in Additive Manufacturing Applications in the Automotive Sector

		Applications	*AM Technology*	*Materials*
Current	Manufacturing process	Prototyping, customised tooling, investment casting	Fused deposition modeling, inkjet, selective laser sintering (SLS), selective laser melting (SLM)	Polymers, wax, hot work steels
	Fluid handling	Pumps, valves	SLM, electron beam melting (EBM)	Aluminium alloys
	Exterior/exterior trim	Bumpers, wind breakers	SLS	Polymers
	Exhaust/emissions	Cooling vents	SLM	Aluminium alloys
Future	Electronics	Embedded components such as sensors, single-part control panels	SLS	Polymers
	Frame, body and doors	Body panels	SLM	Aluminium alloys
	Interior and seating	Dashboards, seat frames	SLS, SLA	Polymers
	OEM components	Body-in-white	SLM, EBM	Aluminium, steel alloys
	Powertrain, drivetrain	Engine components	SLM, EBM	Aluminium, titanium alloys
	Wheels, tires and suspension	Hubcaps, tires, suspension springs	SLS, inkjet, SLM	Polymers, aluminium alloys

Source: Carlota, 2021.

carbon-fiber-reinforced thermoplastics. The current and possible future trends in AM applications in the automotive sector are highlighted in Table 7.1.

7.3 INDUSTRY 4.0

Industry 4.0, or the 4th Industrial Revolution, unlike other previous industrial revolutions is rapidly altering our way of life (i.e., the way people live, work and interact with one another and their surroundings). The emergence of Industry 4.0 has started to revolutionise the manufacturing world due to its comparative advantages over the earlier manufacturing processes. The architecture of Industry 4.0 is designed to enhance efficiency, reduce material wastages, develop high precision components, provide flexibility, reduce downtime, and reduce the human factor in the production line. The evolution optimises the Industry 3.0 manufacturing processes through digital stimuli and physical transformation of industrial activities (Nagy et al., 2018). Industry 4.0 comes with the power of using Internet and phones with a great level of data storage and processing capability to connect people globally. The developmental and technical breakthroughs in the field of IoT, quantum computing, AI, robotics, nanotechnology, rapid prototyping, and so forth are some of the influences of the 4th Industrial Revolution which have altered the way we live, work, interact, produce, market, and transport goods and services.

7.3.1 Additive Manufacturing in the Era of Industry 4.0

The advances currently being witnessed in science and technology have brought about market globalisation. The life span of products is considerably shortened as researchers, engineers, and the production industry continue to work towards more effective and efficient solutions in reducing production period in the development of new products. The application of emerging state-of-the-art technologies in the design and manufacturing process is currently viewed as the most effective solution in products manufacturing. The development in the computing world cutting across IoT, AI, robotics, and others provides the opportunity to shorten realisation time in product development. AM is gaining a step further from rapid prototyping procedure to a more rapid manufacturing technique. Manufacturing procedures of intricate shapes of machine components becomes more possible through AM technologies faster than any other conventional techniques. Its emergence provides possibility for manufacturing freedom and flexibility with less human intervention. The production of customised goods becomes more feasible with the advent of Industry 4.0 with the same or reduced delivery time as that obtained in mass production procedures (Javaid et al., 2022).

AM, an advanced manufacturing technique sometimes referred to as 3D printing, rapid prototyping, or layer manufacturing, is fast gaining wide acceptability as a sustainable and environmentally friendly production technique. AM's ability to fabricate intricate parts through layer-upon-layer deposition with the aid of CAD data using powdery and wire material made it flexible and easy for on-demand production of customised goods. The increasing demand for swift production and supply of customised goods with robust designs can only be achieved with an advanced manufacturing technique. As such, the unique and seamless manufacturing characteristics of AM (with efficient lead time, reduction in material wastage, cost and energy savings nature, use of computing and Internet systems from CAD/CAM model creation, model data transmission, production settings and controls, printing, and post processing to final products) makes it the most suitable choice in the midst of other manufacturing techniques in today's era of the 4th Industrial Revolution.

The influence of AM in the 4th Industrial Revolution cannot be downplayed as it provides the capacity to easily deliver superior goods and services within a short period at reduced cost (Dilberoglu et al., 2017). The AM technology is growing fast due to the increasing demand for customised products as against mass-produced goods. To remain globally relevant due to customers' choice of customised goods, manufacturers and business leaders of industries are encouraged to review and adopt modern operational structures, procedures, and apply effective tools in other to deliver superior goods and services. Pliability and efficiency in on-demand production of customised goods and services are major objectives in today's technological world. The concept of the smart factory is also influenced by AM technology, as 3D printers occupy less space with the ability of replacing several machines employed in the traditional method of production. AM remains a major advanced technology used today to achieve the objectives of the 4th Industrial Revolution.

7.3.2 Future Trends of Additive Manufacturing in Industry 4.0

The recent trend in the on-demand production of customised items makes AM an important part of Industry 4.0. and a likely powerful manufacturing technology of the future. In spite of all the notable advantages associated with AM, low production rate, surface finish quality, and cost of production are some of its limitations that have to be examined. Proper integration of AM into Industry 4.0 can lead to the formation of a smart factory with significant gains in terms of reduction in inventory and labour cost.

The future sustainability of AM in the era of Industry 4.0 remains gloomy, as the technology comes with huge flexibility. The future days will come with customers that will choose to be the designers of their customised items. The designs can then be forwarded through electronic means to manufacturers for production. The future trend can also reveal the designer changing his home into a smart factory or series of network of smart factories. Some arguments revealed that AM as a key component of Industry 4.0 might result in huge success in sustainability especially in terms of production decentralisation (Sreerag et al., 2021). Enhanced and effective decentralised production processes are achievable when AM is properly integrated in Industry 4.0. The location of 3D printing centres close to customers can ensure the elimination of transportation, intermediate production stages, warehousing, and reduction in product delivery time, thereby ensuring the production of smart and customised product models (Krishna et al., 2021).

The future trend of the automotive industry is coming to reality, as most automotive companies now look toward new technologies to ensure time to market in less than two years. The new technologies, mainly including AM, are to shorten product development cycles at lower production costs. Automotive manufacturers are giving keen attention to electric vehicles (EV) in order to remain leading market players in the electrification of vehicles. The development of lightweight components highly critical for EV makes AM a technology of interest as weight tends to have significant effect on battery time. As such, in order to reduce cost and enhance manufacturing capabilities, automobile parts manufacturers are now availing themselves of the available opportunities of AM to develop new products and improve their supply chain.

7.4 SUMMARY

The merging of digital and physical operations in manufacturing industries has indeed changed the face of the industrial activities in the present time leading to the Fourth Industrial Revolution. The emergence of this revolution is happening so fast, which is inevitable and ever-promising beyond just manufacturing. The significant roles that AM technologies are going to play in Industry 4.0 cannot be underestimated with these trends of modern manufacturing processes. The paradigm shift of industrial operations towards embracing these new technologies for rapid prototyping of customised products and services, development of intricate machine components, and advanced printing technology of food items and materials has come to dominate the Fourth Industrial Revolution. More manufacturing companies are already taking advantage of AM technologies with the aim to produce at more effective and efficient manners. The smart factories of the future are here, taking over industrial activities smartly, and are interconnected with greater flexibility with little or no human intervention. It is essential for stakeholders and policymakers to begin to develop initiatives that will promote skills and knowledge acquisitions in this direction. This chapter has provided in-depth views on the roles of AM technologies in Industry 4.0 as well as their interrelationship. It highlights different varieties of AM techniques, principles of operations, and their significance in medical, educational, aerospace, and automobile fields. AM technologies are predicted to dominate the operations of manufacturing processes in the years to come. Therefore, it is important to intensify academic research and skills acquisition in this sector to facilitate adequate growth and development of manufacturing industries.

REFERENCES

Abdulrahman, K. O., Mahamood, R. M., & Akinlabi, E. T. (2022). Additive Manufacturing (AM): Processing technique for lightweight alloys and composite material. In K. Kumar, B. S. Babu, & J. P. Davim (Eds.), *Handbook of Research on Advancements in the Processing, Characterization, and Application of Lightweight Materials* (pp. 27–48). IGI Global. https://doi.org/10.4018/978-1-7998-7864-3

Ameddah, H., & Mazouz, H. (2019). 3D printing analysis by Powder Bed Printer (PBP) of a Thoracic Aorta under simufact additive. In K. Kumar, D. Zindani, & J. P. Davim (Eds.), *Additive Manufacturing Technologies from an Optimization Perspective* (pp. 102–118). IGI Global.

Awasthi, A., Saxena, K. K., & Arun, V. (2021). Sustainable and smart metal forming manufacturing process. *Materials Today: Proceedings*, *44*, 2069–2079. https://doi.org/10.1016/j.matpr.2020.12.177

Balla, V. K., Das, M., Mohammad, A., & Al-Ahmari, A. M. (2016). Additive manufacturing of γ-TiAl: Processing, microstructure, and properties. *Advanced Engineering Materials*, *18*(7), 1208–1215. https://doi.org/10.1002/adem.201500588

Barua, R., Datta, S., Roychowdhury, A., & Datta, P. (2019). Importance of 3D Printing technology in medical fields. In K. Kumar, D. Zindani, & J. P. Davim (Eds.), *Additive Manufacturing Technologies from an Optimization Perspective* (pp. 21–40). IGI Global.

Baudana, G., Biamino, S., Ugues, D., Lombardi, M., Fino, P., Pavese, M., & Badini, C. (2016). Titanium aluminides for aerospace and automotive applications processed by Electron Beam Melting: Contribution of Politecnico di Torino. *Metal Powder Report*, *71*(3). https://doi.org/10.1016/j.mprp.2016.02.058

Bull, G., Chiu, J., Berry, R., Lipson, H., & Xei, C. (2014). Advancing children's engineering through desktop manufacturing. In J. M. Spector, M. D. Merrill, J. Elen, & M. J. Bishop (Eds.), *Handbook of Research on Educational Communications and Technology* (4th ed.). Springer Science+Business Media. https://doi.org/10.1007/978-1-4614-3185-5_54

Bull, G., Haj-Hariri, H., Atkins, R., & Moran, P. (2015). An educational framework for digital manufacturing in schools. *3D Printing and Additive Manufacturing*, *2*(2). https://doi.org/10.1089/3dp.2015.0009

Butt, J. (2020). Exploring the interrelationship between additive manufacturing and industry 4.0. *Designs*, *4*(2). https://doi.org/10.3390/designs4020013

Carlota, V. (2021). The role of AM in the automotive industry. *3D Natives*. www.3dnatives.com/en/the-role-of-am-in-the-automotive-industry/#!

Chen, Y. (2017). Integrated and intelligent manufacturing: Perspectives and enablers. *Engineering*, *3*(5), 588–595. https://doi.org/10.1016/J.ENG.2017.04.009

Dilberoglu, U. M., Gharehpapagh, B., Yaman, U., & Dolen, M. (2017). The role of additive manufacturing in the era of Industry 4.0. *Procedia Manufacturing*, *11*(June), 545–554. https://doi.org/10.1016/j.promfg.2017.07.148

Fina, F., Goyanes, A., Gaisford, S., & Basit, A. W. (2017). Selective laser sintering (SLS) 3D printing of medicines. *International Journal of Pharmaceutics*, *529*(1), 285–293. https://doi.org/10.1016/j.ijpharm.2017.06.082

Gebler, M., Schoot Uiterkamp, A. J. M., & Visser, C. (2014). A global sustainability perspective on 3D printing technologies. *Energy Policy*, *74*(C). https://doi.org/10.1016/j.enpol.2014.08.033

Gibson, I., Rosen, D. W., & Stucker, B. (2010). *Additive Manufacturing Technologies*. Springer. https://doi.org/10.1007/978-1-4419-1120-9

Gibson, I., Rosen, D., Stucker, B., & Khorasani, M. (2021). Introduction and basic principles. In *Additive Manufacturing Technologies* (pp. 1–21). Springer International Publishing. https://doi.org/10.1007/978-3-030-56127-7_1

Huang, J., Qin, Q., & Wang, J. (2020). A review of stereolithography: Processes and systems. *Processes*, *8*(9). https://doi.org/10.3390/pr8091138

Hull, C. W. (2015). The birth of 3D printing. *Research-Technology Management*, *58*(6), 25–30. https://doi.org/10.5437/08956308X5806067

Jandyal, A., Chaturvedi, I., Wazir, I., Raina, A., & Ul Haq, M. I. (2022). 3D printing—A review of processes, materials and applications in industry 4.0. *Sustainable Operations and Computers*, *3*, 33–42. https://doi.org/10.1016/j.susoc.2021.09.004

Javaid, M., & Haleem, A. (2018). Additive manufacturing applications in orthopaedics: A review. *Journal of Clinical Orthopaedics and Trauma*, *9*(3), 202–2–6. https://doi.org/10.1016/j.jcot.2018.04.008

Javaid, M., & Haleem, A. (2019). Current status and applications of additive manufacturing in dentistry: A literature-based review. *Journal of Oral Biology and Craniofacial Research*, *9*(3), 179–185. https://doi.org/10.1016/j.jobcr.2019.04.004

Javaid, M., Haleem, A., Singh, R. P., Suman, R., & Gonzalez, E. S. (2022). Understanding the adoption of industry 4.0 technologies in improving environmental sustainability. *Sustainable Operations and Computers, 3*, 203–217. https://doi.org/10.1016/j.susoc.2022.01.008

Jiang, J., Xu, X., & Stringer, J. (2018). Support structures for additive manufacturing: A review. *Journal of Manufacturing and Materials Processing, 2*(4). https://doi.org/10.3390/jmmp2040064

Khaing, M. W., Fuh, J. Y. H., & Lu, L. (2001). Direct metal laser sintering for rapid tooling: processing and characterisation of EOS parts. *Journal of Materials Processing Technology, 113*(1), 269–272. https://doi.org/10.1016/S0924-0136(01)00584-2

Kim, Y.-W., & Kim, S.-L. (2018). Advances in gammalloy materials—processes—application technology: Successes, dilemmas, and future. *JOM, 70*(4), 553–560. https://doi.org/10.1007/s11837-018-2747-x

Kobryn, P. A., Ontko, N. R., Perkins, L. P., & Tiley, J. S. (2006). Additive manufacturing of aerospace alloys for aircraft structures. *Meeting Proceedings RTO-AVT-139*, 3-1-3-14. www.rto.nato.int/abstracts.asp.

Kosaraju, S., Mohan K. B., & Singh, S. K. (2019). Recent advancement in additive manufacturing. In K. Kumar, D. Zindani, & J. P. Davim (Eds.), *Additive Manufacturing Technologies from an Optimization Perspective* (pp. 1–19). IGI Global.

Krishna, R., Manjaiah, M., & Mohan, C. B. (2021). Developments in additive manufacturing. In M. Manjaiah, K. Raghavendra, N. Balashanmugam, & J. P. Davim (Eds.), *Additive Manufacturing: A Tool for Industrial Revolution 4.0* (pp. 37–62). Woodhead Publishing—imprint of Elsevier.

Kruth, J., Mercelis, P., Van Vaerenbergh, J., Froyen, L., & Rombouts, M. (2005). Binding mechanisms in selective laser sintering and selective laser melting. *Rapid Prototyping Journal, 11*(1), 26–36. https://doi.org/10.1108/13552540510573365

Lee, B. N., Pei, E., & Um, J. (2019). An overview of information technology standardization activities related to additive manufacturing. *Progress in Additive Manufacturing, 4*(3), 345–354. https://doi.org/10.1007/s40964-019-00087-5

Lemu, H. G. (2019). On opportunities and limitations of additive manufacturing technology for industry 4.0 era. In K. Wang, Y. Wang, J. O. Strandhagen, & T. Yu (Eds.), *Advanced Manufacturing and Automation VIII* (pp. 106–113). Springer. https://link.springer.com/book/10.1007/978-981-13-2375-1#toc

Mahamood, R. M., Akinlabi, E. T., Owolabi, G. M., & Abdulrahman, K. O. (2018). Advanced manufacturing of compositionally graded composite materials. In K. Kumar & J. P. Devim (Eds.), *Hierarchical Composite Materials: Materials, Manufacturing and Engineering* (pp. 41–54). Walter de Gruyter.

Martinho, P. G. (2021). Chapter 9—Rapid manufacturing and tooling. In A. S. Pouzada (Ed.), *Design and Manufacturing of Plastics Products* (pp. 381–456). William Andrew Publishing. https://doi.org/10.1016/B978-0-12-819775-2.00008-5

Mwema, F. M., & Akinlabi, E. T. (2020). Basics of Fused Deposition Modelling (FDM). In *Fused Deposition Modeling: Strategies for Quality Enhancement* (pp. 1–15). Springer International Publishing. https://doi.org/10.1007/978-3-030-48259-6_1

Nagy, J., Oláh, J., Erdei, E., Máté, D., & Popp, J. (2018). The role and impact of industry 4.0 and the internet of things on the business strategy of the value chain—the case of Hungary. *Sustainability, 10*(10). https://doi.org/10.3390/su10103491

Pei, E., & Loh, G. H. (2019). Future challenges in functionally graded additive manufacturing. In E. Pei, M. Monzón, & A. Bernard (Eds.), *Additive Manufacturing—Developments in Training and Education* (pp. 219–228). Springer International Publishing. https://doi.org/10.1007/978-3-319-76084-1_15

Peters, M., Kumpfert, J., Ward, C. H., & Leyens, C. (2003). Titanium alloys for aerospace applications. In C. Leyens & M. Peters (Eds.), *Titanium and Titanium Alloys, Fundamentals and Applications*. WILEY-VCH.

Ranjana Kumari. (2015). Advances in gamma titanium aluminides alloys. *International Journal of Metallurgical & Materials Science and Engineering (IJMMSE)*, *5*(4), 1–8. www.tjprc.org/view-archives.php

Rengier, F., Mehndiratta, A., Tengg-Kobligk, H. Von, Zechmann, C. M., Unterhinninghofen, R., Kauczor, H. U., & Giesel, F. L. (2010). 3D printing based on imaging data: Review of medical applications. *International Journal of Computer Assisted Radiology and Surgery*, *5*(4), 335–341.

Sharma, S., & Goel, S. A. (2019). 3D printing and its future in medical world. *Journal of Medical Research and Innovation*, *1*(3). https://jmrionline.com/jmri/article/view/141

Singamneni, S., LV, Y., Hewitt, A., Chalk, R., Thomas, W., & Jordison, D. (2019). Additive manufacturing for the aircraft industry: A review. *Journal of Aeronautics & Aerospace Engineering*, *8*(1). www.longdom.org/open-access/additive-manufacturing-for-the-aircraft-industry-a-review-18967.html

Sreerag, C., Gajjela, R., Manupati, V., & Machado, J. (2021). Additive manufacturing: A thrive for industries. In M. Manjaiah, K. Raghavendra, N. Balashanmugam, & J. P. Davim (Eds.), *Additive manufacturing: A tool for industrial revolution 4.0* (pp. 1–15). Woodhead Publishing—imprint of Elsevier.

Tan, L. J., Zhu, W., & Zhou, K. (2020). Recent progress on polymer materials for additive manufacturing. *Advanced Functional Materials*, *30*(43), 2003062. https://doi.org/10.1002/adfm.202003062

Yang, F., & Gu, S. (2021). Industry 4.0, a revolution that requires technology and national strategies. *Complex & Intelligent Systems*, *7*(3), 1311–1325. https://doi.org/10.1007/s40747-020-00267-9

Chapter 8

Computational Analysis of the Mechanical Compression of Additive Manufactured Lattice Structures

A Numerical Study

Mumtaz Rizwee, Deepak Kumar, and Rahul Kumar

8.1 INTRODUCTION

Lattice structures find widespread utilization across diverse applications owing to their remarkable mechanical properties and significant porosity. These applications encompass lightweight design, surgical implants, sound absorption, noise reduction, protection, and impact resistance [1–5]. Research demonstrated the functionality and exceptional performance of these structures [6, 7]. Notwithstanding, the production of lattice structures remains a formidable task on account of the intricate internal configuration and diminutive dimensions of the struts. Lattice structures can be fabricated through conventional processing techniques such as powder metallurgy, sintering, and space holder [8–10].

Notwithstanding, challenges in term of low porosity, uneven pore size, impurities, and other related issues persist without resolution. In contemporary times, the nascent technology of additive manufacturing has demonstrated its potential to effectively address these issues and is widely regarded as the most appropriate method of fabrication for creating lattice structures [11–16]. The utilization of additive manufacturing presents an opportunity for enhanced design flexibility, allowing for the unit cell size of lattice structures to achieve dimensions on the order of millimeters. As a result, the performance of such lattice structures produced via additive manufacturing has garnered significant interest among scholars and researchers.

The mechanical characteristics of lattices have drawn interest as an essential metric for assessing the macroscopic performance of the lattice structure. For instance, Hedayati et al. [17] developed a stiffness and strength prediction model for an octahedral lattice using the classical beam theory, and ultimately discovered a relationship between the lattice structure's mechanical properties and its geometric parameters. The power–law correlation, as observed by Meza et al. [18], was found to be suitable for predicting the mechanical characteristics of lattice structures, similar to the well-established Gibson–Ashby model [19]. The power–law

DOI: 10.1201/9781003486244-12

147

correlation enabled the elucidation of the factors influencing the mechanical characteristics of the lattice, encompassing the intrinsic material properties, structural arrangement, and relative density. The influence of geometric parameters on the performance of lattice configuration was of utmost significance, regardless of the material employed in their fabrication. Hence, it was of considerable value to investigate the relationship between the microscopic geometric characteristics and the macroscopic properties of the lattice configuration.

In their study, Al-Ketan et al. [20] conducted an investigation on the compressive behaviour of lattices with different topologies and relative densities. Upon initial investigation, it was observed that the mechanical characteristics of the structures displayed a range of variations, which could be attributed to the different topologies and relative densities of the individual cells. The influence of geometric configuration on the mechanical characteristics of structures was observed to be particularly significant in cases where the relative density was reduced. Finally, it had been observed that the deformation mechanism of lattice structures was greatly influenced by the topology of the unit cell. Furthermore, extensive research had been conducted by scholars [21–25] to investigate the lattice configuration with various topologies, emphasizing the significant impact of the unit cell's topology on the structural efficiency.

The mechanical characteristics of the lattice structure are contingent upon the topology of the unit cell. In order to achieve lattice structures that exhibit superior mechanical properties, researchers are persistently investigating novel lattice structures, including those with distorted struts [26, 27] and optimized node structures [28–31]. The lattice type of the rod element governs its force form. In order to accommodate the mechanical characteristics of the structure, it is possible to modify the size of the rod. The available sizes are limited due to constraints in the manufacturing process. Modifying the topological configuration of a structure to align with distinct mechanical response demands is a prevalent practice, albeit one that inevitably amplifies the onus of structural design. Statistical tools (e.g., Taguchi, response surface methodology, analysis of variance, genetics algorithm) can be used to optimized the lattice geometry parameters [32–34].

In this research work a numerical investigation of the mechanical compression and deformation characteristics of various lattice structures produced through additive manufacturing was performed.

8.2 NUMERICAL METHODOLOGY

The utilization of numerical modeling serves as a valuable approach for investigating the intricate mechanical behaviour in relation to various processes. This study employed the finite element method (FEM) to analyze the effect of lattice structure on the mechanical compression and deformation characteristics.

The finite element model utilized a static/implicit computational approach. In order to forecast the mechanical responses of the lattice configuration and examine the stress distribution within the lattice sample during deformation, the finite element analysis was conducted using the commercially available software nTop 4.1.3. A three-dimensional lattice structure model consisting of various unit cells, namely body-centered cubic (BCC), face-centered cubic (FCC), and fluorite, was constructed. The overall dimensions of the model were 9 mm × 9 mm × 9 mm, as illustrated in Figure 8.1. Each individual unit cell within the model possessed dimensions of 3 mm × 3 mm × 3 mm.

The dimension of the lattice structure rod was measured to be 1 mm in thickness. The simulation setup depicted in Figure 8.1 consisted of two plates, each

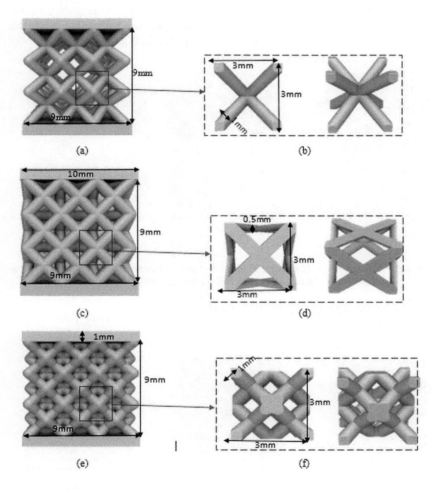

Figure 8.1 (a) Body-centered cubic (BCC) lattice configuration; (b) BCC unit cell; (c) face-centered cubic (FCC) lattice configuration; (d) FCC unit cell; (e) fluorite lattice configuration; and (f) fluorite unit cell.

measuring 10 mm × 10 mm × 1 mm, with a lattice structure sandwiched between them. Both the plate and rod components of the lattice structure are characterized by a triangular mesh with a linear geometry order. Following the completion of the mesh sensitivity analysis, it was determined that the optimal mesh sizes for the plate and rod components of the lattice structure were 0.5 mm and 0.1 mm, respectively.

The tie constant was employed as a means of linking the plate with the lattice structure, as depicted in Figure 8.2, in order to prevent any relative motion between the two components. The researchers opted for an isotropic material (steel) in this investigation. The simulation parameters for the base material included a young modulus of 200 GPa and a Poisson's ratio of 0.3. The specified boundary condition entailed the application of a force (−1000 N) to the top body plate, while the bottom body plate was fully immobilized, as depicted in Figure 8.3.

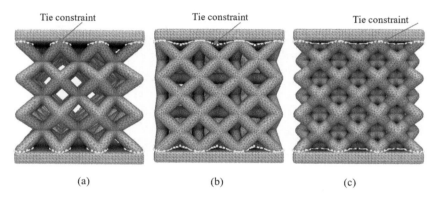

Figure 8.2 Meshing with tie connector in (a) body-centered cubic lattice structure; (b) face-centered cubic lattice structure; and (c) fluorite lattice structure.

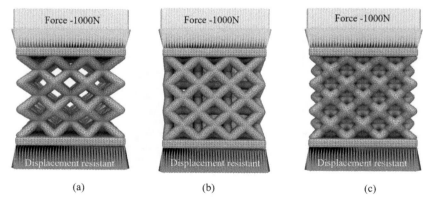

Figure 8.3 Boundary condition for (a) body-centered cubic lattice structure; (b) face-centered cubic lattice structure; and (c) fluorite lattice structure.

8.3 RESULTS AND DISCUSSION

The deformation mode exhibited by the lattice configuration provides valuable insights into the compressive behaviour of the structure, thereby facilitating the analysis of its failure mechanism. By employing numerical compression analysis, one can ascertain that the deformation process of the structure exhibits notable variations. During the implicit analysis, it was determined that the unit cell had a minor effect on the deformation mode of the various lattice structures. Figure 8.4 depicts the simulated deformation analysis of the various lattice structures. The BCC lattice structure exhibited a greater deformation (0.00558 mm) than other lattice structures. During the compressive analysis, the BCC structure demonstrated superior toughness in comparison to other unit cell structures. Due to their higher relative density, the FCC and fluorite lattice structures experienced less deformation than the BCC lattice structures. However, it demonstrated uniform deformation and compression in a layer-by-layer manner, resembling the deformation process found in previous studies of ductile materials [35, 36]. The brittleness of the structure is attributed to the transformation of the lattice structure's unit cell from BCC to FCC and fluorite. Additionally, the deformation modes exhibited by the rods in different regions of the lattice structure were notably distinct.

The upper rods exhibited more pronounced tensile deformation, whereas the lower rods displayed relatively smaller deformations in line with expectations. In the context of practical engineering applications, it is common for the number of lattice unit cells to be significantly large. The mechanical characteristics of the lattice configuration was ultimately determined by the deformation mode exhibited by its internal rod elements. Hence, when considering numerical analysis, it can be concluded that the BCC lattice structure shows greater toughness in comparison to the FCC and fluorite lattice structures.

Figure 8.5 illustrates the mechanical response curve of various lattice configuration during the process of compression leading to densification. The mechanical compression analysis utilized the maximum principal stress theory. It is apparent

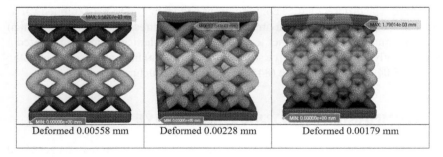

| Deformed 0.00558 mm | Deformed 0.00228 mm | Deformed 0.00179 mm |

Figure 8.4 Compressive deformation analysis of lattice configuration samples: simulation. (*Left to right*) Body-centered cubic, face-centered cubic, and fluorite lattice structure.

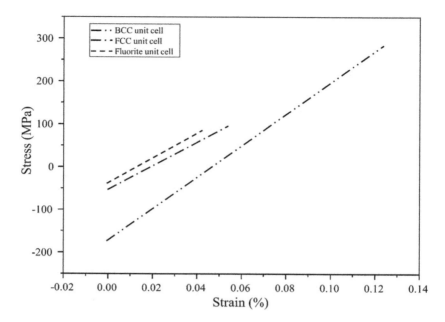

Figure 8.5 Stress–strain curve for different lattice structures.

that the static stress–strain curve exhibited a consistent trend across various lattice structures, albeit with variations in the specific stress and strain values. The lattice structure changed from BCC→ FCC→ fluorite with the raising density of the lattice, and the mechanical characteristics (stress and strain) decreased significantly.

The BCC lattice structure exhibited a prolonged period of strain in comparison to the FCC and fluorite lattice structures, thereby demonstrating favourable toughness, as depicted in Figure 8.5. The fluorite lattice structure exhibited a relatively shorter period of strain, thus displaying characteristics consistent with a brittle structure. The different lattice configurations shown in Figure 8.6 exhibited variations in the development of maximum and minimum stresses as well as maximum and minimum strains at distinct locations. The BCC lattice structure exhibited a significantly higher compressive strength (283.50 MPa) in comparison to both the FCC (98.04 MPa) and fluorite (84.82 MPa) lattice structures.

8.4 SUMMARY AND FUTURE PROSPECTIVE

This study involved the acquisition of various lattice structures characterized by different configurations, achieved through the manipulation of geometric parameters associated with the BCC, FCC, and fluorite unit cell arrangements.

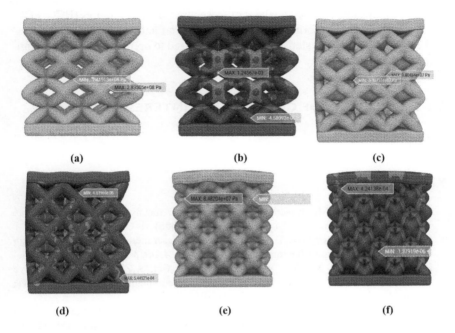

(a)   (b)   (c)

(d)   (e)   (f)

Figure 8.6 Compression stress–strain analysis of lattice structures: simulation. (a) Stress analysis for body-centered cubic (BCC); (b) strain analysis for BCC; (c) stress analysis for face-centered cubic (FCC); (d) strain analysis for FCC; (e) stress analysis for fluorite; and (f) strain analysis for fluorite.

Subsequently, the numerical determination of the mechanical compression and deformation properties of said lattice configuration was conducted using a finite element model.

The compression characteristics of lattice configuration with distinct unit cells exhibit discernible variations. The BCC lattice structure exhibited a greater deformation of 0.00558 mm in comparison to alternative lattice structures. Therefore, the BCC structure exhibited superior toughness in the compression analysis when compared to other unit cell structures. The upper rods of each lattice structure exhibited more pronounced tensile deformation, whereas the lower rods displayed relatively smaller deformations, as expected. The lattice structure changed from BCC→ FCC→ fluorite with the rising density of the lattice, and the mechanical characteristics (stress and strain) decreased significantly. The BCC lattice structure exhibited a prolonged period of strain in comparison to the FCC and fluorite lattice structures, thereby resulting in greater toughness. The BCC crystal structure exhibited a higher compressive strength in comparison to the FCC and fluorite lattice structures. The findings suggest that the BCC structure exhibited superior compressive strength and deformation characteristics in comparison to the FCC and fluorite structures.

In future, dynamic/explicit analysis of these three lattice structures (BCC, FCC, and fluorite) can be performed and their comparison analysis with experimentation can be done. Further statistical tools can be used to optimize the lattice geometry parameter.

8.5 DISCLOSURE OF CONFLICTING INTERESTS

None.

REFERENCES

[1] H.N.G. Wadley, Multifunctional periodic cellular metals, *Philos. Trans. R. Soc. Lond. Ser. A-Math. Phys. Eng. Sci.* 364 (1838) (2006) 31–68.

[2] A.G. Demir, L. Monguzzi, B. Previtali, Selective laser melting of pure Zn with high density for biodegradable implant manufacturing, *Addit. Manuf.* 15 (2017) 20–28.

[3] L. Bai, C. Gong, X. Chen, Y. Sun, J. Zhang, L. Cai, S. Zhu, S.Q. Xie, Additive manufacturing of customized metallic orthopedic implants: Materials, structures, and surface modifications, *Metals* 9 (9) (2019) 1004.

[4] D.-W. Wang, Z.-H. Wen, C. Glorieux, L. Ma, Sound absorption of face-centered cubic sandwich structure with micro-perforations, *Mater. Des.* 186 (2020) 108344.

[5] X. Chen, Q. Ji, J. Wei, H. Tan, J. Yu, P. Zhang, V. Laude, M. Kadic, Light-weight shell-lattice metamaterials for mechanical shock absorption, *Int. J. Mech. Sci.* 169 (2020) 105288.

[6] X. Zheng, H. Lee, T.H. Weisgraber, M. Shusteff, J. DeOtte, E.B. Duoss, J.D. Kuntz, M.M. Biener, Q. Ge, J.A. Jackson, Ultralight, ultrastiff mechanical metamaterials, *Science* 344 (6190) (2014) 1373–1377.

[7] A.A. Zadpoor, Mechanical meta-materials, *Mater. Horiz.* 3 (5) (2016) 371–381.

[8] S.A. Poursamar, J. Hatami, A.N. Lehner, C.L.D. Silva, F.C. Ferreira, A.P.M. Antunes, Gelatin porous scaffolds fabricated using a modified gas foaming technique: Characterisation and cytotoxicity assessment, *Mater. Sci. Eng. C-Mater. Biol. Appl.* 48 (2015) 63–70.

[9] B. Xie, Y.Z. Fan, T.Z. Mu, B. Deng, Fabrication and energy absorption properties of titanium foam with CaCl2 as a space holder, *Mater. Sci. Eng. A-Struct. Mater. Prop. Microstruct. Process.* 708 (2017) 419–423.

[10] C. Torres-Sanchez, J. McLaughlin, A. Fotticchia, Porosity and pore size effect on the properties of sintered Ti35Nb4Sn alloy scaffolds and their suitability for tissue engineering applications, *J. Alloys Compd.* 731 (2018) 189–199.

[11] A.A. Zadpoor, J. Malda, Additive manufacturing of biomaterials, tissues, and organs, *Ann. Biomed. Eng.* 45 (1) (2017) 1–11.

[12] T.D. Ngo, A. Kashani, G. Imbalzano, K.T.Q. Nguyen, D. Hui, Additive manufacturing (3D printing): A review of materials, methods, applications and challenges, *Compos. Pt. B-Eng.* 143 (2018) 172–196.

[13] N.T. Aboulkhair, M. Simonelli, L. Parry, I. Ashcroft, C. Tuck, R. Hague, 3D printing of Aluminium alloys: Additive Manufacturing of Aluminium alloys using selective laser melting, *Prog. Mater. Sci.* 106 (2019) 100578.

[14] M. Rizwee, P.S. Rao, M.Y. Khan, Recent advancement in electric discharge machining of metal matrix composite materials. *Mater. Today: Proceed.* 37 (2021) 2829–2836.

[15] M. Rizwee, S.S. Minz, M. Orooj, M.Z. Hassnain, M.J. Khan, Electric discharge machining method for various metal matrix composite materials. *Int. J. Innov. Tech. Expl. Eng. (IJTEE)* 8 (9) (2019) 1796–1807.

[16] M. Rizwee, P.S. Rao, A review on electro discharge machining of metal matrix composite. *Int. J. Tech. Innov. Mod. Eng. Sci.* 4 (12) (2018) 410–414.

[17] R. Hedayati, M. Sadighi, M. Mohammadi-Aghdam, A. Zadpoor, Analytical relationships for the mechanical properties of additively manufactured porous biomaterials based on octahedral unit cells, *Appl. Math. Model.* 46 (2017) 408–422.

[18] L.R. Meza, G.P. Phlipot, C.M. Portela, A. Maggi, L.C. Montemayor, A. Comella, D.M. Kochmann, J.R. Greer, Reexamining the mechanical property space of three-dimensional lattice architectures, *Acta Mater.* 140 (2017) 424–432.

[19] L.J. Gibson, M.F. Ashby, *Cellular solids: structure and properties*, Cambridge University Press 1999.

[20] O. Al-Ketan, R. Rowshan, R.K. Abu Al-Rub, Topology-mechanical property relationship of 3D printed strut, skeletal, and sheet based periodic metallic cellular materials, *Addit. Manuf.* 19 (2018) 167–183.

[21] S.Y. Choy, C.-N. Sun, K.F. Leong, J. Wei, Compressive properties of Ti-6Al-4V lattice structures fabricated by selective laser melting: Design, orientation and density, *Addit. Manuf.* 16 (2017) 213–224.

[22] L. Zhang, S. Feih, S. Daynes, S. Chang, M.Y. Wang, J. Wei, W.F. Lu, Energy absorption characteristics of metallic triply periodic minimal surface sheet structures under compressive loading, *Addit. Manuf.* 23 (2018) 505–515.

[23] F. Habib, P. Iovenitti, S. Masood, M. Nikzad, Fabrication of polymeric lattice structures for optimum energy absorption using Multi Jet Fusion technology, *Mater. Des.* 155 (2018) 86–98.

[24] K. Hazeli, B.B. Babamiri, J. Indeck, A. Minor, H. Askari, Microstructure-topology relationship effects on the quasi-static and dynamic behavior of additively manufactured lattice structures, *Mater. Des.* 176 (2019) 107826.

[25] L. Bai, J. Zhang, Y. Xiong, X. Chen, Y. Sun, C. Gong, H. Pu, X. Wu, J. Luo, Influence of unit cell pose on the mechanical properties of Ti6Al4V lattice structures manufactured by selective laser melting, *Addit. Manuf.* 34 (2020) 101222.

[26] X. Cao, S. Duan, J. Liang, W. Wen, D. Fang, Mechanical properties of an improved 3D-printed rhombic dodecahedron stainless steel lattice structure of variable cross section, *Int. J. Mech. Sci.* 145 (2018) 53–63.

[27] Z. Meng, J. He, Z. Cai, F. Wang, J. Zhang, L. Wang, R. Ling, D. Li, Design and additive manufacturing of flexible polycaprolactone scaffolds with highly-tunable mechanical properties for soft tissue engineering, *Mater. Des.* 189 (2020) 108508.

[28] F. Liu, D.Z. Zhang, P. Zhang, M. Zhao, S. Jafar, Mechanical properties of optimized diamond lattice structure for bone scaffolds fabricated via selective laser melting, *Materials* 11 (3) (2018) 374.

[29] M. Azmi, R. Ismail, R. Hasan, Investigation on the static and dynamic behavior of BCC lattice structure with quatrefoil node manufactured using fused deposition modelling additive manufacturing, *IOP Conf. Ser.* 788 (1) (2020) 012008.

[30] M. Rizwee, M.F. Ahmad, Investigation of tensile behavior of 0.22% carbon steel with notched specimen subjected to corrosive environment. *SAE Int. J. Mater. Manuf.* 13 (2) (2020) 161–174.

[31] M. Rizwee, M.F. Ahmad, Experimental examination of crack extension in steel with notch under tensile loading and corrosive environment. *J. Inst. Eng. Ser D*. 102 (2021) 55–71.

[32] M. Rizwee, P.S. Rao, M.F. Ahmad, Parametric optimization of electro discharge process during machining of aluminum/boron carbide/graphite composite. *SAE Int. J. Mater. Manuf.* 15 (05-15-01-0007) (2021) 81–89.

[33] M. Rizwee, P.S. Rao, Analysis & optimization of parameters during EDM of aluminium metal matrix composite. *J. Univ. Shanghai Sci. Technol.* 23 (3) (2021) 218–223.

[34] M. Rizwee, P.S. Rao, M.Y. Khan, Experimental investigation and optimization of EDM parameters during machining of Al/B4C/Gr MMC. In R. Singh, S.S. Dhami and B.S. Pabla (Eds.), *Advances in manufacturing technology*. (2022) 55–64.

[35] L. Bai, C. Gong, X. Chen, Y. Sun, L. Xin, H. Pu, Y. Peng, J. Luo, Mechanical properties and energy absorption capabilities of functionally graded lattice structures: Experiments and simulations, *Int. J. Mech. Sci.* 182 (2020) 105735.

[36] H. Yin, Z. Liu, J. Dai, G. Wen, C. Zhang, Crushing behaviour and optimization of sheet-based 3D periodic cellular structures, *Compos. Pt. B-Eng.* 182 (2020) 107565.

Section V

Applications
of Industry 4.0

Chapter 9

Rethinking Manufacturing Workflows for Digital Convergence
The Royal Australian Air Force

Christopher Kourloufas, Luke Houghton,
Balazs Szikszai, Christopher Larkin,
William Sowry, Matthew Jennings, Jennifer Loy,
C. J. Anderson, and Bernard Rolfe

9.1 INTRODUCTION: INDUSTRY 4.0 IN CONTEXT

Industrial engineering involves the design, installation, maintenance, and improvement of integrated systems for mechanical, civil, and electrical engineering applications. These systems involve materials, equipment, people, information, workflow, methods, and energy, and can be very complex. Industry 4.0 predominantly refers to the development of data-driven manufacturing systems, although the term is also used to refer to the range of digital technologies that have matured in recent years, the implications and opportunities arising from their convergence, and their broader use in industry. For this chapter, the focus will be on a definition of Industry 4.0 as data-driven manufacturing systems and the workflow enabled by the convergence of digital technology.

One of the key distinctions between practices exploiting Industry 4.0 capabilities, and those merely adopting digital technologies for manufacturing, is workflow. For companies that add digital technologies to existing practice, without affecting workflow, capability is generally added. However, integrating Industry 4.0 technology whilst rethinking workflow enables new ways of working that create additional benefits, and challenges, for businesses.

Due to recent competitive pressures in global commercial practice, companies have shifted from being 'owners of competencies and resources to becoming integrators of skills, resources, and technologies able to realise complex value creation processes' (Gaiardelli et al., 2021), including developing product service systems to retain their advantage. Much of this shift would not be possible without the application of Industry 4.0 technology, but even with added digital capabilities, businesses are finding it necessary to step back from the linear, one-way conventional, supply chain through to market, approach that has dominated traditional manufacturing and sales for the last century. Instead, value propositions are being refocused towards more responsive market offerings, and a changed customer relationship as a result.

Digital technology, integrated into a connected manufacturing and marketing system, enables a greater emphasis on short-run production and production on demand. The convergence of digital technology also enables the development of interconnectivity between elements, stages, and aspects of manufacturing. This enables real-time monitoring and an unprecedented level of feedback from the product during use (e.g., from sensors in automobiles) that supports the iterative evolution of products, and pre-emptive maintenance. This approach requires a revised support ecosystem, with embedded digital technology skill sets and systems to exploit the flow of information from products, feeding back into the supply chain.

For the Royal Australian Air Force (RAAF), as with other companies globally, the adoption of digital technology systems into the workflow presents numerous challenges. On a basic level, the challenges are around upskilling the workforce. However, at a manufacturing level, the challenges and opportunities in relation to the integration of Industry 4.0 tools is similar to those facing industry more broadly. That is, whilst purchasing additive manufacturing (AM) machines, for example, and training maintenance workers to service the machines and fully exploit the capabilities of them, it is critical to rethink workflows and outputs if the full benefits are to be realised. Although much can be learned from commercial companies undergoing a digital paradigm shift, there are specific considerations in the Defence Force context that require specific thought.

9.2 DIGITAL PLATFORMS FOR THE RAAF CONTEXT

According to Veile et al. (2022), digital platforms, traditionally the domain of customer interaction, are moving into the industrial domain. In their study of different platform types, they identified recurring themes of business model innovation and inter-company connectivity. They argue that, with the flow of data underpinning Industry 4.0, digital platforms customised to production and asset monitoring, as well as marketing and sales, are essential for information sharing. Companies need a digital platform for internal use, as much as one that is external facing.

For the RAAF, a committed adoption of Industry 4.0 principles and technology would result in a paradigm shift in asset maintenance management. As for other organisations, it would require skills in building a RAAF Industrial Internet of Things (IIoT) and data analytics for predictive maintenance, plus a conceptual approach to the use of artificial intelligence (AI) and machine learning (ML) as they apply in the RAAF context. That context does differ from mainstream manufacturers as the lines between industry suppliers and the RAAF are blurred in relation to the maintenance of aircraft and on-base requirements. Manufacturing by the RAAF is limited because of its role predominantly as consumer, rather than producer. It manufactures to repair and maintain, and perhaps evolve, rather than for commercial purposes per se.

There are two levels of digital technology attributed to Industry 4.0 (Dornelles et al., 2021). The first is purely data driven: Internet of Things (IoT), cloud computing, big data, and data analytics. The subsequent layer lies in the cyber-physical realm, encompassing AM, robotics, and mixed reality applications. For Defence, all digital technology systems present security challenges. As digital platforms are increasingly used for asset maintenance management and production monitoring and control, questions around cloud computing, cyber-physical systems, and digital twins are as—if not more—pertinent to Defence than to commercial practice. Where distributed manufacturing is integrated into operations, these become even more of a concern.

9.3 ORGANISATIONAL TENSIONS

Part of rethinking manufacturing for more agile, adaptive practices enabled by converging digital technology involves understanding the need for more collaborative problem-solving and heightened communication methods. Problems are not evenly distributed, nor, in an unpredictable context such as during an active conflict, able to be managed effectively by isolated groups. Problems arise during interactions within a complex world. Therefore, consulting houses, and the World Economic Forum (2022), recommend developing greater collaborative problem-solving.

In addition, creative thinking is highlighted as central to the digital future, because of the unanticipated opportunities and challenges created by digital convergence. Yet, recent research has demonstrated that workarounds proliferate in environments where strict controls or centralised hierarchy is in place (Wibisono et al., 2022). The pressure placed on employees to conform to a standardised system and non-standardised creative process, perhaps in a digitised or highly automated environment, has been increasingly found to create the need to build workarounds. These are designed to alleviate stress caused by the faster pace and scale of commercial interaction enabled by digital communication. They must still meet the need to create fit-for-purpose products, adhere to standard problem-solving schemas, and work within certification processes (Kent et al., 2023).

Recent studies point towards a need to stop thinking about this problem from the point of view of technology, but instead that of job fit and the role of technology (Spierings et al., 2016). As the world in which the organisation exists becomes increasingly complicated, the response must eventually become an adaptable one (Weinzierl et al. 2022). That is, there needs to be a moderator for technology that enables continuous creativity and adaptability considering the ambiguity faced by the corporation, and the pace of change faced by individuals within it. Although this sounds overwhelming for an organisation, such as the RAAF, where structural control is embedded into its culture as well as its hierarchy, it should be the aim. This is because it means the appropriation of technology can be enacted in an agile manner, leading to a distributed network model in which people are working towards a common goal, albeit from very different angles.

The adoption and use of augmented reality and its applications (Ojo, 2019) provides an illustrative example. This personalised type of technology can be utilised to assist workers within manufacturing processes in the use and monitoring of other digital technologies, such as AM. To develop such a capability does not involve simply purchasing the equipment, rather it means adopting the mindset behind the equipment, which could be built on a distributed workflow model (Ojo, 2019). What this means in practice, for example, is that people who access certain points of the supply chain might have access to inventory that is currently being supplied and modelled out by other members of the supply chain. Having a digital twin in place can optimise parts of the supply chain to the point where a person is not needed, with the person's role reimagined to creatively adapt the workflow informed by the digital twin to improve margins of profitability found in those supply chains (Bhandal et al., 2022).

Another example of this can be found in the adoption of AI technologies for modern advertising. These databases could contain millions of people and innumerable patterns that could be analysed by people from any industry at any given time, yet each will only ever see a sliver of the data that is there. However, that does not prevent them using techniques built into these platforms, such as advanced matching, in which broad cross sections of the community are examined for their ability to take a certain action. What used to take marketers considerable time to work out can now be explored within a very short period. By allowing the machine to do the learning and produce a result, this frees up the marketer to focus on creative optimisation. The implications for these new ways of working, and new emphasis on the role of the worker within the organisation, can be evaluated for the Defence context.

9.4 EMERGENT WORKFLOWS

The ways people are interacting with technology during work are evolving at a rapid pace. What is emerging, through research, is the increasing role of machines in assisting human creativity (Marr, 2022). On the downside, this means that certain roles will become redundant, but new roles will also emerge. For society, the future of work integrating digital technology should still have people at their centre. To support this, workflows, for example those involving an AI network, need to share mental models as part of their architecture (Canbaloğlu et al., 2022). Therefore, planning to share mental models as part of workflow should be more readily embedded into practice. For RAAF manufacturing as part of creating a more responsive internal capability, the argument put forward here is that working with digital technology does not solely revolve around technical capabilities. Instead, those capabilities become part of the way in which the technology is made usable, but not its entirety.

A key digital manufacturing technology for more adaptable manufacturing is AM, also known as 3D printing. This technology enables distributed manufacturing, with a decision-making mindset at its core as it allows for production on demand, which provides a good scenario for considering new workflows specific to more agile ways of working in manufacturing. In this sense, the workflow must be viewed as task specific, rather than in a conventional system, where the workflow is more fixed. Creating agile workflows—that is, workflows that can be adapted as needed in real time—is a new challenge, and one that is yet to be mastered.

Newer forms of communication technology need to be built and incorporated into work environments to support ways of working beyond those of a traditional production network, so that they become more accessible, at multiple points, and visible to multiple parts of the organisation. This fosters emergent workflows, where people can potentially share ideas faster to enhance collaboration and creativity. As an example, a worker could create a component part, ready for manufacturing, but then add its digital blueprint to a library where multiple people from anywhere in the organisation could subsequently access that part. This characterises the theory of a distributed manufacturing model, where parts can be accessed in multiple different locations for manufacturing simultaneously. A structured system will require new processes to certify these systems as fit for use, at a speed that delivers real value rather than drags utility back to the level of traditional manufacturing techniques. That is, it may be possible to design, and 3D print, a component much more quickly than via traditional workflow and manufacturing techniques, but if it still takes time to certify that component (particularly if it is a one-off), most of the benefits will be lost.

Another example of this kind of distributed workflow can be found in the use of predictive analytics. Transaction data might be captured by a point-of-sale device in a retail store, but if it is a franchise operation, an aggregated predictive analytics model could also be fed into AI and used for forecasting. Even though the organisational model is not changing, data is being generated at every level, and then aggregated and explored using these technologies. This development creates connected workflows that can remove or reduce organisational barriers (Marr, 2022). An agile manufacturing workflow maximising the opportunities that digital convergence—such as digital manufacturing and communication—offers, relies on the ability to distribute technologies and add more automated processes to achieve outcomes (Figure 9.1). However, as argued in Kent et al. (2023), the more mandated a system is, the more likely pressure will be created to work around it.

It is critical, therefore, to consider organisational reform alongside the introduction of digital technology into the workplace, and to embed changes in approach and cultural practice into the system. This workflow aims not to remove hierarchy,

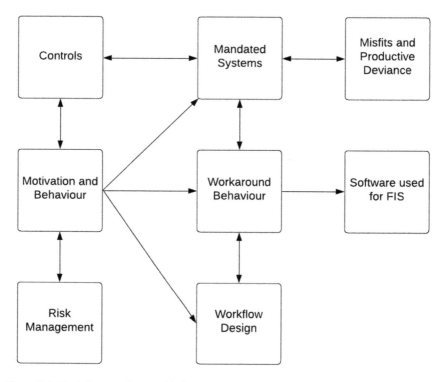

Figure 9.1 Modelling workaround behaviour integration.

but it enables better access to data from multiple different vantage points simultaneously. It proposes a network operating not through the design of the organisational constructs but the creativity of the people who build meaningful nodes within the network. What also makes this approach work, therefore, is harnessing the creative way people share data across the network using platforms, such as with the digital inventory approach enabled by AM.

9.5 AGILE MANUFACTURING

RAAF operations at all levels are based on a traditional hierarchical or 'command and control' type structure. 'Agile' manufacturing is an approach initially described in software development and subsequently adopted into business management (Canda & Gogan, 2012). In contrast to hierarchical management structures, this philosophy is built on adopting a team approach in which minimum viable products are released, and user feedback sought, in a rapid prototyping cycle. The difference between Lean and Agile is that Lean focusses on reducing waste and creating efficiencies that add value, whilst Agile refers to being able to be more responsive to pain-points throughout the process and ultimately to customer needs. Therefore, a process may be both Lean and Agile.

In the United States, the Department of Defense has adopted 'Agile' with its team approach, 'sprints', and 'scrum-masters' for project management, as a way of creating a competitive advantage in response to the natural agility that smaller organisations, less constrained by legacy systems and processes, and legislation, may operate (Fogarty & Franz, 2021). The process is characterised by continuous evaluation and feedback, including the active identification of risks and problems, and the enabling and empowering decision-making at levels determined by the task, not the conventional organisational structure and concurrent development and supply. This again is not a conventional approach for Australian Defence Force logistics.

What enabled Agile to evolve in information technology was the typically distributed nature of information systems and software development where the approach originated, and its ability to be rapidly deployed in a digital environment. Digital convergence has sped up the prototyping cycle for broader applications, enabling products to be developed more quickly. As argued by Weinzierl et al. (2022) distributed technologies, such as AM, bridge the need for workarounds because they more closely match work patterns. Workarounds are creative (Kent et al., 2023) and are methods for stopping the gap between poorly constructed processes and the creativity needed to get work done. The nature of this technology lends itself to a significant mindset shift (Leonardi & Neeley, 2022). Most organisations still conform to the hierarchical model. Given that organisational reform and transformation projects currently still largely fail in relation to digital transformation (Vaia et al., 2022), it is important to think how gains in agile processes can be effectively deployed.

By having a ready parts library on hand for 3D printing, for example, the organisation would not need to restructure itself around the technology, which has frequently been identified as the mistake in the past. Instead, it can have a distributed model where people can collaborate around the platform, without having to leave their roles or even move into some kind of cross-functional arrangement. The business process, in essence, stays the same, but the creativity used within that process evolves around the use of the technology and the results can be scaled and shared across the organisation in different areas.

The promise of these technologies is that it takes the human right into the centre of creative development and manufacturing and moves the technology to the background where information and parts can be shared in real time. Previously, material flow and utilisation levels of material and machines were the essential components feeding a digital monitoring system. However, as interconnected systems become more autonomous, then their monitoring becomes more around the operating systems and their decision-making than the individual components

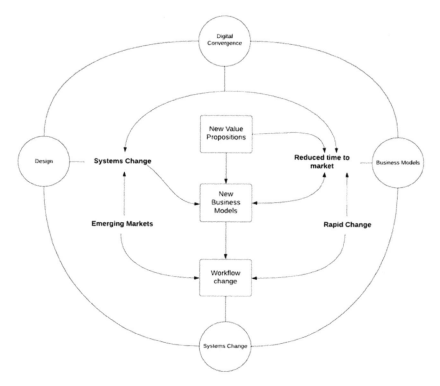

Figure 9.2 Modelling the pressures created by digital convergence.

(Bendul & Blunk, 2019). Control authority is now central to digital platforms and systems and represents a critical shift in thinking needed for the RAAF.

A network distributed model for an AM Agile environment could work as in Figure 9.2. For example, in a humanitarian logistics context, if certain parts were able to be 3D printed remotely, such as replacement parts for critical services (Loy et al., 2016), then the blueprint could simply be shared with a local 3D printer operator. The workflow of the future is likely to be distributed because it aligns with the emerging megatrends (Naughtin et al., 2022), but more critically, that is the nature of the technological revolution Industry 4.0 is shaping. Technologies can be used by people for different purposes across the organisation, but if that knowledge is able to be shared, for example using complementary apps, not constrained by conventional organisational structures built for customer relationship management and other enterprise purposes, then actual sustainable agility would be more likely to be achieved. There needs to be an agile entry process that matches the agile design and production process. In addition, a key element is the organisational trust that must be placed in any such library, and in the designed parts contained within it.

According to most change management theory, early adopters of any kind of technology tend to be leaders in their own right (Bianchi et al., 2017). This means they not only adopt technology but also use it for innovative purposes well before people in the system realise it is happening. As society moves into an integrated digital world, where information will be omnipresent, it can be argued that adapting workflows to these technologies, rather than creating versions of the technology for existing workflows, is a necessary reverse in thinking for organisations. This switch in approach could well create the backbone of flexible and agile organisations of the future.

Usability and ease of use in these systems is already increasing. The adaptability of being able to 3D print parts on demand, for example, has the potential to create radical new business models, but use cases are still being shoehorned into organisations that are yet to understand the distributed mindset behind the effective use of these technologies (Loy et al., 2023). The way forward is to have technologies that can be used for agile purposes by more operators within an organisation, thereby opening up a distributed mindset across the workforce to create the potential for added value. However, the challenge organisations face when enabling this technology is that the distributed mindset behind it will inevitably challenge the existing hierarchy. If the hierarchy is not able to adapt to the speed of these technologies, it is time to create a more distributed model of control. What follows is a proposal for rethinking the workflow of the future and how digital technologies could be used in a distributed way, aiming as a starting point, to be not too disruptive to the existing organisational structure, whilst increasing the opportunity for creativity of the individual and support their productivity.

9.6 SMART MANUFACTURING

The research underpinning this chapter considers developments in advanced manufacturing that have emerged from Industry 4.0 through an adoption lens use case for the RAAF. As research in Industry 4.0 has progressed, it has become increasingly clear that companies and organisations will have to not only rethink their technical workflow to incorporate advances in manufacturing machinery, but also rethink their working practice to exploit the opportunities this technology brings. Concepts of Industry 4.0 tend to be studied within a specific area of research, recently the focus on smart manufacturing only (and siloed) has lessened (Meindl et al., 2021).

The 'Four Smarts model of Industry 4.0' (Frank et al., 2019) describes a broader definition of Industry 4.0 than much of the literature, which involves the integration of Smart Manufacturing, Smart Products and Services, Smart Supply Chain and Smart Working. Complex organisations with a social remit and responsibility, such as in Defence where the stakes are highest, will need to drive the development and adoption of advances in manufacturing that sit within a connected workflow. Otherwise, the digital thread connectivity of a workflow will be directed at efficiencies and outcomes that are industry driven, rather than shaped by the requirements of the Defence future force. The highest level of the German Academy of Science and Technology (ACATECH) Industry 4.0 maturity index is represented by autonomous production systems. For Defence, system complications, such as the potential of breaches to security in autonomous production, must still be mitigated by human oversight. Balancing responsibility and efficiencies to create effective but accountable systems is a challenge.

Whilst there are many drivers for developing advanced manufacturing capabilities for Defence, shaping many different industry briefs, three factors are creating the foundation for a new way of working that could influence the further development of Defence Industry 4.0 manufacturing towards smart manufacturing. The first, and most critical, is the changing nature of conflict. An influential publication for Defence in Australia, 'Prototype Warfare' by Dr Peter Layton (2018), describes the need for a more responsive workforce and operations in an increasingly grey zone context, in which challenges need to be tackled in a more agile, bespoke manner. Prototyping for manufacturing in this context refers to the ability to iteratively develop products to more quickly bring them to a resolution, which is an approach that the bespoke capability of digital fabrication provides. It can also be translated into the need to build digital systems for product development that allow for bespoke production on demand. Where traditional manufacturing relies on an upfront investment in tooling, reducing the ability to create different instances of a part, digital fabrication technology, such as AM, does not require tooling. This shifts the production paradigm from mass production to mass customisation. Mass customisation requires the facility to collect data for a specific need, which involves different ways of working. However, for an organisation of the size of Defence, with the scale of its operations, the move towards mass customisation would then impact the way in which those part iterations and instances were managed, validated, and distributed.

The second factor is digital convergence. Until recently, the development pathway of emerging digital technologies could be tracked individually, and fell under the auspices of specific disciplinary research, such as digital twins under information and communication technology (ICT) and AM under mechanical engineering. However, in the last few years, digital convergence has merged the advances in manufacturing and ICT to create capabilities that are difficult to categorise. Digital communication is an underlying enabler in much of the changes in practice, but combinations of digital technology also include 3D scanning and data analytics, sensor technology and augmented reality, and more. Essentially, new opportunities are constantly emerging that combine different fields of research to create transdisciplinary outcomes.

The third factor is the realisation that these new, transdisciplinary capabilities are changing the experience for users, and therefore new ways of working with the technology need to be determined. The challenge for an organisation is stepping back far enough to view digital convergence technology and consider objectively its use in their situation, or the change in practice—and workflow—it necessitates.

The need for a distributed knowledge framework within organisations, in this context, is high. There are many use cases where employees, or users, of software programs create groups to share workarounds, yet this is rarely formally documented or shared, even as it starts to become a part of the company's intellectual property. There is also rarely time allocated within a job to document and share alterations to established workflows, as in most cases it is not a billable hour that can be justified. When operational teams start to embed or think about adding new systems they should, as a starting point, build a current workflow for how their company uses its systems in reality, rather than in theory.

With the shift to flexible workflows based on tasks, rather than a fixed (but adapted) workflow, personalised workflows of the future should allow greater operability between multiple workspaces or modelling systems. Routine or mundane tasks could be reduced through an acceptance of a more flexible workflow that allows for workarounds rather than ignores them, for example allowing teams to automate certain processes. Interestingly, with the current emergence of AI and chat-based AI systems, there is already evidence of people without a coding skill set now being able to build specific workarounds for software platforms they have had for some time. This ability to allow people who previously did not have a coding background or skill set to solve their own problems should see an increase in digital convergence–based practice. This is at odds with one-size-fits-all systems where everything in a business must adapt and conform to a single system (including, for example, how files are managed, owned, and even named).

Navigating these changes, and having businesses allow users to control the way they work—enabled by rapidly evolving software—will be the new frontier. In highly complex 3D modelling packages and simulations, where there is a large amount of data to be continually updated with every tweak and change, giving programming operability to the software users will change the way in which systems are created. All these point to a new way of working, building the opportunity to integrate workarounds, or bridges, between administration systems and creative or engineering systems.

Just as Agile has emerged from software development, so this industry is arguably at the forefront of enabling a more agile, collaborative mindset to problem-solving, enabled by online forums. A knowledge sharing mindset is arguably key to creating a prototype warfare capability for Defence. However, due to the high level of security needed during this work, inevitably operations tend to stay within silos built which retain and manage expertise but also constrain the utility of the innovation. Knowledge might not be shared around or across bases, other forces, or with allies. To break this down, there needs to be a way of sharing best practice in a distributed knowledge framework but contain the critical security elements of practice.

The workflow of the future needs more adaptable and agile thinkers, people who do not rely on any specific tool for their outcome (but understand how the tools work), as with the current trajectory for development of software tools with the emergence of AI suggests, the ability for users who have limited knowledge of the operation of a particular software's features will be able to easily navigate complex operations through text-based input. The need in terms of design, engineering, and manufacturing in the future shifts to having creatives who understand material and manufacturing processes rather than the need for software experts. This is so that the users can explore and push the boundaries of what the process and material are capable of, rather than pushing the boundaries of what the individual software is capable of. The training will need to focus on lateral and divergent thinking in ambiguous situations allowing people to use their knowledge as a base starting point and the ability to use it in divergent ways.

9.7 DIGITAL CONVERGENCE

The convergence of digital technologies and processes will continue to give unprecedented scope to users, allowing a new generation to create and handle even more complex data than the previous generation, and so it is imperative that the way in which these technologies converge is designed to benefit a broader audience. These processes speak to what is termed Industry 5.0, and the reintegration of the person into process, by allowing a curation of thought unconstrained to traditional capabilities of technological prowess. In the data-driven nature of Industry 4.0, as there is more data captured, the focus shifts to how data is used.

A key question within this new reality is whether the data being collected in these new systems is the right data for each specific input and/or output, and how workflows are adapted to track and check in real time (as much as is realistic). This is to allow for a responsive system and the ideal of enabling constant change. An example of where this matters, would be in the traditional documentation stages of manufacturing. For large assemblies, there is the need for each new drawing set to be continually updated as any slight change is introduced. This results in considerable file management (typically driven by a particular software's cloud-based storage, e.g., Vault[1] for Autodesk) to 'up rev' each individual drawing.

These programs are designed to optimise processes and enable working across teams in different locations, and point towards new practice, but with limitations. For example, where a new program is used in conjunction with this platform, such as if a surface model derived from an external 3D computer modelling program falls outside the purview of the main platform. There are various workarounds and macros that have been developed for this but are typically not available to a broader audience as they are developed on a case-by-case basis by the user who understands the issues they aim to solve. This type of data set can be missed without capturing workflows and workarounds that could enhance a specific sector.

In a more recent example, with advances in extended reality (XR) there are processes being developed to adapt stages of a conventional manufacturing workflow to allow workers along the process, from design to manufacturing, to affect aspects of the process they may not previously have been able to access. There is research looking at removing the physical documentation phase of manufacturing from a paper-based document trail and instead map it to a workflow based within an augmented reality (AR) model. The intent is that this can be worked on simultaneously by a technical design team, fabrication team, and installation team in 3D, allowing live updates and feedback from each stage. This can feed technical design back into a responsive digital twin. This has the potential to allow for a more fluid, accessible conversation between the people and the processes of each stage of manufacturing, and the data capture of changes can arguably be analysed closer due to the digital nature of the updates, manufacturing, and installation.

AR documentation allows a digital model to be overlaid on the piece being fabricated to ensure its accuracy in an accessible manner. This can reduce miscommunications when working with changing team members. This process allows for a potentially robust review process for all stages, as each change and communication can be embedded in the digital model, showing within each phase the requirements that are needed for future outcomes. This allows the installation phase and any challenges or changes that could help workflows to be documented live in a 3D model, giving the technical designer an opportunity to make the changes for future production. This shift in practice aligns with the development of AM workflows, as each model can be 3D scanned upon completion of the 3D print and fed back into the digital version allowing any deviations, no matter how small, or incremental changes to be tweaked prior to the next iteration. AI could be used in this context to automate quality control through the detection of anomalies (Ruiz-Real et al., 2020).

Advances in associated digital technology, such 3D scanning allow a data-driven, production workflow that monitors every part, and feeds back into an AI-enabled system to assess the optimal printing settings and processes (e.g., Bamboo X1,[2] which uses LiDar scanning to ensure the initial print layers are successful, as well as ensuring the model does not fail at any stage. This also controls and calibrates material flow). This workflow would enable updates to the model and making changes within parameters set by a technical designer. This ability to have data work in a way in which efficiencies are driven by the manufacturing process itself will require different skill sets to operate effectively. This suggests the future user be a curator of information, and the system more accessible.

The focus for research into digital convergence tends to be on the complex challenges of integrating multiple technological capabilities for a system that transcends conventional practice. However, the effect on people management and the role of individuals within an increasingly complex system should not be overlooked. Training employees on the use of emerging technology involves learning not only the technicalities of its operation but also the changed work practices that the technology creates. This then requires that the management of workers operating within a changed work practice and new system be reimagined. This may not be straightforward, as the types of new ways of working enabled by digital convergence can create different operating priorities and skills. For example, where augmented reality for remote installation activities replaces conventional paper-based diagrams or video instructions, abilities such as good special awareness and active learning may supersede the ability to research or synthesise different sources of information. How to effectively manage these emerging skill sets is yet to be determined.

Another management issue with regards to changing skills sets is recruitment. Established organisations have recruitment streams that have been built over time, with an identified set of skills and abilities prioritised. Once changes are made to accommodate new ways of thinking and new skill requirements, there is a knock-on effect on human resources. This aspect of adapting to new technology can be overlooked, yet without it, the potential for the successful adoption of digital technologies is reduced.

9.8 PREVENTATIVE TO PREDICTIVE MAINTENANCE

Operating large fleets of aircraft and other kinds of machinery involves expensive maintenance in a highly regulated environment. The maintenance of mechanical systems, machines, and vehicles has historically been bound to a predetermined schedule as defined by the manufacturer. This schedule is often developed to allow a system to perform over a reasonable period in a manner in line with warranties, customer expectations, or contractual obligations. Manufacturers cannot always predict the exact usage and environmental operating conditions for each example of their product in the field, which can lead to a scenario where maintenance schedules become less than ideal. This can lead to excessive downtime potential and cost implications due to unnecessary maintenance, or failures and down time due to damage, accelerated wear, and/or insufficient maintenance. This can cost millions in lost time to maintenance schedules, which could be devastating in a conflict situation.

The RAAF operates a large variety of mechanical and electronic assets where maintenance is required for continued reliable operation. Beyond aircraft, the principles presented in this report can also be applied to ground vehicles, generators, pumping systems, operations centres, information technology infrastructure, and HVAC units. Beyond direct-cost saving implications of scheduling the right maintenance at the right time, significant non-monetary costs can also be avoided by removing the possibility of unforeseen or unexpected asset failure. Unplanned failure can extend to prolonged unavailability of that asset, particularly if:

- Replacement parts are unavailable onshore and need to be sent by an OEM.
- Replacement parts are out of stock or need to be manufactured by an OEM.
- Replacement parts are unavailable or out of manufacture.
- Part failure leads to a cascade failure (e.g., bearing failure can lead to catastrophic failure inside a reciprocating engine).

Digitisation, improved simulation tools, and the availability of scalable computing power have also provided an opportunity for the use of digital twins to develop potential predictive maintenance (PdM) models where an integrated system is cost prohibitive or cannot be integrated. Assets can be 'mimicked' as a virtual replica with states, sensor readings and inspection data being fed to the model, allowing observation of simulated behaviour to produce predictions. Notably, General Electric (GE) implemented digital twins for this type of analysis on wind farms (Ochella et al., 2021). This approach can be used as part of a phased implementation strategy to reduce risk, representing a lower cost/first phase implementation for RAAF without the need for significant physical asset integration.

There are many differences between preventative and predictive maintenance. While the two terms are similar in both the ethos and meaning, the big difference lies in what digital technologies and digital convergence can do for maintenance. For example, in the RAAF context, a preventative schedule for maintenance for aircraft determines what the engineers do. That is, aircraft engineers must perform certain duties at certain times that enable them to create schedules to know how and when maintenance can occur. This kind of approach is 'preventative' because it is relying on existing schedules of maintenance from manuals, or perhaps from the manufacturer, to perform the required duties.

The digital approach, however, is predictive. This is where preventative maintenance is translated into a data-driven process by using the tools provided in digital convergence to create the basis for an IIoT and a predictive maintenance system where actions are based on predicted condition rather than time. This approach does not rely just on schedules but on any available data from any number of possible sources. This approach can take thousands of points of data and build analytics-driven models not only to enable the prevention of mechanical failure, but to be able to predict when it is likely to happen and ostensibly prevent it. The overall advantage of this approach is that it reduces the probability of mechanical failure because it uses all the data available, both from the manufacturer and other engineers, to build complex predictive models that will warn maintenance engineers and others involved in the process exactly when something could go wrong. This is not just based on the use of AI, but also to the use of a complex network of technologies that are digital in nature.

The following example shows ways in which a predicted maintenance schedule, built on digital convergence, is entirely different to preventative maintenance schedule and would enhance the RAAF's ability to build a new kind of example of how to do 'digital maintenance'.

9.9 PREDICTIVE MAINTENANCE SCHEDULING

What follows is an example of how predictive maintenance schedule would work and what the benefits of using it could be.

9.9.1 Artificial Intelligence

AI can be used to generate insights from deep learning, ML, and several data points from both primary and secondary sources. For example, AI could be used to predict machinery breakdowns by looking at existing patterns from maintenance and operational data that is available from past service records or from the OEM themselves (Ochella et al., 2021).

To examine the condition of any kind of equipment, data could be collected from in-machine sensors and then sent to solutions operators whose results will turn up on the screen, letting them know that maintenance was required because data shows that over time certain parts can wear out. The AI model can reduce the cost associated with a scheduled maintenance and increase safety (Startus Insights, 2023). A preventative schedule would simply be a list of things that could be done to the aircraft, or any machinery that is required by the manufacturer, whereas a predictive schedule could draw on a much wider dataset to help prevent disaster in the future.

9.9.2 Data Analytics

Predictive analytics enable solutions to be analysed from unstructured data sources, including, for example, past reports and sensor ratings, as well as environmental parameters and other data imports to help predict failures. Again, the major difference here between the digital approach, as opposed to the traditional approach, is that this data can be synthesised and customised, then explored to introduce new and undiscovered factors relating to maintenance. Preventative maintenance simply just explores the areas that the manufacturer or other engineers believe important, whereas the data produced by analytics would enable big data platforms to improve the transparency of systems, health, and other related conditions that the preventative schedule will not find. Search insights are typically referred to as data-driven insights, because they provide real-time predictions for better business decisions and thereby reduce turnaround times for maintenance. Not only that, but they enable data to be examined in real time and unexplored areas of maintenance to be added to the schedules.

Further to this, schedules could be created on the fly by analytics, and dashboards could be produced to maintenance engineers, so it would be possible to work on things before they even become a problem, or even known in preventative schedules. By being able to forecast when maintenance is required through these analytics, the maintenance team could mitigate risk and introduce programs to extend the life of assets. This is a cost saving at a benefit that is often overlooked in maintenance schedules because the majority of the focus is on prevention and not prediction.

9.9.3 Internet of Things and Sensor Data

One of the most interesting developments in data is the development of IoT-driven sensor data. Already in use, this approach allows predicted maintenance to occur by connecting and monitoring existing sensors in real time to produce data for analytics dashboards mentioned in the previous section. Smart sensors allow maintenance teams to explore data such as operating temperature, oil quality, or voltage levels, for example, or acceptable limits on technology infrastructure, such as wall pressure limitations. This data is gathered in real time and enables machine failures to be de-risked substantially. This is because the data is collected in real time as it monitors potential failures and then data can be collected about the levels and acceptable limits that could be breached. For example, if a piece of equipment has an operating temperature that is critical, the sensors will enable an engineer to be able to quickly go in and look at the problem and collect data. This data can be used for multiple purposes, including forecasting for the future, and shared with other maintenance teams.

9.9.4 Digital Twins

One of the most promising technologies in the field of predictive maintenance is the creation of digital twins. Digital twins can provide a model that tracks the dynamic, changing conditions of operating environments and equipment by generating a virtual replica of physical equipment, physical processes, and tasks created by operators. Digital twins can enable manufacturers to continually monitor actual working conditions of people using and visualising operations and create analytics around future possible predictive maintenance scenarios. The benefit of digital twinning is it is able to predict data of real-time anomalies and problematic areas that cause breakdowns to be recognised and therefore replicable at scale. Again, contrasting this with the problem of preventative maintenance, this type of predictive maintenance can be scaled digitally.

As an example, a digital twin could predict maintenance and simulate different scenarios and understand what kind of risk factors are involved in a single maintenance chain, and therefore that could be scaled and replicated to others. Simulation, which would entail looking at all the aspects of maintenance across the length of the supply chain would find areas of optimisation and maintenance service, overlooked by operators because they're relying on preventative manuals. For example, digital twins can understand these anomalies and share them with others. Digital twins can help predictive maintenance by mitigating problems by advancing the understanding of risks that exist in an operating environment. This is done through simulating the processes and then replicating them.

One of the most popular uses of digital twins in in the racing car industry. Formula One racing teams have a digital twin of a car that creates a feedback loop between the real car and the one used in simulations. This feedback loop creates a safe test environment to look at riskier elements of driving and to try to understand some of the more complex areas of maintenance that are required in these vehicles. The racing digital twin also provides a testing environment for trials and improving the speed and aerodynamics of the vehicle, which event failed in the actual vehicle itself.

The digital twin, therefore, provides a safe operating environment for experimenting, but also for taking that knowledge and using it in the real world in real time. The RAAF has an extensive range of maintenance schedules due to the number of platforms it operates. A feedback loop could be created and then replicated using a digital twin to enable an operator to create a virtual environment for optimisation and predicted maintenance. When combined with the other digital technologies, such as sensors and AI previously mentioned, a robust dashboard becomes available where prediction becomes significantly easier, informing an effective maintenance strategy. The use of digital visualisation tools, such as AR, provide a new level of sophistication in communication to the use of digital twins. 3D scanning supports the development of accurate information for on-site inspections, maintenance, schedules, failure, documentation, building, installations at a distance, and so forth. AR can then be used to inform and guide operators on site.

9.9.5 Collaboration Platforms

The shift from mass production to mass customisation, and bespoke digital inventory for a specific use case, informed by sensor data visualised using a digital twin, enables on-demand fabrication. However, the level of complexity this approach allows requires the addition of facilities for communication, collaboration, and decision-making that complement the forms in which information is shared. Interacting with digital data in a 3D environment, and collaborating with others online, needs to be managed within an appropriate online platform.

There are different collaborative platform profiles currently available that illustrate the potential to create new ways of working in the 3D digital environment for the Royal Australian Air Force, but as yet none is designed to meet their specific requirements. One of the main barriers is security. Managing even a traditional intranet within a Defence context is fraught with problems. Adding 3D visualisation and live data streaming and analytics is a challenge yet to be resolved. However, from a strategic perspective, building experience of working within emerging 3D environments would support their introduction in the near future.

There are three types of immersive 3D environment. The first is through an online server, such as is used for building massively multiplayer online games (MMOG). These do not require the use of virtual or augmented reality headsets but rely instead on the use of avatars. These platforms, such as Microsoft Mesh,[3] allow the user to navigate the environment and interact with other uses and objects within the space. These virtual spaces support multiple users, interactive products, and spacial renderings. A key advantage of this type of 3D environment is that it is cross-platform and can be operated with no additional hardware. This might be important in a remote communication scenario, where headsets are not available, which could be relevant to the RAAF context. The second type involves the use of augmented reality to overlay projected objects onto the real world. For these, additional hardware, such as headsets and handheld devices, are required although it is also possible to use iPhones for limited applications. These platforms could be relevant to the RAAF to promote remote installation practices, and training personnel on their use is happening in industries such as construction.

The final type of platform uses virtual reality to fully immerse the user in the 3D virtual environment. For Defence, these are currently used to de-risk training, for example for firefighting. In addition to simulations, they are also used with robots for safe, remote access to assets in challenging areas, for example, under the sea (e.g., Raytracer[4]). They do require specialised hardware and a significant level of investment in creating specialised environments and objects. However, their use would enable collaboration across Squadrons on the development of site-specific or mission-specific parts in a 3D online environment. Examples such as Aveva Extended Reality[5] provide for digital twins, IIoT, AI-infused analytics, in a virtual collaborative space, as well as the opportunity to overlay information in 3D on a real-world environment. This is a sophisticated facility, enabling the connection of multiple data sources to a digital twin that allows the visualisation of an operations life cycle.

Working with collaborative, cloud-based platforms is in its infancy. Rules for interaction in these online spaces are still being written. For Defence, there are heightened security concerns, such as the need to verify the identity of users, the protection of shared data and cyber-security needs to protect the platform itself from being hacked and its intent subverted. However, in addition, for the tool to be used effectively, workflows to operate within the digitally enhanced environment that maintain the advantages it brings will need to be developed. With AM, the technology itself is as a rule more expensive to use than conventional manufacturing unless the parts being produced are designed to exploit the specific advantages it provides. Similarly, with an online collaborative system, enhanced by live data and visualisation systems, unless the parts being produced exploit the advantages the system provides, then the added complications of shifting to this system would not be worthwhile. Developing new ways of working, new ways of sharing data and products, for example through distributed manufacturing, and new ways of collaborating, such as through a more dispersed system of decision-making, needs to be fundamental to the adoption of genuinely digital communication systems.

Operating the practice outlined in Figure 9.3, would involve multiple different digital technologies used for a variety of purposes. The service it visualises integrates a 'virtual platform' into the system and is used as a model to enhance collaboration and support the concept of 'virtual trades' (Kourloufas, 2022)—an initiative within RAAF where personnel were upskilled in digital literacy for emerging technologies, particularly AM. This involved a series of workshops introducing digital technology relevant to changes to practice in manufacturing, such as 3D scanning, but also workshops on how these technologies could change practice. Participants from across the RAAF, the Australian Army, and the Australian Navy identified how and where they could see bespoke manufacturing could add value in their own situations, and where they imagined it

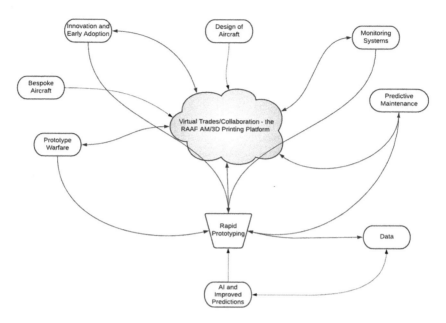

Figure 9.3 A digital convergence platform for the RAAF.

could create broader opportunities for Defence. For the virtual trades to operate, a distributed manufacturing platform would help leverage all of the technologies discussed earlier and in turn create efficiencies and optimisations not
realised before at scale. For distributed manufacturing, AI could calculate the
optimised distribution of parts across a network and the logistics of their delivery for assembly at a use-site. In addition, arguably it can recalculate logistics in
real time as unexpected events occur.

An example of a response to prototype warfare using this model could be to
rapidly 3D print drones on demand across different scenarios, much as is being
demonstrated in Ukraine. An engineer could specify the payload of a drone, select
a design, and send a blueprint/file to a facility located as near to the conflict as
possible for printing in that location. The newly printed and assembled drones
could be fitted with sensors, providing information on their performance to feed
back into the overall system. Deep ML enables further predictions that engineers
can use to adjust their approach for efficacy. This results in a smart strategic and
somewhat distributed approach that complements the main Defence Force capability. On a larger scale, a new drone could be under development by an internal,
sovereign capability factory inside an airbase. The designer working with the engineer, perhaps not even in the same location, could pull up an existing parts digital
inventory. Both put on headsets and gloves and in the virtual environment move

the drone around to investigate particular elements of design and construction. The file for the final design is sent digitally for fabrication, with sensors built into the output for tracking.

Whilst the interest in creating adaptable products for crisis situations is growing, the greatest potential of these technologies at this time is for 'predictive maintenance as a service' (Zhang et al., 2019). The benefit of having an established system is that they create a platform for people to use that develops a service that can be scaled digitally across the RAAF using a combination of technologies into a consistent process. It also builds capability in the use of digital systems and technology across the workforce. The kind of data feeding this type of digital system is not symmetrical; that is, it does not come from one place but from many places. The role of these technologies separately does not necessarily give the engineer any benefits, but when combined into a service model, the reality of digital convergence becomes apparent. The real issue here is one not of scale but of applicability. Much of the system and machinery would require investment, but use cases are repeatable, bringing costs down over time. The end result is a service to the whole of an organisation that produces an optimised, measurable, and trackable product, and then informs would-be engineers of its maintenance requirements all in one setting.

9.10 CONCLUSION

Complex organisations with a social remit and responsibility, such as in Defence where the stakes are highest, will need to drive the development and adoption of advances in manufacturing that sit within a connected workflow. Otherwise, the digital thread connectivity of a workflow will be directed at efficiencies and outcomes that are industry driven, rather than shaped by the requirements of the Defence future force. Integrating behavioural models into workflow planning is critical because of the holistic perspective and structure that digital convergence provides.

A responsive system, encompassing supply, design, manufacturing, and use, where constant feedback drives predictive maintenance over preventative maintenance, requires a rethink of workforce development and management. Where real-time responses are generated, decision-making is dispersed and access to multiple nodes within the system by multiple actors on the system needs a rigorous development model and preparation. With the opportunities provided by digital convergence—that integration of digital technologies from different fields combined to created new ways of working that transcend siloed practice—comes the responsibility and challenge to develop tools and culture supportive of distributed decision-making and creative problem-solving. Managing the technical and workforce processes individually is difficult; combining the two synergistically to maximise their potential is the ambition.

9.11 DISCLAIMER

The research informing this chapter involved a collaboration between the Government of Australia (represented by the Royal Australian Air Force) and Griffith University, Australia (with Deakin University, Australia), through a Defence Science Partnership Agreement. While the research included in this chapter was informed by the work undertaken in collaboration with the Royal Australian Air Force, the views expressed herein are those of the authors and not the official view of the Royal Australian Air Force.

NOTES

1 www.autodesk.com.au/products/vault/features
2 https://bambulab.com/en/x1
3 www.microsoft.com/en-us/mesh
4 www.raytracer.co
5 www.aveva.com/en/solutions/digital-transformation/xr/

REFERENCES

Bendul, J. & Blunk, H. (2019), The design space of production planning and control for industry 4.0. *Computer in Industry*, 105, 260–272.

Bhandal, R., Meriton, R., Kavanagh, R.E. & Brown, A. (2022), The application of digital twin technology in operations and supply chain management: A bibliometric review. *Supply Chain Management: An International Journal*, 27(2), 182–206.

Bianchi, M., Di Benedetto, A., Franzo, S. & Frattini, F. (2017), Selecting early adopters to foster the diffusion of innovations in industrial markets. *European Journal of Innovation Management*, 20(4), 620–644.

Canbaloğlu, G., Treur, J. & Roelofsma, P. H. (2022), Computational modeling of organisational learning by self-modeling networks. *Cognitive Systems Research*, 73, 51–64.

Canda, A. & Gogan, L. (2012), Taking the leap to agile manufacturing: From intention to a successful paradigm shift. *Managerial Challenges of the Contemporary Society*, 3, 77–80 Cluj-Napoca 2012.

Dornelles, J., N'Estor, A. & Alejandro, G. (2021), A smart working in industry 4.0: How digital technologies enhance manufacturing workers' activities. *Computers & Industrial Engineering*, 163, 107804.

Fogarty, I. & Franz, G. (2021), Agile product management: How to build weapons faster and better. *Breaking Defense*, March 5. https://breakingdefense.com/2021/03/agile-product-management-how-to-build-weapons-faster-better/

Frank, A., Dalenogare, L. & Ayala, N. (2019), Industry 4.0 technologies: Implementation patterns in manufacturing companies. *International Journal of Production Economics*, 210, 15–26. https://doi.org/10.1016/j.ijpe.2019.01.004.

Gaiardelli, P., Pezzotta, G., Rondin, A., Romera, D., Jarrah, F., Bertoni, M., Wiesner, S., Wuest, T., Larsson, T., Zaki, M., Jussen, O., Boucher, X., Bigdeli, A.Z. & Cavellieri,

S. (2021), Product-service systems evolution in the era of Industry 4.0. *Service Business: An International Journal*, 15(1), 177–207

Kent, S. (Stace), Houghton, L. & Licorish, S. (2023), Towards an understanding of the relationship between institutional theory, affective events theory, negative discrete emotions, and the development of feral systems when using human resource information systems. *Computers in Human Behavior Reports*, 9, 100264. https://doi.org/10.1016/j.chbr.2022.100264

Kourloufas, C. (2022), Additive manufacturing air and space power concept development, air and space power conference: Resilience and innovation in air and space, 22–23 March. https://airpower.airforce.gov.au/sites/default/files/2022-11/Air%20and%20Space%202022%20Proceedings.pdf p83.

Layton, P. (2018), Prototype warfare and the fourth industrial age. *Air and Space Power Centre*, Australia. https://airpower.airforce.gov.au/sites/default/files/2021-03/AP36-Prototype-Warfare-and-the-Fourth-Industrial-Age-Peter-Layton.pdf

Leonardi, P. & Neeley, T. (2022), Developing a digital mindset. *Harvard Business Review*, June, 50–56. https://web.p.ebscohost.com/ehost/pdfviewer/pdfviewer?vid=0&sid=4a4a292f-05df-4260-ab7d-8ad7ce8c34f0%40redis

Loy, J., Novak, J. & Diegel, O. (2023), *3D printing for product designers: Innovative strategies using additive manufacturing*, Routledge.

Loy, J., Tatham, P., Healey, R. & Tapper, C. (2016), 3D printing meets humanitarian design research: Creative technologies in remote regions. *Creative Technologies for Multidisciplinary Applications*, IGI Global, pp. 54–75.

Marr, B. (2022), *Future skills: The 20 skills and competencies everyone needs to succeed in a digital world*, Wiley.

Meindl, B., Ayala, F., Mendonça, J. & Frank, A. (2021), The four smarts of Industry 4.0: Evolution of ten years of research and future perspectives. *Technological Forecasting & Social Change*, 168, 120784.

Naughtin, C., Hajkowicz, S., Schleiger, E., Bratanova, A., Cameron, A., Zamin, T. & Dutta, A. (2022), *Our future world: Global megatrends impacting the way we live over coming decades*, CSIRO.

Ochella, S., Shafiee, M. & Dinmohammadi, F. (2021), Artificial intelligence in prognostics and health management of engineering systems, *Science Direct*. https://doi.org/10.1016/j.engappai.2021.104552

Ojo, A. (2019), Next generation government—hyperconnected, smart and augmented. *Working Conference on Virtual Enterprises*, 285–294. https://doi.org/10.1007/978-3-030-28464-0_25

Ruiz-Real, J., Uribe-Toril, J., Torres, J. & De Pablo, J. (2020), Artificial intelligence in business and economics research: Trends and future. *Journal of Business Economics and Management*, 22(1), 98–117; 99.

Spierings, A., Kerr, D. & Houghton, L. (2016), Issues that support the creation of ICT workarounds: Towards a theoretical understanding of feral information systems. *Information Systems Journal*. https://doi.org/10.1111/isj.12123

Startus Insights. (2023), Top predictive maintenance trends & innovations you should follow in 2023. *Startus Insights*. www.startus-insights.com/innovators-guide/predictive-maintenance-trends-innovation/

Vaia, G., Arkhipova, D. & DeLone, W. (2022), Digital governance mechanisms and principles that enable agile responses in dynamic competitive environments. *European*

Journal of Information Systems, 31(6), 662–680. https://doi.org/10.1080/09600 85X.2022.2078743

Veile, J. W., Schmidt, M. & Voigt, K. (2022), Toward a new era of cooperation: How industrial digital platforms transform business models in Industry 4.0. *Journal of Business Research*, 143(2022), 387–405.

Weinzierl, S., Wolf, V., Pauli, T., Beverungen, D. & Matzner, M. (2022), Detecting temporal workarounds in business processes: A deep-learning-based method for analysing event log data. *Journal of Business Analytics*, 5(1), 76–100. https://doi.org/10.1080/ 2573234X.2021.1978337

Wibisono, A., Sammon, D. & Heavin, C. (2022), Opening the workaround black box: An organisational routines perspective. *Journal of Decision Systems*, 271–283. https:// doi.org/10.1080/12460125.2022.2073647.

World Economic Forum. (2022), *Jobs of tomorrow: The triple returns of social jobs in the economic recovery*. www.weforum.org/reports/jobs-of-tomorrow-2022%0AJobs.

Zhang, W., Dong Yang, D. & Wang H. (2019), Data-driven methods for predictive maintenance of industrial equipment: A survey, *IEEE Systems Journal*, 13(3). DOI: 10.1109/ JSYST.2019.2905565

Chapter 10

State of the Art on Hybrid Harvesting for Sustainable Micro-Energy Generation in the Industry 4.0 Era

Subhransu Kumar Panda and J. Srinivas

10.1 INTRODUCTION

The Fourth Industrial Revolution, called Industry 4.0, is considered as a blend of electronics and information technology boosted the industrial production systems considerably. Industry 4.0 encompasses technologies such as artificial intelligence (AI), 3D printing, the Internet of Things (IoT), cybersecurity, unmanned aerial systems, big data analytics, cloud computing, sensors and actuators, and so forth. With the growing world population, the demand for fossil fuels is constantly increasing. For energy production in future decades, there are several alternative energy sources such as solar, wind, tidal, and geothermal. Even though such sources are available abundantly on the earth, their utilization is not an easy task for start-up firms and is not economical due to high setup costs. Apart from large-scale energy storage and retrieval, and residential and industrial scenarios in the modern era, there is a tremendous demand for alternative battery energy sources as wireless sensors, actuators, smart homes, and wearable electronics. Remote monitoring and control of objects through data transmission and reception capabilities are the main motives behind IoT technology. To drive the power circuits of such systems, micro-power generation units from ambient energy sources are quite useful in comparison with replaceable battery sources. The micropower demands of such devices can be achieved with ambient energy harvesters (EHs), where the surrounding vibrations, sounds, heat, or chemical energy sources are converted into useful electrical forms. In automobiles, for example, the sensor-based vehicle tire monitoring system makes use of wireless sensors powered using strain-based energy harvesting (Lee et al., 2015; Lee & Choi, 2014; Esmaeeli et al., 2019). Oudenhoven et al. (2012) found many advancements to increase the energy harvesting capability for a range of tire monitoring applications. Some of the important performance and safety parameters like temperature, pressure, and acceleration can also be measured by these sensors. Such natural small-scale energy sources dissipate energy from the equipment as heat or internal damping forces.

Ambient vibration and acoustic sources such as equipment, machinery, automobiles, and aircraft systems resulting in considerable mechanical energy that

DOI: 10.1201/9781003486244-15

can be converted into electric form by proper means of harvester design. Over the last two decades, different configurations of vibration-based EHs have been reported. It was proved that mechanical vibration-based EHs are more efficient than other energy sources like solar, thermal, strain-based, bioenergy, and acoustic. Vibrations occur from machinery as well as wind-excited systems, including bluff and streamlined bodies. Additionally, mechanical vibrations can be obtained from moving bodies like humans, vehicles, bridges, and structures. These sources of vibration have greater energy harvesting capability due to their versatility, availability, and high power density. A comparison among these sources is much more important in terms of energy harvesting capability and is depicted in Table 10.1.

In many applications, advanced battery sources have to be replaced or recharged regularly due to their limited life span. On the other hand, piezoelectric (PM;Guo & Lu, 2017), electrostatic (Lu et al., 2016), electromagnetic (EM; Khan et al., 2010), and triboelectric (Shi et al., 2019; Ahmed et al., 2019; Parida et al., 2019) energy conversion mechanisms convert energy from ambient vibrations more conveniently. These EHs are capable of providing efficient and low-maintenance energy solutions. Zuo and Tang (2013) concluded that vibration-based energy harvesting are capable of providing the required operating power for industrial sources. In the PE energy harvesting system, the mechanical strain or displacement is converted into electrical voltage by using certain materials like piezoceramics and lead–zirconate–titanium (PZT) patches (Pradeesh & Udhayakumar, 2019). The PE energy conversion mechanism (transduction) is most popular due to its relatively larger output power with minimum surrounding vibrations. On the other hand, in an EM harvesting system, a moving magnet in a copper coil induces electric current in the circuit. EM harvesters are intended for low frequency applications.

There are different means of enhancing the output from an EH. Introducing nonlinearities widens the resonance frequency band to capture more displacement. On the other hand, by adding multiple transduction mechanisms into a single system, the output power can be enhanced. A combination of multiple modes of energy conversion facilitates continuous energy harvesting potential and improves the output power for biasing a sensor. Few research works reported such harvester

Table 10.1 Comparison of Different Energy Sources

Source of Energy	Power Density
Vibration (Ringeisen et al., 2006)	$(10–300) \times 10^{-3}\,W/cm^3$
Solar (Hande et al., 2007)	$15 \times 10^{-3}\,W/cm^3$
Wind (Nayyar & Stoilov, 2015)	$(0.1–0.5) \times 10^3\,W/m^2$
Photovoltaic (Ibn-Mohammed et al., 2017)	$10 \times 10^{-6}\,W/cm^2$
Battery (Li-Ion) (Wang et al., 2013)	$90 \times 10^{-3}\,W/cm^3$
Human motion	$(0.1–1) \times 10^{-3}\,W/cm^3$
Thermoelectric (Raghunathan et al., 2005)	$0.04 \times 10^{-3}\,W/cm^3$
Acoustic noise (100–160 dB) (Horowitz et al., 2006)	$96 \times 10^{-8}\,W/cm^3$

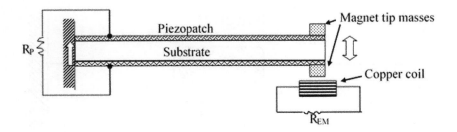

Figure 10.1 Simple configuration of piezo-electromagnetic energy harvester.

designs employing PE, photovoltaic, and radio frequency sources to power bio-medical electronic devices. Different variants of these hybrid system designs are available. In solar power applications, both photovoltaic and solar thermal genera-tors can be used simultaneously. Sang et al. (2012) concluded that PE and EM har-vester hybrid systems enhance the output power considerably. Figure 10.1 shows a configuration of a hybrid harvester making use of a PE cantilever with magnetic tip masses surrounded by a copper coil.

As the beam vibrates with base excitation, the tip masses start to move into the copper coil and induce the electric current. Simultaneously, the PE patches help in the conversion of surface strains from beam deflections into an equivalent electric voltage. Thus, the total output is augmented.

Alternatively, the copper field coil can be kept as a tip mass and magnets are arranged at fixed locations. There are different configurations of the system for low-frequency ranges. Gure et al. (2017) described various kinds of such clas-sic and novel hybrid energy harvesting systems available in the literature. Many other models of hybrid PE–EM harvesters are available in the literature (Peng et al., 2021; Rexy et al., 2021; Schlögal et al., 2021; Alhumaid et al., 2021; Ali & Khan, 2021). Narita et al. (2019) developed a PE-based hybrid EH by combining carbon-fiber-reinforced polymers (CFRP) composite laminates. Above 50 mV of output, the potential was generated due to the impact load on the samples. These kinds of structures give another dimension to the field of energy harvesting with the development of lightweight and efficient EHs. Figure 10.2 shows the model of Li et al. (2015), where a magnet is placed on a fixed beam with PE layer and coils placed under the magnet.

More detailed research on PE–EM hybrid harvester designs are noticed in the literature. Xia et al. (2017) presented a design of a tunable hybrid energy harvesting system. Toyabur et al. (2018) considered a PE–EM hybrid harvester based on mul-tiple degrees of freedom. It allows for achieving multiple close resonant frequen-cies. A polyacrylate beam was employed as a substrate so that the higher modes were brought to a lower frequency range. The prototype has four PZT patches, and NdFeB magnets were fabricated. At the third resonant mode of vibration (17 Hz) and under base acceleration of 0.4 g, a single PE generator is capable of producing

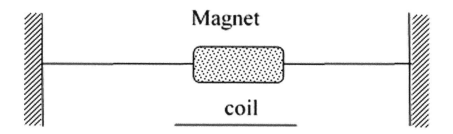

Figure 10.2 Fixed beam with a central magnet.

250 µW power. Here, the circuit resistance is maintained at 90 KΩ. Similarly, a single EM generator is capable of harvesting 244 µW power at a very small circuit load (10 Ω). Rajarathinam and Ali (2018) proposed a hybrid vibration energy harvesting system with PE and EM transduction. An oval-shaped hybrid EH modelled by Jung et al. (2020) produced an output power of 25 mW at input vibration and acceleration of 60 Hz and 0.5 g, respectively. Here, the EH is combined with both PE and EM generators. Lallart and Lombardi (2020) employed a hybrid nonlinear interface for energy harvesting. To enhance the output voltage, a scheme called 'synchronized switch harvesting' on an EM system was developed with an EM transducer. Li et al. (2019) presented hybrid PE and EM EHs for low frequency surrounding vibrations. Piezo and two sets of magnets and coils were inserted into the system. The strain was enhanced with a truss mechanism and impact load was induced with a stopper. Using this setup, an array of 99 LEDs was lighted. Qi et al. (2021) developed a PE–EM wave EH for self-powering in sea-crossing bridges. There was a storage module also. The wave motion hit the PE sheets and core, moving back and forth within a fixed coil. Power of 162 mW was noticed from the storage system. Rajarathinam et al. (2020) developed a hybrid PE–EM EH coupled with magnetic oscillators and compared the results with the linear model. The magnetic oscillators were provided to introduce nonlinearity to the system. Khan (2020) fabricated and tested a vibration-based hybrid EH. Here a polyvinylidene difluoride membrane was used to model the PE part, whereas the EM system was modelled with a permanent magnet, planar, and coil. Liu et al. (2021) presented a review of the role of vibration and thermal EHs in the field of hybrid EHs. For this purpose, they explained the configurations, mechanisms, performance, and advantages of different hybrid energy harvesting systems. They introduced the effect of PE, thermoelectric, and EM transduction. Li et al. (2020) proposed a hybrid EH mounted on a vehicle to harvest wind and vibration energy while driving. Xu et al. (2019) modelled a hybrid EH by combining the natural wind energy and magnetic field to improve the energy harvesting capability and reliability of conventional harvesters. Lee et al. (2020) modeled a controlled hybrid triboelectric–PE nano-generator to harvest random and irregular vibration from the

human feet. The hybrid harvester was capable of harvesting 127 µW power. The power generated from the shoe was capable of lighting LEDs and different wireless sensors. Lai et al. (2021) found that hybrid piezo–dielectric wind EH can be used to harvest vortex-induced vibration from wind. PE sheets and vibro-impact dielectric elastomer generators are the two energy conversion processes in hybrid EH. Jiang et al. (2020) designed a harvester as a hybrid of thermal and kinetic energy from thermal droplets by using combined pyroelectric and triboelectric EH. Similarly, the dynamics of the droplets also play an important role in the performance of the EH. Zhang and Jin (2021), in their recent work, illustrated an improvement in hybrid harvester performance by introducing the stochastic dynamics in the form of colored Lévy noise that describes most surrounding excitations.

Optimization of the harvester design is an important step from an industrial engineering perspective. Usually, efficiency and output electric power are considered as objective functions, while the stresses induced in the beam, the circuit heat generated, and the geometrical and material properties of the substrate structure are selected as constraints. The variables of optimization include the dimensions, environmental conditions, and so forth. It is often a nonlinear multi-objective optimization problem, which can be solved by modern non-conventional metaheuristic optimization techniques like genetic algorithms, particle swarm optimization, simulated annealing, and so on. A brief overview of these aspects will be discussed in the last section. The remaining portion of the chapter is organized as follows: section 10.2 presents the mathematical modeling of PE–EM hybrid harvester systems; section 10.3 describes a few notable optimization approaches in improving the output of hybrid harvesting systems; and conclusions and future scope of this research are given in section 10.4.

10.2 ELECTROMECHANICAL MODELING OF HYBRID SYSTEMS

When the output electrical power is harvested from mechanical energy using multiple conversion processes, the overall output increases considerably. Three such cases are explained next.

10.2.1 Hybrid Cantilever Piezoelectric System with a Hanging Magnet

The system consists of a PE cantilever beam with tip mass m_t, and a magnet (of mass m_2) is allowed to hang at the tip using a spring of stiffness k_2. The system is like an absorber attached to a cantilever (Rajarathinam & Ali, 2018). The magnetic mass moves within the solenoid made of copper coil, which is coupled with the beam base. Figure 10.3 shows the simplified two degrees-of-freedom model of this hybrid harvesting system.

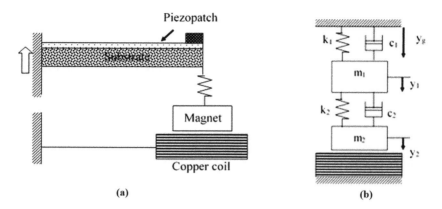

Figure 10.3 Simplified coupled system under consideration ($m_1 = m_t + 33\ \rho AL/140$): (a) original system; (b) simplified model.

Here k, c, and m are stiffness, damping, and mass parameters, respectively, while the suffixes 1 and 2 indicate the PE beam and magnetic mass systems, respectively. The load is applied at the base of the cantilever, where it is attached to the vibrating object. The simplified equations of motion for this lumped parameter system are given here:

$$m_1\ddot{y}_{r1} + c_1\dot{y}_{r1} + c_2\left(\dot{y}_{r1} - \dot{y}_{r2}\right) + k_1 y_{r1} + k_2\left(y_{r1} - y_{r2}\right) + \theta_p v_p = -m_1\ddot{y}_g \qquad (10.1)$$

$$m_2\ddot{y}_{r2} + c_2\left(\dot{y}_{r2} - \dot{y}_{r1}\right) + k_2\left(y_{r2} - y_{r1}\right) = -m_2\ddot{y}_g \qquad (10.2)$$

where $y_{r1} = y_1 - y_g$ and $y_{r2} = y_2 - y_g$ are relative displacements of masses m_1 and m_2. The PE coupling equation is given as:

$$-\theta_p\dot{y}_{r1} + C_p\dot{v}_p + \frac{v_p}{R_p} = 0 \qquad (10.3)$$

The EM output voltage is given as:

$$v_{em} = -BL_c\dot{y}_{r2} \qquad (10.4)$$

Here B, L_c, C_p, R_p, and θ_p are, respectively, magnetic flux density, the effective length of copper coil, electrical capacitance of the circuit, resistance of the circuit, and the EM coupling coefficient. Therefore, the system has three unknowns, y_{r1}, y_{r2}, and output voltage v_p, which are a function of time and depend on the input base excitation acceleration $\ddot{y}_g$. The amount of power harvested in the PE circuit is given from v_p as v_p^2/R_p, and that in the EM harvester circuit is given as v_{em}^2/R_{em}. Figure 10.4 shows the total power history obtained with base harmonic

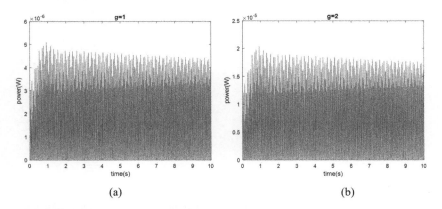

Figure 10.4 Total power harvested as per the available data (a) at g = 1 and (b) at g = 2.

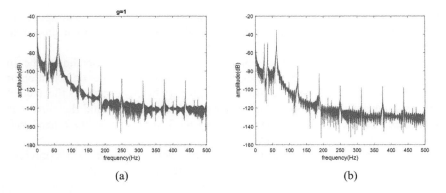

Figure 10.5 The corresponding power spectra (a) at g = 1 and (b) at g = 2.

acceleration amplitudes (g = 1 and g = 2) by solving simultaneously the previous equations.

Figure 10.5 shows the corresponding power spectra obtained. In comparison with a pure PE beam configuration, the overall power harvested has improved.

10.2.2 Hybrid Harvester with Intermittent Nonlinearities

In practice, the input excitation of the harvester is like a narrow-band random load, nonlinear magnetic force, or wind-induced vortex force instead of harmonic signals as occur in machinery. Such intermittent inputs deteriorate the output power. To enhance the resonance frequency band, several nonlinearities can be introduced. Zhao et al. (2018) proposed a similar setup, but a gap was maintained

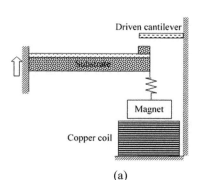
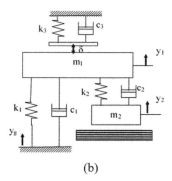

(a)   (b)

Figure 10.6 (a) Hybrid piezoelectric–electromagnetic nonlinear energy harvesting system (m₁: piezoelectric beam, m₂: magnetic system) and (b) the simplified model of the harvesting system.

between a driven cantilever and the tip mass along with a magnetic suspension. Figure 10.6 shows the schematic diagram of their system along with a simplified mathematical model.

As the input base excitation is applied, the cantilever vibrates, leading to the tip mass hitting another (driven) cantilever tip. This results in a larger deformation of the attached suspension situated beneath the primary beam surface. As the magnet moves again inside the copper coil, it cuts the magnetic flux and the current is generated. The PE voltage on one hand, and the EM current on the other hand, enhance the output power from the system.

The simplified mathematical model of the system is similar to the previous linear model. The equations of motion of the system are written as:

$$m_1\ddot{y}_{r1} + c_1\dot{y}_{r1} + k_1 y_{r1} + k_2\left(y_{r1} - y_{r2}\right) + c_2\left(\dot{y}_{r1} - \dot{y}_{r2}\right) + \theta_p v_p + f = -m_1\ddot{y}_g \qquad (10.5)$$

$$m_2\ddot{y}_{r2} + c_2\left(\dot{y}_{r2} - \dot{y}_{r1}\right) + k_2\left(y_{r2} - y_{r1}\right) + \theta_{em}I_{em} = -m_2\ddot{y}_g \qquad (10.6)$$

$$-\theta_p\dot{y}_{r1} + C_p\dot{v}_p + \frac{v_p}{R_p} = 0 \qquad (10.7)$$

$$-\theta_{em}\dot{y}_{r2} + L_{em}\dot{I}_{em} + R_{em}I_{em} = 0 \qquad (10.8)$$

where L_{em} is the inductance of the coil, R_{em} is the total resistance of the coil, I_{em} is the induced current, θ_p is the PE coupling coefficient, θ_{em} is the electromechanical coupling coefficient, R_p is external resistance across the PE circuit, and $y_{r1} = y_1 - y_g$ and $y_{r2} = y_2 - y_g$ are relative displacements of masses m₁ and m₂. Also, the contact force $f = k_3\left(y_{r1} - \delta\right) + c_3\dot{y}_{r1}$ exists whenever $y_{r1} \geq \delta$. Interestingly, here the

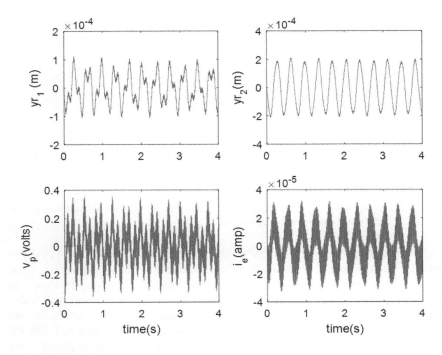

Figure 10.7 Responses of base accelerated (g = 1) primary cantilever (δ = 1.8 mm, k_3 = 4940 N/m).

fourth EM equation was also coupled with the displacement field. Thus, there are four unknowns, y_{r2}, y_{r1}, v_p, and I_{em}, which are all functions of time. The input base acceleration is considered as harmonic, so that $\ddot{y}_g = Y_g e^{i\omega t}$. But due to the contact force term, the resultant equations in the time domain are converted into six state-space equations and solve with zero initial conditions. Wang et al. (2014) adopted equivalent data of the system from the literature (Wang et al., 2014). Figure 10.7 shows the time responses of all four variables.

Figure 10.8 shows the frequency spectra of output power with only a PE circuit in comparison with a combined PE and EM circuit. The maximum power output has increased from 0.16 mW to 0.27 mW. The computations are made with base excitation coinciding with the first subsystem natural frequency. In addition, the system has nonlinearity in terms of the force applied intermittently, whenever the cantilever displacement exceeds a gap distance. This broadens the frequency band and has an opportunity to harvest at multiple frequencies also. As the performance of linear EH is limited to a narrow band of frequencies, the nonlinear properties inherent in the system could be effectively utilized during the design stage. Non-linear parameters should be selected carefully to ensure smooth operation.

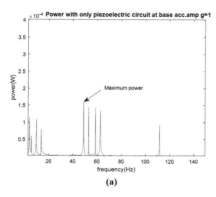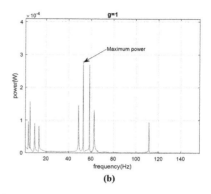

Figure 10.8 Power spectra (a) with only piezoelectric (PE) circuit; and (b) combined power of PE and electromagnetic circuits.

Nonlinearities improve the bandwidth of the system. Zhou et al. (2018) in another work proposed a nonlinear hybrid PE and EM energy harvesting fixed beam with a central magnetic tip mass operated by a Gaussian color noise signal. A snap-through mechanism is another approach to harvest power over wider bandwidths. Yang and Cao (2019) adapted a bimorph cantilever structure with tip mass attached to a discontinuous oscillator connected at the free end. The PE cantilever with a tip mass works with frequency matching ambient loads, while the EM system mounted at the cantilever tip was modeled with a nonlinear damping force model.

The equations of motion for a simplified model of such a system are:

$$m\ddot{x} + kx + \left(c_1\dot{x} + c_3\dot{x}^3 + c_5\dot{x}^5\right) + Bil + \theta_v v = -m\ddot{y} \tag{10.9}$$

$$C_p\dot{v} + \frac{v}{R_p} - \theta_v\dot{x} = 0 \tag{10.10}$$

$$L_e i + Ri - Bl\dot{x} = 0 \tag{10.11}$$

where m is the tip mass, k is the total stiffness, $\ddot{y}$ is the base acceleration, v is the output voltage, I is the output current from the PE and EM circuits, R_p is the PE circuit resistance, R is the total resistance of the EM circuit including load resistance, and l is the length of the coil.

10.2.3 Experimental Studies

Fabrication and experimental work on the hybrid EH is an important aspect to know its practical performance. Various elements like the alternative current to

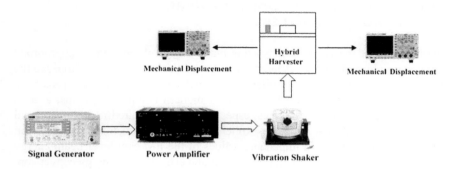

Figure 10.9 Experimental setup for measurement of output power.

direct current converters, resistors, and capacitors are used in the design of power circuits. All these elements absorb or release a certain amount of energy in between the conversion into useful power. The circuit elements have limited conversion efficiency also. Initial laboratory testing on the prototypes is needed to identify the actual output. Figure 10.9 shows the experimental setup for output measurement.

The setup usually consists of a vibration exciter (shaker) receiving a modulated signal from a function generator. As the beam system is vibrated, the PE and EM circuits generate output power. Since the output from a PE circuit requires rectification, a bridge-diode circuit is often employed. An accelerometer is used to measure the mechanical vibrations from the structure, while the EM circuit output is indicated in other oscilloscopes. From a micro-electromechanical systems point of view, the module is erected in a small casing and output power is directly utilized in running a sensor system. Vibrations from the mini wind turbine have been likewise employed with the hybrid energy augmentation process by Zhao et al. (2019). The entire harvester hardware occupies a small space on the vibrating substrate. Cao et al. (2021) experimentally analysed the performance of a flow-induced PE EH with magnetic force. A frequency sweep experiment has been carried out to obtain the resonant frequency. The effect of the magnetic force on the frequency response has been obtained at the resonant frequency. The magnetic force has the capability to improve the performance of the EH. Mohammadnia et al. (2020) considered a hybrid EH to enhance the energy harvesting performance from solar irradiation. The harvester comprised a solar concentrator, cavity, Stirling engine, concentrated photovoltaic, beam splitter, and solar thermoelectric generator. Kim et al. (2021) proposed a smart-pen PE energy harvester which is capable of harvesting energy while writing, when the PE materials are polarized in both d_{31} and d_{33} modes. The cantilever-type EH was capable of harvesting 1.5 µW at 3 Hz writing frequency and 12.5 mm writing length. Similarly, for an impact-type EH, the power output increases to 2.6 µW. The device successfully collects the energy from writing and will be helpful for powering the smart pen without a battery. From the experimental studies, Hu et al. (2021) found that folded-beam EH designs were capable of producing more output potential compared to the array-structured designs.

10.3 OPTIMIZATION STUDIES OF HYBRID ENERGY HARVESTERS

Optimization of the harvesting systems plays a key role in finding appropriate parameter values of cantilever length, width, and thickness. Also, to improve the power efficiency in an EM controller, the optimal controller data can be predicted. Due to the high computational potential of modern computer systems, a good number of optimization techniques, especially nature inspired non-conventional methods, are noted in solving the explicitly defined formulations. Cai and Zhu (2020) presented optimum impedance values of the EM cantilever beam energy harvesting system for maximizing the power and efficiency of energy conversion.

Geometric, material, and electrical parameters can be optimally selected to enhance the output power from the hybrid harvester. Foong et al. (2020) reported the considerations for optimizing the structural parameters of a single degree-of-freedom EM vibration harvester which provided improved power output with increased volume for constant beam thickness. In addition, when constraints like stress and damping are considered, the power output was found to be larger by adopting the load resistance as an input parameter, rather than an optimum resistance. The power limitation occurs as the coupling coefficient becomes very high. More recently, Li et al. (2023) employed coil and magnetic array in EM vibration energy harvester and achieved an optimal power density of 106.68 μW/cm^3 with six magnets.

In coupled systems, both electrical and mechanical parameters have an influence on the optimum electrical output. The maximum power output, in general, is achieved when the excitation frequency matches well with the natural frequency and the electrical and mechanical damping becoming identical. Tai and Zuo (2017) proposed optimization of EM and PE energy harvesting systems from base-excited vibration. Two variable optimization analyses for maximum power were illustrated. The expression for steady-state complex voltage and average power for PE harvester can be written by substituting $\ddot{y} = \ddot{Y}e^{j\omega_1 t}$ and $x = Xe^{j\omega_1 t}$ (where ω_1 is the base excitation frequency) as:

$$\frac{V}{\ddot{Y}} = \frac{j\theta_p m\omega_1}{\left[i\theta_p^2\omega_1 + \left(\dfrac{1}{R_p} + jC_p\omega_1\right)\left(\omega_n^2 - \omega_1^2 + 2j\zeta_m\omega_1\omega_n\right)\right]} \tag{10.12}$$

$$F(X) = P = \frac{1}{2}\frac{V^2}{R_p} \tag{10.13}$$

Therefore, power output or sometimes power density (power per unit volume of harvester) is a function of load resistance R_p and the frequency $\omega_n = r\sqrt{\dfrac{k}{m}}$, when other parameters are considered constant. For the EM harvester system also, the power expression in a similar way can be derived separately. The previous expression for power can be maximized by providing optimum values of variables by iterating in certain variable bounds. For a hybrid energy harvesting system also, likewise the total power was optimized. Due to the nonlinear nature of the problem, often several metaheuristic optimization schemes are implemented for solving the problems. For more realistic situations, multiple objectives, such as maximizing power, minimizing weight, and maximizing the bandwidth by proper selection of nonlinear parameters under various constraints can be formulated. Once an optimum solution is obtained, the 3D computer-aided design model can be developed, and the output power is numerically computed using a finite element model. Topology optimization techniques can be used for optimizing multi-resonant EMs.

Wang et al. (2021) coupled an EM EH and a triboelectric EH to model a nonlinear hybrid EH to harvest energy from vibration at ultralow frequency. In this analysis, the effect of linearity, zero stiffness, and bi-stability on the energy harvesting capability was calculated. It is important to study the non-linearity and design of any kind of system to optimize the performance of EMs. Jung et al. (2020) presented a formulation for hybrid EMs by minimizing mechanical damping and improving electrical damping. Sun et al. (2020) fabricated eco-hybrid EMs. Jiang et al. (2023) presented a low-frequency hybrid PE-EM harvester using two parallel cantilevers with a permanent magnet connected to the beams via springs. The output power is maximized numerically. The parameter selection and formulation of constrained optimization problem in hybrid energy harvesting systems is still an open research area.

10.4 CONCLUSIONS

This chapter presented a summary of hybrid vibration energy harvesting systems for sustainable micro-power generation in Industry 4.0 applications like wireless communication network systems. The output power of the electromagentic harvesters is considerable, with low frequency vibrations, while piezoelectric energy harvesters are effective at high-frequency input waves. Therefore, to maintain the output requirements over a broadband frequency, hybrid PE–EM harvesters are useful. Both harmonic and random vibrations from machinery, automobiles, and other equipment can be employed along with surrounding air stream vibrations in energy conversion. Some coupled electromechanical models of these hybrid harvesters were studied in detail. Industry 4.0 principles have increased flexibility with mass customization using big data analytics. From this point of view, self-powered sensor systems are required to transmit the data in future. Future applications may include high-power output devices (or arrays of such devices) deployed at remote locations to serve as reliable power stations for large systems. The use of artificial intelligence methods in economizing the harvested power is a future challenge. Exploiting other conversion mechanisms together with nonlinearity considerations in low-frequency random excitation conditions may give a further improved designs.

REFERENCES

Ahmed, A., Hassan, I., Mosa, I. M., Elsanadidy, E., Phadke, G. S., El-Kady, M. F., . . . and Kaner, R. B. (2019). All printable snow-based triboelectric nanogenerator. *Nano Energy, 60,* 17–25.

Alhumaid, S., Hess, D., and Guldiken, R. (2021). Energy regeneration from vehicle unidirectional suspension system by a non-contact piezo-magneto harvester. *Engineering Research Express, 3*(1), 015033.

Ali, T., and Khan, F. U. (2021). A silicone based piezoelectric and electromagnetic hybrid vibration energy harvester. *Journal of Micromechanics and Microengineering, 31*(5), 055003.

Cai, Q., and Zhu, S. (2020). Unified strategy for overall impedance optimization in vibration-based electromagnetic energy harvesters. *International Journal of Mechanical Sciences, 165,* 105198.

Cao, D., Ding, X., Guo, X., and Yao, M. (2021). Improved flow-induced vibration energy harvester by using magnetic force: An experimental study. *International Journal of Precision Engineering and Manufacturing-Green Technology, 8,* 879–887.

Esmaeeli, R., Aliniagerdroudbari, H., Hashemi, S. R., Alhadri, M., Zakri, W., Batur, C., and Farhad, S. (2019). Design, modeling, and analysis of a high performance piezoelectric energy harvester for intelligent tires. *International Journal of Energy Research, 43*(10), 5199–5212.

Foong, F. M., Thein, C. K., and Yurchenko, D. (2020). Important considerations in optimising the structural aspect of a SDOF electromagnetic vibration energy harvester. *Journal of Sound and Vibration, 482,* 115470.

Guo, L., and Lu, Q. (2017). Potentials of piezoelectric and thermoelectric technologies for harvesting energy from pavements. *Renewable and Sustainable Energy Reviews, 72,* 761–773.

Gure, N., Kar, A., Tacgin, E., Sisman, A., and Tabatabaei, N. M. (2017). Hybrid energy harvesters (HEHs)—A review. *Energy Harvesting and Energy Efficiency: Technology, Methods, and Applications,* 17–61.

Hande, A., Polk, T., Walker, W., and Bhatia, D. (2007). Indoor solar energy harvesting for sensor network router nodes. *Microprocessors and Microsystems, 31*(6), 420–432.

Horowitz, S. B., Sheplak, M., Cattafesta, L. N., and Nishida, T. (2006). A MEMS acoustic energy harvester. *Journal of Micromechanics and Microengineering, 16*(9), S174.

Hu, S., Bouhedma, S., Schütz, A., Stindt, S., Hohlfeld, D., and Bechtold, T. (2021). Design optimization of multi-resonant piezoelectric energy harvesters. *Microelectronics Reliability, 120,* 114114.

Ibn-Mohammed, T., Koh, S. C. L., Reaney, I. M., Acquaye, A., Schileo, G., Mustapha, K. B., and Greenough, R. (2017). Perovskite solar cells: An integrated hybrid lifecycle assessment and review in comparison with other photovoltaic technologies. *Renewable and Sustainable Energy Reviews, 80,* 1321–1344.

Jiang, B., Zhu, F., Yang, Y., Zhu, J., Yang, Y., and Yuan, M. (2023). A hybrid piezoelectric and electromagnetic broadband harvester with double cantilever beams. *Micromachines, 14,* 240. https://doi.org/10.3390/mi14020240.

Jiang, D., Su, Y., Wang, K., Wang, Y., Xu, M., Dong, M., and Chen, G. (2020). A triboelectric and pyroelectric hybrid energy harvester for recovering energy from low-grade waste fluids. *Nano Energy*, *70*, 104459.

Jung, I., Choi, J., Park, H. J., Lee, T. G., Nahm, S., Song, H. C., . . . and Kang, C. Y. (2020). Design principles for coupled piezoelectric and electromagnetic hybrid energy harvesters for autonomous sensor systems. *Nano Energy*, *75*, 104921.

Khan, F. U. (2020). A vibration-based electromagnetic and piezoelectric hybrid energy harvester. *International Journal of Energy Research*, *44*(8), 6894–6916.

Khan, F. U., Sassani, F., and Stoeber, B. (2010). Copper foil-type vibration-based electromagnetic energy harvester. *Journal of Micromechanics and Microengineering*, *20*(12), 125006.

Kim, J. H., Cho, J. Y., Jhun, J. P., Song, G. J., Eom, J. H., Jeong, S., . . . and Sung, T. H. (2021). Development of a hybrid type smart pen piezoelectric energy harvester for an IoT platform. *Energy*, *222*, 119845.

Lai, Z., Wang, S., Zhu, L., Zhang, G., Wang, J., Yang, K., and Yurchenko, D. (2021). A hybrid piezo-dielectric wind energy harvester for high-performance vortex-induced vibration energy harvesting. *Mechanical Systems and Signal Processing*, *150*, 107212.

Lallart, M., and Lombardi, G. (2020). Synchronized switch harvesting on electromagnetic system: A nonlinear technique for hybrid energy harvesting based on active inductance. *Energy Conversion and Management*, *203*, 112135.

Lee, D. W., Jeong, D. G., Kim, J. H., Kim, H. S., Murillo, G., Lee, G. H., . . . and Jung, J. H. (2020). Polarization-controlled PVDF-based hybrid nanogenerator for an effective vibrational energy harvesting from human foot. *Nano Energy*, *76*, 105066.

Lee, J., and Choi, B. (2014). Development of a piezoelectric energy harvesting system for implementing wireless sensors on the tires. *Energy Conversion and Management*, *78*, 32–38.

Lee, J., Oh, J., Kim, H., and Choi, B. (2015). Strain-based piezoelectric energy harvesting for wireless sensor systems in a tire. *Journal of Intelligent Material Systems and Structures*, *26*(11), 1404–1416.

Li, J., Liu, Z., Hu, H., Hu, J., and Wang, J. (2023). Theoretical and experimental investigation of magnet and coil arrays optimization for power density improvement in electromagnetic vibration energy harvesters. *Energy Conversion and Management*, *293*, 117411.

Li, P., Gao, S., and Cai, H. (2015). Modeling and analysis of hybrid piezoelectric and electromagnetic energy harvesting from random vibrations. *Microsystem Technologies*, *21*, 401–414.

Li, X., Li, Z., Bi, C., Liu, B., and Su, Y. (2020). Study on wind energy harvesting effect of a vehicle-mounted piezo-electromagnetic hybrid energy harvester. *IEEE Access*, *8*, 167631–167646.

Li, Z., Li, T., Yang, Z., and Naguib, H. E. (2019). Toward a 0.33 W piezoelectric and electromagnetic hybrid energy harvester: Design, experimental studies and self-powered applications. *Applied Energy*, *255*, 113805.

Liu, H., Fu, H., Sun, L., Lee, C., and Yeatman, E. M. (2021). Hybrid energy harvesting technology: From materials, structural design, system integration to applications. *Renewable and Sustainable Energy Reviews*, *137*, 110473.

Lu, Y., O'Riordan, E., Cottone, F., Boisseau, S., Galayko, D., Blokhina, E., . . . and Basset, P. (2016). A batch-fabricated electret-biased wideband MEMS vibration energy harvester with frequency-up conversion behavior powering a UHF wireless sensor node. *Journal of Micromechanics and Microengineering, 26*(12), 124004.

Mohammadnia, A., Rezania, A., Ziapour, B. M., Sedaghati, F., and Rosendahl, L. (2020). Hybrid energy harvesting system to maximize power generation from solar energy. *Energy Conversion and Management, 205*, 112352.

Narita, F., Nagaoka, H., and Wang, Z. (2019). Fabrication and impact output voltage characteristics of carbon fiber reinforced polymer composites with lead-free piezoelectric nano-particles. *Materials Letters, 236*, 487–490.

Nayyar, A., and Stoilov, V. (2015). Power generation from airflow induced vibrations. *Wind Engineering, 39*(2), 175–182.

Oudenhoven, J. F. M., Vullers, R. J. M., and van Schaijk, R. (2012). A review of the present situation and future developments of micro-batteries for wireless autonomous sensor systems. *International Journal of Energy Research, 36*(12), 1139–1150.

Parida, K., Xiong, J., Zhou, X., and Lee, P. S. (2019). Progress on triboelectric nanogenerator with stretchability, self-healability and bio-compatibility. *Nano Energy, 59*, 237–257.

Peng, Y., Zhang, D., Luo, J., Xie, S., Pu, H., and Li, Z. (2021). Power density improvement based on investigation of initial relative position in an electromagnetic energy harvester with self-powered applications. *Smart Materials and Structures, 30*(6), 065005.

Pradeesh, E. L., and Udhayakumar, S. (2019). Effect of placement of piezoelectric material and proof mass on the performance of piezoelectric energy harvester. *Mechanical Systems and Signal Processing, 130*, 664–676.

Qi, L., Li, H., Wu, X., Zhang, Z., Duan, W., and Yi, M. (2021). A hybrid piezoelectric-electromagnetic wave energy harvester based on capsule structure for self-powered applications in sea-crossing bridges. *Renewable Energy, 178*, 1223–1235.

Raghunathan, V., Kansal, A., Hsu, J., Friedman, J., and Srivastava, M. (2005, April). Design considerations for solar energy harvesting wireless embedded systems. In *IPSN 2005. Fourth International Symposium on Information Processing in Sensor Networks, 2005* (pp. 457–462). IEEE.

Rajarathinam, M., and Ali, S. F. (2018). Energy generation in a hybrid harvester under harmonic excitation. *Energy Conversion and Management, 155*, 10–19.

Rajarathinam, M., Malaji, P. V., and Ali, S. F. (2020). A nonlinear hybrid energy harvester. In *Advances in Rotor Dynamics, Control, and Structural Health Monitoring: Select Proceedings of ICOVP 2017* (pp. 605–614). Springer.

Rexy, A. I., Mary, J. N., Priyaadarshini, K. G., and Rachael, T. (2021). Hybrid energy harvesting based on piezoelectric and electromagnetic systems. *Journal of Physics: Conference Series, 1921*(1), 012060.

Ringeisen, B. R., Henderson, E., Wu, P. K., Pietron, J., Ray, R., Little, B., . . . and Jones-Meehan, J. M. (2006). High power density from a miniature microbial fuel cell using Shewanella oneidensis DSP10. *Environmental Science and Technology, 40*(8), 2629–2634.

Sang, Y., Huang, X., Liu, H., and Jin, P. (2012). A vibration-based hybrid energy harvester for wireless sensor systems. *IEEE transactions on Magnetics, 48*(11), 4495–4498.

Schlögl, M., Schneider, M., and Schmid, U. (2021). Design and simulation of a scalable hybrid energy harvesting device for low frequency rotations. *Journal of Physics: Conference Series, 1837*(1), 012007.

Shi, Q., Qiu, C., He, T., Wu, F., Zhu, M., Dziuban, J. A., . . . and Lee, C. (2019). Tribo-electric single-electrode-output control interface using patterned grid electrode. *Nano Energy*, *60*, 545–556.

Sun, Y., Lu, Y., Li, X., Yu, Z., Zhang, S., Sun, H., and Cheng, Z. (2020). Flexible hybrid piezo/triboelectric energy harvester with high power density workable at elevated temperatures. *Journal of Materials Chemistry A*, *8*(24), 12003–12012.

Tai, W. C., and Zuo, L. (2017). On optimization of energy harvesting from base-excited vibration. *Journal of Sound and Vibration*, *411*, 47–59.

Toyabur, R. M., Salauddin, M., Cho, H., and Park, J. Y. (2018). A multimodal hybrid energy harvester based on piezoelectric-electromagnetic mechanisms for low-frequency ambient vibrations. *Energy Conversion and Management*, *168*, 454–466.

Wang, C., Li, Y., Chui, Y. S., Wu, Q. H., Chen, X., and Zhang, W. (2013). Three-dimensional Sn–graphene anode for high-performance lithium-ion batteries. *Nanoscale*, *5*(21), 10599–10604.

Wang, H. Y., Tang, L. H., Guo, Y., Shan, X. B., and Xie, T. (2014). A 2DOF hybrid energy harvester based on combined piezoelectric and electromagnetic conversion mechanisms. *Journal of Zhejiang University Science A*, *15*(9), 711–722.

Wang, K., Ouyang, H., Zhou, J., Chang, Y., Xu, D., and Zhao, H. (2021). A nonlinear hybrid energy harvester with high ultralow-frequency energy harvesting performance. *Meccanica*, *56*, 461–480.

Xia, H., Chen, R., and Ren, L. (2017). Parameter tuning of piezoelectric–electromagnetic hybrid vibration energy harvester by magnetic force: Modeling and experiment. *Sensors and Actuators A: Physical*, *257*, 73–83.

Xu, X., Han, Q., and Chu, F. (2019). Hybrid energy harvesting from the natural wind and magnetic field. *IOP Conference Series: Materials Science and Engineering*, *531*, 012007.

Yang, T., and Cao, Q. (2019). Dynamics and energy generation of a hybrid energy harvester under colored noise excitations. *Mechanical Systems and Signal Processing*, *121*, 745–766.

Zhang, Y., and Jin, Y. (2021). Colored Lévy noise-induced stochastic dynamics in a tri-stable hybrid energy harvester. *Journal of Computational and Nonlinear Dynamics*, *16*(4), 041005.

Zhao, D., Liu, S., Xu, Q., Sun, W., Wang, T., and Cheng, Q. (2018). Theoretical modeling and analysis of a 2-degree-of-freedom hybrid piezoelectric–electromagnetic vibration energy harvester with a driven beam. *Journal of Intelligent Material Systems and Structures*, *29*(11), 2465–2476.

Zhao, L. C., Zou, H. X., Yan, G., Liu, F. R., Tan, T., Zhang, W. M., . . . and Meng, G. (2019). A water-proof magnetically coupled piezoelectric-electromagnetic hybrid wind energy harvester. *Applied Energy*, *239*, 735–746.

Zhou, X., Gao, S., Liu, H., and Jin, L. (2018). Nonlinear hybrid piezoelectric and electromagnetic energy harvesting driven by colored excitation. *Energies*, *11*(3), 498.

Zuo, L., and Tang, X. (2013). Large-scale vibration energy harvesting. *Journal of Intelligent Material Systems and Structures*, *24*(11), 1405–1430.

Index

For Product Safety Concerns and Information please contact our EU
representative GPSR@taylorandfrancis.com
Taylor & Francis Verlag GmbH, Kaufingerstraße 24, 80331 München, Germany